In the Shadow of the Manhattan Project

In the Shadow of the Manhattan Project

Radium, Fraud, and Secrecy at Eldorado

PATRICIA I. McMAHON
AND ROBERT BOTHWELL

UBCPress · Vancouver

Printed in Canada, this book is made of FSC-certified and recycled (forest-based) material. The FSC-certified materials meet FSC's standards for responsible forestry, and recycled materials are used instead of virgin forest materials. www.fsc.org.

UBC Press is an eBOUND Digital Certified publisher. The epub version of this book meets stringent accessibility standards, ensuring it is available to people with diverse needs.

Library and Archives Canada Cataloguing in Publication

Title: In the shadow of the Manhattan Project : radium, fraud, and secrecy at Eldorado / Patricia I. McMahon and Robert Bothwell.
Names: McMahon, Patricia I., author | Bothwell, Robert, author
Description: Includes bibliographical references and index.
Identifiers: Canadiana (print) 20260220388 | Canadiana (ebook) 20260220396 | ISBN 9780774873949 (softcover) | ISBN 9780774873956 (PDF) | ISBN 9780774873963 (EPUB)
Subjects: LCSH: Eldorado Mining and Refining Limited – Corrupt practices. | LCSH: Manhattan Project (U.S.) | LCSH: Radium industry – Corrupt practices – Canada – History – 20th century. | LCSH: Fraud – Canada – History – 20th century. | LCSH: Fraud investigation – Canada – History – 20th century. | LCSH: World War, 1939-1945 – Diplomatic history.
Classification: LCC KE8973 .M36 2026b | LCC KF9365 .M36 2026b kfmod | DDC 345.71/0263—dc23

UBC Press gratefully acknowledges the financial support for our publishing program of the Government of Canada, the Canada Council for the Arts, and the British Columbia Arts Council.

UBC Press is situated on the traditional, ancestral, and unceded territory of the xʷməθkʷəy̓əm (Musqueam) people. This land has always been a place of learning for the xʷməθkʷəy̓əm, who have passed on their culture, history, and traditions for millennia, from one generation to the next.

UBC Press
The University of British Columbia
www.ubcpress.ca

Contents

Illustrations

Preface and Acknowledgments

In 1984, the University of Toronto Press brought out Robert Bothwell's *Eldorado: Canada's National Uranium Company*. The book was an official history of a Crown corporation, and many research tangents had to be trimmed or, in some cases, left aside. That was especially true of the investigation and prosecution of Boris Pregel, Carl French, and Marcel Pochon over an astonishingly audacious case of fraud and theft at Eldorado. While the settlement of the case was described, the details were left to another occasion.

This book marks that occasion. When the official history was published, there were no police files, intelligence records, or biographical materials available on the three perpetrators, all of whom were closely involved with the company. Even after almost four decades, there were many unanswered questions about how the three men had stolen so much. In 2018, the University of Toronto held a workshop on nuclear policy at which Bothwell delivered a keynote speech on this fascinating wartime crime. Patricia McMahon, the director of the Osgoode Society for Canadian Legal History oral history program, had her curiosity piqued because of the lawyers involved. John Robinette stood out in particular, and the Eldorado case was significant enough to have been captured in his 1987 interview for the Osgoode Society program. It was time to team up.

Together, we decided to see what more could be discovered. The story turned out to be even better than expected, and there is much about its telling that involves luck and coincidence.

Building on the research done for the earlier publication, and with the help of a small group of talented research assistants, we secured documents from archival collections in Canada, the United States, the United Kingdom, France, and Belgium. Given the concerns about national security that surrounded the investigation – it did, after all, involve the highly classified pursuit of an atomic bomb – we expected to find records dominated by worries about security and espionage. We were wrong. From the beginning, every agency, whether Canadian, British, or American, treated this as an ordinary criminal investigation, albeit one pursued in exceptional wartime circumstances and shrouded in secrecy.

When Eldorado Mining and Refining closed down, records concerning the company were transferred to the National Archives of Canada (now Library and Archives Canada, or LAC), where they are available to researchers as R1220-0-5-E (RG 134 at the time of our research). The most important component as far as this book is concerned is found in the Glassco Commission files, informally known as the Glassco report after the principal in the government's investigation, J. Grant Glassco. Glassco was an accountant hired by C.D. Howe, the minister responsible for Eldorado, to investigate apparent financial improprieties at the company. His report is probably the most important single document in our findings.

In 1984, after *Eldorado* was published, the Royal Canadian Mounted Police (RCMP) began to compile a file containing documents totalling around 1,500 pages that collectively match the Glassco report in importance by giving depth and credibility to its analysis. This was in response to a lawsuit for nuisance against the federal government filed by Waste Not Wanted Inc. (WNW), a not-for-profit corporation created by a group of Scarborough, Ontario, residents who wanted to prevent the relocation of soil contaminated with radioactive materials to their neighbourhood. That soil came from a nearby subdivision whose homeowners, led by George Heighington, had filed their own lawsuit in 1983 for damages arising from the contamination of their properties. In late September 1988, Heighington, requested these documents under Canada's *Access to Information Act* (ATIA). The administration of ATIA is frequently obstructive and vastly time-consuming. That was not the case here. The RCMP produced the documents that had been prepared for the WNW lawsuit and promptly declassified them, all for the cost of copying: $45.60.

The WNW lawsuit was eventually dismissed for want of standing because the corporation did not have title to the contaminated land, although some of the documents were produced as part of the discovery process that allows parties to litigation to examine the records of the opposite side. The file compiled for Heighington came too late for the civil suit he championed, the trial having been held in mid-1987. We were much more fortunate; the full record we obtained is a researcher's dream and provided an essential source for the events described here. The file is labelled according to the group requesting it, Waste Not Wanted Inc. (WNW). We are grateful for the assistance of Glenn Wright for procuring it as the file was not otherwise listed through the LAC collections catalogue. As always, we are indebted as well to Paul Marsden, who helped us gain access to and copy related records. His extraordinary efforts are also responsible for securing many of the images that appear throughout the book. The *Heighington* civil suit produced transcripts of the trial testimony, which were included in the file before the Court of Appeal for Ontario and proved to be beneficial for this book.

It was a piece of great good fortune to obtain the RCMP file, but it was even more extraordinary that it survived at all. Typically, the RCMP retains documents related to security investigations but not police investigations. In the case of fraud at Eldorado, however, the file was flagged for retention because of the investigators who were involved. Terrence Guernsey, who served as the superintendent in charge of security intelligence until his retirement in 1960, was a young detective corporal in 1945. Originally, he was responsible for doing employee security checks at key companies, including Eldorado after it became a Crown corporation. That was how he first came across the trio of French, Pregel, and Pochon. In 1945, he was involved with the criminal investigation of the company, along with Corporal William McElhone. Even though this was a criminal investigation, because of Guernsey's involvement, the file was classified erroneously as a security matter and retained. For that, we are grateful. Much of this story would remain untold without it.

In addition, the current work makes extensive use of interviews conducted for the 1984 book with six individuals who figure in this history: W.J. (Bill) Bennett, who was C.D. Howe's secretary and executive assistant (1935–46), then executive vice-president of Eldorado (1946–47), and finally the company president (1947–58), and who knew most of the individuals mentioned here; Bertrand (Bert) Goldschmidt, William (Bill) McElhone, and Terrence (Terry) Guernsey of the RCMP; and Major Phillip Merritt and Major General Kenneth Nichols of the Manhattan Project. Their recollections were revealing and instructive. Interviews of key lawyers undertaken and housed by the Osgoode Society for its oral history program were also invaluable. Margaret Gowing, the official historian of the British atomic effort, the Tube Alloys nuclear weapons research and development project, offered insights into Boris Pregel, whose personality lingered in the British official mind.

The British official records were neither as useful nor as accessible as Professor Gowing. In late 2018, shortly after research began for the current book, the British government withdrew from the National Archives approximately 100,000 files related to the country's nuclear program (the AB and ES series), as attested to by the UK Information Commissioner's Office, *Decision Notice,* Reference no. IC-317526-G0C5, 16 September 2024. The files were withdrawn at the instruction of the UK's Nuclear Decommissioning Authority without any warning to researchers, thereby removing many records that had been open for more than thirty years. Additionally, the National Archives had lost Gowing's annotated copy of her book *Britain and Atomic Energy* (London: Macmillan, 1964). Fortunately, some notes and copies were preserved from research conducted in 1982 for *Eldorado* and were of use for the current project. As well, thanks to the efforts of our talented research assistant Angus Lee, material that had been freely available in the 1980s was recovered by 2024. In spring 2025, the last requested records were delivered (Eldorado Fraud Investigation, 1946, National Archives, United Kingdom, AB16/748), although they turned out to contain little more than gossipy news from Lesslie Thomson to Bill Akers about the 1946 investigation. Included in a letter dated 18 March 1946 was a copy of Boris Pregel's protestation of innocence, read by Arthur Slaght in open court a month earlier.

Lee also copied the papers of the late Dr. Vilma Hunt at the Arthur and Elizabeth Schlesinger Library on the History of Women in America, Radcliffe Institute for Advanced Study at Harvard University. Dr. Hunt was an American environmental scientist who became fascinated by, and admired, Boris Pregel, despite his apparent penchant for radioactive contamination. As part of her research, Hunt conducted extensive interviews with Pregel's younger brother, Alexander. Among other things she wrote a play about Pregel, and drafts of a book on the search for and marketing of uranium. To Dr. Hunt, we offer a retrospective thanks for her work, some of which was very helpful.

The exceptional efforts of the researchers who reviewed European archival collections in Belgium and France must be acknowledged. Victoire MacNaughton tackled the papers of the Union Minière du Haut-Katanga (UMHK) at the Belgian State Archives, the contents of which are managed by the Association pour la valorisation des archives d'entreprises/Vereniging voor de Valorisatie van Bedrijfsarchieven. The documents related to the

UMHK are fully available and open for public consultation. Julia Guennou assessed and retrieved important materials from the Institut Curie in Paris. Venia Veselovsky provided invaluable assistance with Russian-language materials, particularly in reviewing and interpreting Sophia Pregel's work and in discussions with other relatives of Pregel, including his niece, Julia Gauchman, who lived in Chicago.

This book also makes extensive use of the collection of records of the Manhattan Project, RG 77, in the National Archives and Records Administration (NARA) at College Park, Maryland. The records have been open for many years, so archivists tread a well-marked path in guiding researchers to the most important documents, and we relied on materials obtained previously for *Eldorado*. This time, however, the brief was for something different: documents bearing on internal surveillance and intelligence, not spies but criminals. Thanks to the RCMP files, it was clear that surveillance had occurred, and a précis of US transcripts of Pregel's conversations was available. Moreover, the intelligence files were cited in the excellent official US Army history of the Manhattan Project, Vincent Jones's *Manhattan, the Army and the Atomic Bomb* (Washington, DC: Center of Military History, US Army, 1985). But efforts by local researchers, including A.J. Daverede, to track down intelligence files originating from the US Army proved fruitless. As a result, this book contains what is in effect the RCMP's version of the missing intelligence. Given a subsequent US government–ordered purge of the archives, those files are likely to remain missing for a long time, perhaps permanently.

We benefited as well from the work of others, particularly Robert Norris. His biography of Leslie Groves, *Racing for the Bomb: General Leslie R. Groves, the Manhattan Project's Indispensable Man* (South Royalton, VT: Steerforth Press, 2002), was helpful to this account, as were the research materials he deposited in his personal papers, housed at the Hoover Institution Library and Archives, Stanford University. Although Norris did not discuss Boris Pregel in his book, he maintained a file on him. It turned out to be a treasure trove of important documents, many of which are no longer easily obtainable. Thanks to Richard Groves, grandson of General Leslie Groves, for reading part of the manuscript and spotting an error.

We also appreciate the efforts of Katie Davis, whose work at the Franklin D. Roosevelt Presidential Library at Hyde Park, New York, and on the Henry Wallace Papers at the University of Iowa Special Collections and University Archives added significant dimension to our understanding of the relationship between Pregel and the US vice president. Thanks, too, to A.J. Davidson, who undertook painstaking work reviewing collections of *The Northern Miner, Saturday Night* magazine, and assorted other periodicals and newspapers. Thanks to his diligence, we learned what was truly secret and what was merely said to be secret. His work on historical understanding of the relevant *Criminal Code* provisions was invaluable. Kevan Graham provided enormous assistance in the final stages of this manuscript, helping to locate and secure the necessary permissions for some of the images in this book.

We are most grateful for the support of Ira Gluskin, the sponsor of the May Gluskin Chair in Canadian History at the University of Toronto. Income from the chair paid for our talented students who served as research assistants and travelled to archives in Canada, France, Belgium, and Great Britain. Their work broadened and deepened the evidence for our history.

Additionally, we consulted memoirs of participants. Boris Pregel, Carl French, and Marcel Pochon unsurprisingly left no accounts of their achievements, although Pregel was a past master in self-promotion, as his articles, speeches, and interviews showed. We eventually concluded that truth and exaggeration were equally balanced in these. Leslie Groves and Kenneth Nichols, both of whom were involved in the US effort to develop the atomic bomb, did provide a record. Groves's *Now It Can Be Told: The Story of the Manhattan Project* (New York: Harper, 1962) was self-serving and shed little light on the Pregel affair. Of greater assistance was Nichols's *The Road to Trinity: A Personal Account of How America's Nuclear Policies Were Made* (New York: William Morrow, 1987). Nichols covers Pregel briefly but accurately and handles relations with Canada sensitively and perceptively. Bertrand Goldschmidt covers and re-covers atomic affairs in several books. The compact English version of his *Pionniers de l'atome* is *Atomic Rivals* (New Brunswick, NJ: Rutgers University Press, 1990), which contains some Canadian material not found in the French editions.

Some institutional histories have already been mentioned, especially the excellent British official history by Margaret Gowing and the equally meritorious American army history by Vincent Jones. Like Eldorado, the UMHK has its own history: René Brion and Jean-Louis Moreau, *De la mine à Mars: La genèse de Umicore* (Tielt, Belgium: Lannoo, 2006). It furnished valuable information and context for the activities of the company.

This account benefited from access to various court records. Unlike archival records subject to access to information legislation, court records are presumptively open to the public. Locating them can be challenging, however, because they are known by registry number, not case name, and there is no digital registry with that information. In Ontario, Superior Court records are moved from the judicial system to the provincial archives after thirty years. Thankfully, we were able to review this file in late February 2020. This was another piece of luck: any later, and the archives would have been closed due to the COVID-19 pandemic. The court file for the *Heighington* case included many sources that could be cross-referenced with the RCMP file. We also secured access to the records of the Court of Appeal from 1989, reviewing them in the basement of Osgoode Hall in Toronto at the end of February 2020. We appreciate the efforts of the court records staff who helped us locate decades-old records that had not yet been sent to the archives.

We express our collective thanks to the countless people who have read this manuscript or participated in workshops and discussions about the book, including the Legal History Workshop at the University of Toronto in late 2019 and the faculty workshop at Osgoode Hall Law School in early 2023. We appreciate the thoughtfulness and thoroughness of their comments, especially those of the two anonymous reviewers. Thanks as well to our editors at UBC Press – Randy Schmidt, Ann Macklem, and Camilla Blakeley – for their care in shepherding the manuscript to publication, and their commitment to bringing this story to a wider audience.

Finally, a personal note. Patricia McMahon is grateful to her family for their unwavering enthusiasm for this project. Her husband, Kevin Ackhurst, deserves special thanks for his eagle-eyed review of the manuscript – and, like their children, Jack and Max, for cheerfully tagging along on side trips to sites connected to the events in this book. For years, Robert Bothwell's late wife Gail patiently put up with tales of old Eldorado. She would be happy to see them finally settled. We dedicate this book to our families.

Playbill

The Players

Wallace Akers. Former chemical company executive who functioned as director of the British atomic project Tube Alloys, and who also directed the organization's relations with the Canadians and Americans during the war.

George Bateman. Canada's metals controller, and later Minister of Munitions and Supply C.D. Howe's emissary in Washington, representing the country on the Combined Development Trust.

J.E. Beckett. Accountant who worked for the Glassco investigation of financial impropriety at Eldorado Mining and Refining and was the supervising auditor for the associated investigation of Radium Luminous Industries.

John Joseph (Joe) Bench. Canadian Liberal senator and member of Boris Pregel's Canadian defence team. Bench also represented Dial and Instrument Finishers Ltd. as a corporate entity in the Foreign Exchange Control Board investigation, as well as Carl French in his personal capacity as company president.

W.J. (Bill) Bennett. Executive assistant to Minister of Munitions and Supply C.D. Howe. Bennett managed Howe's office from the mid-1930s through the Second World War, and in 1946 became executive vice-president of Eldorado Mining and Refining, making company president Gilbert LaBine largely a figurehead. Bennett served as Eldorado's president from 1947 to 1958.

Vannevar Bush. Director of the US Office of Scientific Research and Development, with oversight for wartime military research and development and thus early administration of the Manhattan Project. Bush was co-director of the project with James Bryant Conant.

Winston Churchill. Conservative politician, prime minister of the United Kingdom from 1940 to 1945.

James Bryant Conant. Harvard University president who became chair of the US National Defense Research Committee in 1941, with civilian oversight for the Manhattan Project. Conant was co-director of the project with Vannevar Bush.

William A. Consodine. Lawyer who became a wartime officer in the US Army Corps of Engineers and was a key figure in the American investigation of Boris Pregel.

Leslie Cook. Chemist at the Canadian National Research Council who worked as a technical adviser to the RCMP and investigators, especially with respect to understanding the hazards associated with radium.

Marie Curie. Polish-French chemist who discovered radium and won the Nobel Prize twice, first in physics and then in chemistry. Curie devised the refining process for radium later used by Eldorado.

Pierre Curie. Husband of Marie Curie and co-winner with her of the Nobel Prize in physics.

Carl B. French. American-born businessman who served as secretary-treasurer of Eldorado Mining and Refining and oversaw day-to-day operations. He also owned, operated, and held a significant number of shares in numerous radium-related companies, often in connection with Boris Pregel. French was at the heart of the investigation into financial impropriety at Eldorado.

J. Grant Glassco. Chartered accountant hired by the Canadian government to investigate apparent financial improprieties at Eldorado Mining and Refining and prepare a report to help determine whether to prosecute the responsible individuals.

Bertrand Goldschmidt. French chemist and student of Marie Curie who fled Vichy France where, as a Jew, he was in great danger. An acquaintance of Boris Pregel, he worked briefly at Eldorado in Port Hope, and then at the Montreal laboratory. He was later head of the French atomic energy agency.

J.H. (Jack) Greenberg. Lawyer for Eldorado Mining and Refining in the late 1930s.

Leslie Groves. A regular officer in the US Army Corps of Engineers, Groves directed the Manhattan Project nuclear research and development program, once it was turned over from civilian administration, from 1942 to 1946. Starting as a colonel in 1940, Groves was successively appointed brigadier general in 1942 and major general in 1944.

Terrence (Terry) Guernsey. RCMP sergeant tasked with investigating personnel at Eldorado Mining and Refining.

C.D. Howe. American-born Canadian engineer, academic, and politician in Liberal cabinets from 1935 to 1957. He served as William Lyon Mackenzie King's minister of munitions and supply from 1940 to 1945 and subsequently minister of reconstruction and supply.

Nicholas Ivanenko. Employee of Carl French who worked with his wife on a farm in Scarborough, a suburb of Toronto, to refine radium. The Ivanenkos owned the farm, where considerable quantities of radioactive waste were found.

Guy M. Jarvis. Canadian lawyer who worked as counsel for the Department of Munitions and Supply.

Frédéric Joliot-Curie. Successor to Marie Curie as director of her laboratory in Paris. Joliot took the name Curie when he married Marie and Pierre's daughter Irène, with whom he shared the Nobel Prize in chemistry.

Irène Joliot-Curie. Daughter of Marie and Pierre Curie and co-winner of the Nobel Prize in chemistry.

William Lyon Mackenzie King. Liberal politician and prime minister of Canada for three terms: 1921–26, 1926–30, and 1935–48.

Charlie LaBine. Elder brother of Gilbert LaBine, fellow prospector, and co-founder of Eldorado Gold Mines Ltd.

Gilbert LaBine. Prospector, storyteller, discoverer of high-grade pitchblende at Great Bear Lake. LaBine founded and presided over Eldorado Gold Mines Ltd., which he turned into a uranium-radium firm after his pitchblende discovery. LaBine defied the odds to create both a mine and a radium refinery in Canada but proved more successful at launching a company than running one. His negligent management style permitted the fraud and theft described in this tale.

Gustave Lechien. Socially well-connected Belgian engineer and director of Radium Belge, the marketing arm of Union Minière du Haut-Katanga. Lechien settled in the United States in 1940 after UMHK moved its operations there from Belgium, but fled to Guatemala in 1941 after apparently embezzling company funds and stealing radium.

Malcolm MacDonald. Former cabinet minister who was appointed British high commissioner in Ottawa and leader of the British delegation to petition Canadian prime minister William Lyon Mackenzie King for supplies of Canadian uranium.

C.J. (Chalmers James "Jack") Mackenzie. President of the Canadian National Research Council and a former student of C.D. Howe. Howe relied on Mackenzie as an emissary in Washington and London.

William McElhone. RCMP sergeant specializing in preparing complex financial cases for trial. McElhone worked with the Foreign Exchange Control Board and already had an excellent relationship with prosecutor John J. Robinette by the time the Eldorado investigation was launched. McElhone was promoted sergeant in November 1945, and resigned from the RCMP in January, 1947.

W.H. (William Henry) McGuire. Canadian Liberal senator from Ontario. McGuire was president of International Uranium Mining Company, and subject to the Glassco investigation.

Phillip Merritt. Geologist and wartime officer in the US Army Corps of Engineers who worked on the Manhattan Project. Merritt's knowledge of Canadian mining gave him valuable insights about Canadian uranium supply.

J.P. (Jay Pierrepont) Moffat. American diplomat, diarist, and historian who served as US minister to Canada during the Second World War.

Eger V. Murphree. American chemist who served as an engineer with the Manhattan Project and was tasked with buying Canadian uranium. In that capacity, Murphree had contact with Eldorado Mining and Refining and with Boris Pregel.

Kenneth Nichols. Colonel in the US Army Corps of Engineers and Leslie Groves's deputy in the Manhattan Project. A regular officer with a PhD in hydraulic engineering, Nichols was involved in negotiations for various contracts to purchase uranium from Union Minière du Haut-Katanga and Eldorado Mining and Refining. He began the war as a captain, and was successively promoted to major (1941), lieutenant colonel (1942), colonel (1943), and brigadier general (1946).

Michael Perrin. Chemist in the Tube Alloys British atomic program. Perrin was deputy to Wallace Akers and in that capacity was involved in diplomatic missions and liaison.

W.H. (Winston) Pickett. Wartime officer in the US Army Corps of Engineers who was part of the American team involved with the Eldorado investigation.

Marcel Pochon. French chemist who trained with Marie Curie. After developing a radium treatment facility at the South Terras Mine in Cornwall during the 1920s, he was recruited by Gilbert LaBine in 1931 to work as Eldorado's chief chemist and radium specialist. Pochon was involved in several of Boris Pregel's ventures, becoming a salaried employee of the Canadian Radium and Uranium Corporation in 1942 while still employed at Eldorado.

Alexander Pregel. Younger brother of Boris Pregel and connected to several of the latter's business ventures.

Alexandra Pregel. Second wife of Boris Pregel and a very well-known artist in 1930s Paris.

Anna Pregel. Wife of Alexander Pregel.

Boris Yulievich Pregel. Russian-born entrepreneur, refugee, patron and practitioner of the arts, self-promoter, fraudster, and radium sales agent extraordinaire. Educated as an engineer in Belgium and fluent in at least four languages, Pregel served as an officer in the Imperial Russian Army and then as an officer in the counter-revolutionary White Army. Pushed into exile in 1920, Pregel had a wide-ranging business life in Europe, where he was a freelance sales agent for Radium Belge, a subsidiary of the Union Minière du Haut-Katanga. As a Jew he was in great danger when the Germans conquered France, and fled to New York in 1940. Repudiated by Edgar Sengier, he set up independently in New York to broker radium deals and became universal sales agent for Eldorado in 1940.

Klara Pregel. Sister of Boris Pregel.

Sofia Gruzenberg Pregel. First wife of Boris Pregel.

Sophia Pregel. Sister of Boris Pregel and well-known Russian literary figure.

John J. Robinette. Toronto lawyer selected as lead prosecutor in the criminal case involving fraud at Eldorado Mining and Refining. By the time of the Eldorado investigation, Robinette had a history of prosecuting cases for the Foreign Exchange Control Board.

Franklin D. Roosevelt. Democratic politician, and president of the United States from 1933 to 1945.

Joseph Sedgwick. Criminal lawyer and second to Arthur Slaght's lead in the defence of Boris Pregel and Bay Securities. Sedgwick also represented Carl French in the Foreign Exchange Control Board investigation.

Edgar Sengier. Belgian engineer who rose through the ranks at Union Minière du Haut-Katanga to become director of African operations. He moved to the United States in 1939–40 and became the effective head of the company, operating from New York after the German conquest of Belgium. Sengier dismissed Boris Pregel as a UMHK sales agent, though the two never completely broke off contact. Sengier sold the company's uranium stock to the Manhattan Project and was consequently greatly esteemed by the Americans.

Arthur Slaght. Liberal member of Parliament from 1935 to 1945 and lead lawyer in Boris Pregel's Canadian defence team. Slaght also represented Carl French in the Foreign Exchange Control Board investigation.

Harry Snyder. American oil magnate, big game hunter, rancher, explorer, and speculator. Snyder invested heavily in Eldorado Mining and Refining, becoming the company's treasurer, earning a seat at the board table, and securing de facto control of operations before his abrupt departure in 1940.

G.P. (George Paget) Thomson. British physicist, Nobel Prize–winner, and head of the MAUD committee, a British scientific working group formed to determine if the atomic bomb was feasible. Thomson was stationed in Ottawa in 1941–42 and was a member of the British delegation that asked for Canadian help on the Tube Alloys project.

Lesslie Thomson. Special assistant to Minister of Munitions and Supply C.D. Howe. Trained as an engineer, and with a background in academia, Thomson was a key confidant and adviser to the minister.

Sir Henry Tizard. British chemist and adviser to the Royal Air Force in charge of radar. In 1939, he discussed the possibility of an atomic bomb with Edgar Sengier but postponed buying the Union Minière du Haut-Katanga's uranium stock.

James Tully. New York lawyer who spearheaded civil litigation against Boris Pregel on behalf of Eldorado Mining and Refining in the Southern District of New York.

Lowell Wadmond. New York lawyer retained by Boris Pregel as counsel in the civil lawsuit brought against Pregel by Eldorado Mining and Refining in New York.

Henry Wallace. Agronomist, Democratic politician, and vice-president of the United States from 1941 to 1945. Wallace was fascinated by the potential of radiation for agriculture, and was cultivated by Boris Pregel as a useful and prestigious contact.

A.E. Whitaker. US Army officer who worked under Leslie Groves in the Manhattan Project. Whitaker had been a member of the Secret Service before the Second World War and had worked with RCMP sergeant William McElhone before the Eldorado investigation.

W.H. Williams. RCMP inspector who worked as coordinating security officer for the Canadian nuclear project.

The Companies

African Metals Corporation (Afrimet). Fully owned subsidiary of Belgian parent company Union Minière du Haut-Katanga. Afrimet was established in 1926 to handle all non-radium sales in the United States and served as Edgar Sengier's corporate base while he lived in New York.

American Luminous Industries Inc. New York–based subsidiary of the Canadian Radium and Uranium Corporation, founded by Boris Pregel to manufacture luminous compounds in the United States. Carl French became a board member in 1941.

American Radium Industries Inc. New York–based subsidiary of Canadian Radium and Uranium Corporation, founded by Boris Pregel. Carl French was a board member.

Bay Securities Ltd. Toronto-based brokerage and investment company concerned principally with the promotion and sale of shares of International Uranium Mining Company Ltd. Carl French was the company's secretary-treasurer and director. He and Pregel were significant shareholders in Bay Securities, as was J.H. Greenberg.

Canadian Radium and Uranium Corporation (CRUC). New York–based company founded by Boris Pregel to facilitate radium and uranium deals. With the knowledge and consent of Eldorado Mining and Refining president Gilbert LaBine, Carl French became a CRUC board member and paid director in September 1941. Marcel Pochon was also on the board and served as a paid company adviser. Eldorado filed a civil lawsuit against CRUC, Pregel, and French in the Southern District of New York in 1946.

Central Trading Corporation. Subsidiary established by Edgar Sengier and Gustave Lechien to handle marketing for Union Minière du Haut-Katanga in the United States. Central Trading owned a stockpile of uranium ore stored on Staten Island.

Chemical Services Ltd. British subsidiary of Boris Pregel's Société Anonyme Demetra. The company's only dealings with Eldorado Mining and Refining were in connection with services performed on the latter's behalf in the United Kingdom.

Dial and Instrument Finishers Ltd. Company established to apply luminous compounds to dials and instruments. Founded by Carl French, who was also its principal shareholder, the company operated out of 103 Church Street in Toronto.

Eldorado Mining and Refining Ltd. Canadian company founded as Eldorado Gold Mines Ltd. in 1926 by brothers Gilbert and Charlie

LaBine, initially to prospect for gold and then to mine and refine pitchblende discovered at Great Bear Lake, Northwest Territories. Eldorado was the sole Canadian uranium producer during the Second World War and the only company available to the Allied powers for refining uranium for the Manhattan Project during the Second World War. Between 1942 and 1944, Eldorado was quietly nationalized on national security grounds, changing its name in 1943 and officially becoming a Crown company in January 1944.

Gunnar Gold Mine (later Gunnar Mining Ltd.). Mining venture established by Gilbert LaBine during his tenure as Eldorado Mining and Refining president. The company became involved with uranium mining once LaBine left Eldorado.

Industrial Radium Corporation. Chicago-based company established in 1943. Its only transaction of significance was the purchase of more than 21 grams of radium from Boris Pregel, who was the company's principal shareholder. Carl French and his family also had financial interests in the company. In 1945, its capital stock was acquired by Chicago-based Radium Luminous Industries Inc. and the company was then dissolved.

International Rare Metals Refinery Inc. Company owned and operated by Boris Pregel to refine radium at Mount Kisco, New York. Carl French was a board member and earned a salary from the company, as did Marcel Pochon, unbeknownst to Gilbert LaBine and the Eldorado Mining and Refining board of directors. Anna Pregel, Alexander's wife, was paid great sums for work she was said to have undertaken for the company in relation to a series of dubious transactions involving Radium Luminous Industries.

International Uranium Mining Company Ltd. Toronto-based company whose shares were listed on the Toronto Stock Exchange and which held mining claims at Contact Lake, near Great Bear Lake, in the Northwest Territories. The claims were said to contain radioactive ores and were purchased from companies owned by Carl French and Boris Pregel. Marcel Pochon also became a shareholder in International Uranium Mining.

Radium Belge. Marketing arm of Union Minière du Haut-Katanga, created by Edgar Sengier and directed by Gustave Lechien. Radium Belge employed Boris Pregel as its chief sales agent from 1923 to 1940.

Radium Luminous Industries Inc. Chicago-based company established by Carl French and used by him to evade excise taxes on shipments of radium from Canadian company Radium Luminous Industries Ltd.

Radium Luminous Industries Ltd. Toronto-based company founded by Carl French in 1941 and formally incorporated in 1942. Its offices were located at 103 Church Street in Toronto, and French used the company to purchase and sell radium stolen from Eldorado.

Société Anonyme Demetra (Demetra SA). Zurich-based holding company established by Boris Pregel to organize his various business enterprises.

Société Générale. Belgian industrial and financial conglomerate in which the Belgian royal family was a major investor. The Société was the majority shareholder in the Union Minière du Haut-Katanga.

Standard Chemical Company. Pennsylvania-based radium producer. The US company was a competitor to Union Minière du Haut-Katanga and dominated the global radium market in the 1920s until UMHK tried to bankrupt it. Instead, Standard Chemical agreed to become UMHK's sales agent for radium in the United States and abandoned its own production.

Union Minière du Haut-Katanga (UMHK). Belgian mining company with mineral interests in the Belgian Congo, notably copper, tin, cobalt, silver, and radioactive ores. Much larger and richer than Eldorado, UMHK forced the latter into a marketing cartel in 1938. The company's administrative operations were moved from German-occupied Belgium to New York with the outbreak of the Second World War.

X-Ray and Radium Ltd. Company dealing with the medical use of radioactive substances. The enterprise was founded by Carl French after the war, and operated out of a building on Davenport Road in Toronto, resulting in radioactive contamination at the site that was discovered in 1975. French sold the company to Westinghouse in the late 1960s.

The State Actors

Atomic Energy Control Board (AECB). Canadian federal agency established in 1946 to oversee the development, application, and use of nuclear energy, including responsibility for radioactivity testing and clean-up.

Combined Development Trust (CDT). Entity established to coordinate uranium supply for the Manhattan Project between the United States, the United Kingdom, and Canada.

Combined Policy Committee (CPC). Entity tasked with governing Anglo-American relations within the project to develop the atomic bomb. Canada was also represented on the committee.

Department of Munitions and Supply. Canadian government ministry responsible for the procurement and oversight of supply during the Second World War, including uranium. Its functions were absorbed into the Department of Reconstruction, which then became the Department of Reconstruction and Supply at the beginning of 1946 to help the Canadian economy make the transition from wartime to a peacetime footing.

Foreign Exchange Control Board (FECB). Canadian federal agency established in 1939 to regulate transfers of money between Canada and the rest of the world, with statutory powers ranging from controlling foreign currency holdings to restricting capital exports.

Home Ownership Made Easy (HOME) Plan. Program created in 1967 to provide affordable housing to low-income families. The province of Ontario owned the land and arranged for houses to be built. The government then offered low-interest loans to cover house purchases, while the land was leased to homeowners with an option to buy.

Manhattan Engineering District (MED). Entity created by the US Army for the purpose of conducting the Manhattan Project to develop the atomic bomb. The MED was named after the US Army Corps of Engineers district in which it was located, Manhattan.

Ministry of Economic Warfare (MEW). British government department tasked with targeting enemy resources and trade during the Second World War, specifically by preventing the flow of raw materials in order to hinder industrial output.

National Research Council. Canadian government agency dedicated to science and technology research and development.

Office of Scientific Research and Development (OSRD). Civilian agency established by the US government in 1941 to mobilize scientific research for military purposes. The OSRD coordinated work on uranium fission from 1941 to late 1942, when that effort was transferred to US Army control through the Manhattan Project.

Ontario Housing Corporation. Canadian provincial agency established in 1964 to manage social housing, including by providing subsidized mortgages that enabled renters to buy their own homes.

US Army Corps of Engineers. US military branch that ran the Manhattan Project and maintained control over American atomic weapons research and production from 1942 until the United States Atomic Energy Commission was established in 1947.

In the Shadow of the Manhattan Project

Introduction

When John J. Robinette, QC, took the witness stand on 25 May 1987, the eighty-year-old had already been a courtroom giant for decades. Described as the Grand Old Man of the Ontario Bar, the six-foot-tall Robinette had "a tendency to plumpness" but was best known for a "theatrical sense of timing and gesture" that made him one of the country's most respected litigators.[1] Roy McMurtry, the only person to have served as the province's attorney general and then chief justice, called him "the most distinguished barrister in the history of our country."[2] He was an advocate with an air of invincible gentility, the kind judges listen to with rapt attention.[3] By 1987, he had dominated Canadian courtrooms for more than five decades, having represented a who's who of the country's corporate elite as well as the federal government in a range of high-profile constitutional cases. His longevity was such that his first appearance before the Supreme Court of Canada, in the 1930s, involved a case under the 1865 *Colonial Laws Validity Act*, while his last was argued under the *Canadian Charter of Rights and Freedoms* in 1984.

Justice Richard Holland presided over Ontario's High Court of Justice that day in 1987. A transplanted Englishman, the sixty-two-year-old Holland was a former commercial and personal injury lawyer and an experienced judge, having served on the bench since 1972. He had recently overseen a landmark trial between International Corona Resources Ltd. and Lac Minerals Ltd. over the theft of confidential information about mining rights on a parcel of land, and Robinette knew him well enough to have written the foreword to his recently published book on advocacy.[4]

That the two knew one another outside the courtroom is not to suggest collusion but simply reflects the collegiality of the bar in Toronto at a time when there were considerably fewer lawyers than there are now.

But on that late spring day, Robinette had a different task from his usual business before the court. He was the lead witness on behalf of more than forty individual plaintiffs, homeowners who were suing the province. They wanted money from the Government of Ontario to compensate them for buying homes on land contaminated with radium. The payment they sought was not to make up for any ill health effects but because their homes were now practically worthless. Dutifully, from the witness box, Robinette recounted his involvement in a criminal matter from the Second World War, a spectacular case of fraud that had cost a Crown corporation and the federal government millions of dollars.

Having served as the Crown's lead prosecutor, Robinette was the perfect witness. He had first-hand knowledge of the investigation and great credibility before the court. Mere months away from a dementia diagnosis, he offered damning oral testimony bolstered by a raft of historical records that carefully documented what had happened at the corporation during the war. In support of the plaintiffs' case, Robinette methodically took the court through convincing evidence that laid out who knew what and when they knew it, including federal and provincial government knowledge of the contamination. This book explores the clever plot – to defraud a company of millions – that improbably led to the contamination and more.

The civil lawsuit in which Robinette now appeared as star witness stemmed from several well-intentioned albeit ill-considered decisions of the Ontario government.[5] In 1967, with inflation and interest rates reaching record highs, the province created a program to help lower income families buy homes. One of the largest subdivisions in the Home Ownership Made Easy plan (naturally advertised as HOME) was Malvern, located in the east end of Toronto in what was then the borough of Scarborough. Under the plan, builders leased lots from the province, which were then assigned to buyers with whom they contracted to construct houses at set prices. Homeowners would own the buildings but lease the land. The plan proved to be so popular that the Ontario Housing Corporation had to choose a lucky few to become residents from among more than 30,000 applicants in the fall of 1973.[6] Within three years, Ontario had sold the leased lots to the tenants at market value, with the province financing the entire purchase with interest-free mortgages. At a time when mortgage rates were higher than 11 percent, it was a terrific offer, too good to pass up for many.

But all was not as it seemed.

On 22 February 1975, the front pages of *The Globe and Mail* and *The Toronto Star* reported that radiation had been found earlier in the week inside a building at 103 Church Street in downtown Toronto. The stories did not identify the name of the company responsible for the contamination but simply reported that the site had been occupied by a radium luminous dial painting company between 1943 and 1947. A photographer who had moved into the building several months earlier made the discovery when he noticed that his film was becoming heavily fogged during development. He knew enough to suspect it must have come into contact with radiation and called the provincial Ministry of Health for help. Investigations quickly followed. The results of the tests were shocking. As the newspapers reported, radiation emissions in the building were eight hundred times greater than levels considered to be safe. By Monday, another contaminated building had been found at a different location.

Radium is like calcium in bones. If it gets into the body, it can settle in bones permanently and increase the risk of developing leukemia. But radium also generates gases, including radon, which when inhaled can settle in the lungs. If it does, it can bombard your lungs for the rest of your life.

The news was sensational and made it all the way to *The New York Times* several days later.[7] To the extent that readers did not understand the potential effects of exposure to radiation, the paper reminded them, recounting two classic examples. The first involved young women who had painted luminous watch dials in the 1920s and developed a range of ailments related to radiation sickness, including bone cancer. They had ingested radium while using their lips to shape paint brushes to a point. The second involved film fogging, just like the case in Toronto. Following the first tests of the atomic bomb in July 1945, customers of the Eastman Kodak Company in the United States started to notice fogging on the company's X-ray film. The culprit turned out to be the strawboard stiffeners used in the film's packaging, which included straw harvested hundreds of kilometres away from the nuclear test site in New Mexico. As the *Times* explained, its own investigation had determined that radioactive debris had been found as far west as Arizona and as far north and east as Maryland.

Clearly, the news was alarming for Toronto residents. The newspapers urged anyone who had worked in the building since 1943 to get in touch with the provincial Ministry of Health in Toronto, and two federal agencies in Ottawa: Health and Welfare Canada and the Atomic Energy Control Board, more commonly known as the AECB. The ministry had already contacted the AECB to test and clean up the property. Health is ordinarily a provincial responsibility, but radioactivity and its clean-up fall within the federal government's mandate, no matter how or where it is found. Investigators knew the radiation was coming from concrete beneath the floor tiles of an office adjacent to where the photographer stored his film. Worried officials began to look for old tenants, but because the floor plan had changed so many times in the past thirty years, they couldn't identify everyone who might have been exposed to radiation and urged former tenants to get in touch. Word spread, and soon almost a hundred former tenants came forward.

How radiation ended up in downtown Toronto became clear once investigators realized which company had been operating in the building in 1943 and who owned it: Carl French. In 1975, the American-born French was a seventy-two-year-old retired businessman who had earned a fortune selling his company, X-Ray and Radium Ltd., to Westinghouse several years earlier. He was well known for philanthropic endeavours in the fight against cancer, serving as the Canadian Cancer Society's first national fundraising campaign chair and working internationally to do the same. But during the Second World War, French owned and operated a company named Radium Luminous Industries Ltd. out of the building on Church Street. The company, whose name left nothing to the imagination, used radium-infused paint to manufacture luminous instrument dials for aircraft cockpits. It all made sense. The source of the radiation was luminous paint that had spilled during the production process.

As ministry officials dug deeper, they learned that French had owned other properties in and around the city. Soon, they found out that he had stored materials on a 10-acre parcel of farmland in Scarborough owned by a friend.[8] In 1945, Scarborough was a borough beyond Toronto's eastern city limits. Eight years later, the province expropriated the land to prepare for the increased demand for housing with the postwar baby boom underway. It was an investment, retained for future urban development. That time arrived two decades later, when the land was transferred to the Ontario Housing Corporation. The AECB, duly informed, went to investigate the property, which was now part of the Malvern subdivision, the very same development that was part of the HOME program.

AECB staff were cautious in their approach to the investigation. Dozens of young families lived in the subdivision, and no one wanted to cause unnecessary upset. Not wanting to alarm homeowners by asking permission to test backyards, they decided to limit their sampling to public property near the houses. To the relief of AECB officials, there were no abnormal results.[9]

Alas, the results were misleading. In November 1980, residents awoke to read the disturbing news in *The Globe and Mail* that their affordable homes had been built on land contaminated with radium in the very subdivision the AECB had cleared just five years earlier. Only then did the residents of McClure Crescent learn the truth, that their homes were on a hotspot. There was some public debate between local officials about whether they had known about the AECB's testing in 1975. In 1980, the local member of Parliament, Paul Cosgrove, was also the minister of public works in Ottawa. In 1975, he had been the mayor of Scarborough. He denied knowing anything about the tests. Keith Fitzgerald, an official with the provincial Ministry of Health, recalled it differently, telling reporters that he had personally told the mayor about the tests when they were done.[10] Regardless, it was clear that residents had been kept in the dark even about the tests being done.

How could something like this happen?

At the heart of the story is a company called Eldorado, whose business was mining and refining uranium and radium. It was government owned because it was central to the Manhattan Project, the American venture that produced the atomic bomb. The making of the bomb was probably the greatest secret of the Second World War. Masked by that secrecy, three key men associated with Eldorado embezzled over $2.5 million in cash and in kind (equivalent to more than $50 million in current terms).[11] Carl French not only owned and operated Radium Luminous Industries during the war but also – and more significantly – served as Eldorado's secretary-treasurer, giving him access to the company's materials. He conspired to defraud the company with Marcel Pochon, the company's chief chemist, and Boris Pregel, the universal sales agent charged with selling the company's radium and uranium.

This book fits within several historical genres. It is a legal history about both white-collar crime and the wartime regulation of export markets and currency. It discusses the extent to which civil proceedings might better serve victims of fraud by following the criminal investigation and efforts to prosecute French, Pregel, and Pochon. Those charges were eventually stayed when the company settled a New York civil suit against French and Pregel, brought to disgorge profits and return stolen radium.

This is also a business history about a company that contributed significantly to the dawn of the atomic age and made Canada an important part of the global nuclear industry, one that involves understanding the way in which the Canadian economy worked before and during the Second World War, especially with respect to natural resources and what we now call rare earth minerals. In that sense, it is a case study on the radium and uranium trade from the 1920s through the early post-war period.

This is a diplomatic history about the delicate balance among friends, allies, and imperial relations between Canada, Great Britain, and the United States during the Second World War and the early years of the Cold War. Finally, it is also a glimpse into some of the professions in Canada – lawyers, accountants, and engineers – and their wartime work.

Business and diplomacy share a bond: the conduct of both depends on relationships. This book involves a cast of colourful men. There was Gilbert LaBine and his brother, Charlie, the men behind Eldorado. There were the three men who exploited their position with the company: French, Pregel, and Pochon. Then there were the men responsible for investigating what happened: accountant J. Grant Glassco and lawyer John Robinette, along with Terrence (Terry) Guernsey and William (Bill) McElhone of the Royal Canadian Mounted Police (RCMP). They worked with military intelligence and security officials under General Leslie Groves, who oversaw the Manhattan Project and became obsessed with bringing the Eldorado trio to justice. (Groves was given the temporary rank of major general in March 1944 but bookended the war as a brigadier general and retired as a lieutenant general.) At one point he had twenty intelligence agents following and recording Pregel, French, and Pochon.

We begin with an overview of the discovery of radium and the development of the lucrative trade that ensued, including the rise of the dominant actor in the field, the Belgian company Union Minière du Haut-Katanga (UMHK), which had a rich supply of radium from Africa. We then trace the discovery of radium in Canada, the development of Eldorado, and trade through the golden years of the 1930s before the company almost collapsed under the weight of ferocious competition from the UMHK. Next, we outline the race to build the atomic bomb during the Second World War and the role that Eldorado played, including the efforts of French and Pregel to arrange sales of uranium to the US Army Corps of Engineers and the Manhattan Project. This discussion situates the work of the company within the broader context of international diplomacy and wartime conduct to show how easily French, Pregel, and Pochon could steal radium. The narrative then details growing suspicions about fraud once Eldorado was nationalized, and the efforts of Glassco and Robinette to investigate and prosecute it. Discussion of the criminal charges and surrounding publicity, including the work of defence counsel Arthur Slaght and Joseph Sedgwick, follows next. Eldorado's civil suit, filed in the Southern District of New York, is the subject of the final chapter, as is the ultimate decision to settle the lawsuit and withdraw the criminal charges.

This book serves as a cautionary tale about what can happen when preoccupations with secrecy and national security take priority over open courts and concerns about justice. The three men eventually settled a civil suit in New York, agreeing to disgorge the profits and return the fraudulently obtained radium, but they were never tried in open court – or, as they liked to point out, convicted. What follows is, in some senses, the trial that never was.

1
The Most Valuable Metal on Earth

Radium is a metal, atomic number 88 in the periodic table of elements. Pure radium is silver in colour, but when exposed to air it turns black on the surface as it bonds with nitrogen and becomes radium nitride. Though it exists naturally, radium cannot be seen in nature. It must be laboriously separated from other elements, and even then, it is exceedingly rare and dangerous because it emits radiation in the form of particles and rays. More simply, it releases energy through nuclear decay – radioactivity. The energy takes the form of alpha, beta, and gamma rays, named after the first three letters of the Greek alphabet. The emission of energy makes radium and other radioactive elements, such as polonium, unstable.

To contextualize what happened at Eldorado during the Second World War, it's necessary to understand where, when, and how radium was found, its qualities, and what made it so valuable. Also helpful is a grasp of the early radium trade and the rise of its dominant purveyor, the Union Minière du Haut-Katanga (UMHK) from Belgium, along with two of its most significant employees: Edgar Sengier and Boris Pregel.

Uranium, atomic number 92, was already known well before the Second World War, having been discovered in 1789 by German chemist Martin Klaproth, who extracted a black powder from a composite rock called pitchblende. As it turned out, the black powder was not pure uranium but uranium dioxide. Pure uranium was not produced until 1841.

Marie Curie, 1912 | Photo by Henri Manuel, Nobel Foundation Archive

Pierre Curie, 1903 | Photo by R. Moreau, Nobel Foundation Archive

Radium was discovered and named in 1898 by Maria Skłodowska, better known as Marie Curie, who was working in tandem with her husband, Pierre. Their research involved what would be called *radioactivité,* from the Latin *radius,* meaning ray, and French *actif,* for active. A substance that emits rays is, therefore, radioactive. Marie Curie discovered several radioactive elements, including one that she called simply *radium*. But radioactive substances are subject to decay. In 1899, the Curies discovered that radium decayed into radon, a colourless gas, an element with the atomic number 86.

It was known that uranium contained energy in and of itself, and the Curies began their work knowing that uranium was radioactive – it emitted rays – but it would be a few years before there was any agreement about what radioactivity was.

Uranium had to be extracted from pitchblende, a waste product that was available literally by the ton. It came from a mine in Bohemia, then part of Austria. The Austrian government had no problem donating it to the Curies' French laboratory, which unaccountably wanted it, for merely the price of the shipping.

Using instruments designed by Pierre, Marie focused on extracting uranium from pitchblende, only to discover that another substance in pitchblende was more radioactive than uranium. As a result, she had to devise a method to remove the uranium. Using a lengthy and complicated process of fractional crystallization, in which the pitchblende was "ground, dissolved, boiled, stirred, filtered, poured, and cooled," she produced samples of thirty different minerals.[1] Two, polonium and radium, were notably radioactive, and both were previously unknown but chemically closely associated with other elements: bismuth and barium. From bismuth it was possible to isolate polonium, named for Marie's native Poland, while barium acted as a carrier for radium. Of the two, the Curies decided that radium was more powerful and more practicable to work with, and thus better suited to continue their work. Conveniently, the English word *ray,* the French *rayon,* and the Latin *radius* are all mutually comprehensible, while French *radioactivité* and English *radioactivity* are just about the same. The discovery was announced to the Académie des Sciences in Paris in December 1898.

The next discovery came from Canada. Ernest Rutherford, a McGill University scientist, theorized that radioactive elements spontaneously changed into other elements. Rutherford's identification of the product resulting from radium's decay met the definition – indeed helped to frame it.

Rutherford discovered something else. The energy released in the decay of radium was greater than any known energy source. A gram of radium released no less than 100 million calories of energy as it decayed, and probably closer to a hundred times that – 10 billion calories per gram. One nuclear historian has described it as "astounding."[2]

The first thing a lay person would notice about a radioactive substance is that it glows in the dark, hence the term *radioluminescence*. This is not unique to radioactivity. Fireflies, for example, exhibit *bioluminescence,* while a substance like phosphorus absorbs energy and retransmits it in a process known as *photoluminescence*. A chemical reaction can also produce light through the interaction of two substances. But only radioactive materials retain their light. The rest fade after a few hours.

Luminescence appealed to all manner of people. It charmed the Curies, who liked to gaze at glowing objects in their laboratory. "One of our joys," Marie wrote, "was to go into our workroom at night; we then perceived on all sides the feebly luminous silhouettes of the bottles or capsules containing our products. It was really a lovely sight and always new to us. The glowing tubes looked like faint fairy lights."[3] It did not take long for radioluminescence to acquire commercial value, first as a spectacle, and then more practically, on machinery dials and watches. The next decade was filled with news about radium. Radium fancifully became a conduit to health and beauty, harmless for the most part, because the radioactive products and treatments were imaginary. Much of the publicity was mere commercial advertising for some quite imaginative "radium" products; in most cases, reading the word *radium* on the package was as close as the buyer got to radioactivity.

Radioactivity was a serious matter. It could be a tool of medicine, as with X-rays, discovered by German physicist Wilhelm Röntgen in 1895, which allowed physicians to see into the body and record the image. Very early on, Röntgen himself noted that exposure to X-rays also reddened the skin, and extensive exposure gave an effect similar to a burn. So did radium. In fact, it could destroy tissue. When this was noticed, one scientist pointed out that this property could be used to heal as well as harm. In particular, it could destroy cancerous tissue because the cancer was more susceptible to radiation than the healthy tissues around it. Overexposure to radioactivity would destroy them too, but not if the radiation was applied precisely under strictly controlled conditions. Radium was thus a miracle, one of the very few weapons in the fight against cancer.

Early radium therapy operated by trial and error. Gradually, science and medicine arrived at a rough understanding of how much radium could be used, for how long, and in what form. The errors, while in retrospect unavoidable given the lack of knowledge and experience, were stark and often fatal reminders of the dangers and limitations of the treatment. Pierre Curie discovered radon gas, which occurs naturally without any processing, but also realized that it decays very quickly. Radon's half-life – the time it takes for half of the atomic nuclei in a radioactive sample to decay – is just 3.8 days. Its utility as a medical tool was accordingly limited. Radium, on the other hand, had a half-life of 1,600 years. Perhaps most important, the quantities of radium needed for treatment were minuscule.

As early as 1902, some doctors had started to specialize in what was quickly labelled radiotherapy. Soon, they realized that radiotherapy had its risks as well as benefits. Properly applied to a tumour, it could cure, but no one really knew what was appropriate in any given circumstance. One thing gradually became clear: repeated use or careless handling of radiation posed a danger to scientists and medical practitioners. After the Curies jointly won the 1903 Nobel Prize in physics, Pierre used his address to the committee in 1905 to praise the effects of radium, notably in the treatment of diseases such as lupus, cancer, and nervous conditions, but also cautioned against exposure. Even a tiny amount of radium could produce first skin reddening and then a sore that was difficult to heal. More serious or prolonged contact, he warned, "could lead to paralysis and death. Radium must be transported in a thick box of lead."[4] By 1910, protective measures were beginning to appear: lead shields, lead aprons for patients, and reductions in the length of exposure. An X-ray that might have been focused on a patient for fifteen minutes in 1896 was reduced to seconds.

Pierre died in 1906 at age forty-six, not from radioactive poisoning but because he was run down by a horse and cart in a Paris street. That does not mean he was in perfect health before his death. Far from it. Before he died, Pierre suffered from severe pain in his hips and legs, which some have conjectured were manifestations of radiation sickness.[5] Marie was equally exposed but carried on prominently and productively, dying in 1934 at the age of sixty-six.

Marie Curie kept radium isotopes in her desk drawer, carried them around, and admired the glow they projected. Radiation may well have contributed to her death, but in the later opinion of a French scientific commission, her unprotected exposure to X-rays while engaged in war work during the First World War probably did the most damage. In the commission's view, only direct ingestion of radium, not merely handling it, would cause illness and death.[6] Nevertheless, the Curies' surviving papers, books, and other artifacts from as far back as the 1890s are kept in lead-lined containers, and researchers consulting them must wear protective gear.[7]

In an age of male supremacy, Marie Curie's achievements gave the lie to the myth that science was the property of the male mind. If doubt remained – and it did in many circles – her pre-eminence was sealed when she won a second Nobel in 1911, this time in chemistry. The only person to win in two different scientific fields and an icon of science triumphant, she devoted the rest of her life to the study and science of radiation. Undaunted by publicity, she understood its uses not just in securing her own reputation but in forwarding research. She exploited her fame to bludgeon the University of Paris into building her a first-class laboratory, in which she trained a generation of students in the ambiguities of radiation. According to one student from the late 1920s, the atmosphere was like a religious convent, but the piety was mitigated by Madame Curie's natural charm, her simplicity, and her attention to what even the most junior student was saying or doing.

Although the important work in atomic physics was carried on elsewhere, especially at Cambridge University, the discovery of radium was the central pillar of Marie Curie's Radium Institute, remaining the heart and soul of her labour as she sought to improve on her discoveries at the turn of the century with the help of her students. "She continued," according to Marcel Guillot, "to have the discovery of new radioactive elements as her principal object, and that by crystallizations or fractionated precipitations, thus remaining faithful to the method of work which had been fruitful in her hands at the beginning."[8] Her students learned about the benefits of radium, and also something of its hazards, but what Curie taught, and what she believed, ignored some of those dangers.

Anyone Can Make Radium

All Marie Curie's students learned how to make radium, which she regarded as a routine accomplishment. "Anyone can make radium," she is known to have said, and probably repeated many times.[9] Soon the development of radium transcended the pots and vats of the Curies' modest laboratory, and moved to a factory owned by the Société Centrale des Produits Chimiques, which could manage the heavy work of devising a reliable and regular process for converting pitchblende into radium and uranium.[10] The process was the "méthode Curie" – available to everyone, since the Curies had refused to patent it. A production line equipped with vats ranged from large to small, and heating equipment to boil the various stages, replicated on a grand scale the Curies' fractionating of the first tiny amount of radium.

As radium's fame spread and demand expanded, the price of pitchblende rose because its known sources were few. Soon, the Austrian government embargoed the export of pitchblende from Bohemia. No more free tons for the Curies; instead, the Austrians gave them a low price. A search for alternative sources began.

By 1905, uranium ore was known to exist in Portugal, and pitchblende could be found in Cornwall, England. But the most important radioactive minerals were found in the mountains of Colorado. The United States had the material, the labour force, the mining experience, the scientific know-how, and the necessary capital. By 1913, American companies were processing radium, and from that time forward, the United States dominated radium production.[11]

The demand for radium increased with the outbreak of war in 1914. Armed conflict is fertile ground for technological innovation and the Great War, as it was then called, was no exception. Warfare brought forth the development of tanks, poison gas, and military aircraft. In 1914, it was impossible to read dials on war machinery without striking a match and lighting a lamp. Doing so naturally gave away one's position to the enemy, and combustible lamps were impossible to use on aircraft. Luminous paint, containing radium mixed with a phosphor such as zinc sulphide, offered a solution. At first its adoption was unofficial: British newspapers carried ads designed to attract soldiers who could afford to buy watches with painted luminous dials. It was an enormous market, and so was the drain on radium supply.[12]

By the end of the war, consumption outran supply. In 1918, the British government banned the use of radium outside of hospitals, other treatment facilities, and its own military purposes.[13] With the end of the war, the government found itself with 5 grams of surplus radium, which was sold off at a steeply discounted $64,000 per gram. Once the windfall of war surplus had abated, however, the price of radium soared again, reaching more than $100,000 per gram.

Thus far we have focused on demand and supply, but what about the internal economics of radium? Anyone can make radium – in theory. In practice, anyone with a lot of money and access to a secure supply of radioactive ore could make radium. Those conditions were significant limitations.

Cost and sale price depended on geology. Pitchblende can contain a kaleidoscope of other minerals, ranging from silver to lead. The best possible had a grade of 80–85 percent uranium trioxide. The radioactive ore found in Colorado, the centre of American radium production, had a grade lower than 1 percent. The higher the uranium content, or grade, the less ore had to be mined and transported, and the less time it took to process, with fewer expensive chemicals. Inversely, the lower the grade, the more expensive it was to make radium. To produce a single gram, the main American radium producer, Standard Chemical Company of Canonsburg, Pennsylvania, now a suburb of Pittsburgh, took "500 tons of carnotite, 500 tons of chemicals, 1 million liters ... of water, 1000 tons of coal, and the labor of 150 men."[14] Few could afford to buy it, and Standard Chemical sold most of its radium in Europe at extravagant prices.

And then things changed.

Enter the Belgians

In 1913, two geologists working for a Belgian mining company found pitchblende in a hilly region in central Africa. They were not actually looking for it. The company's main interest was in copper, and it also mined cobalt, zinc, cadmium, manganese, silver, gold, and tin. All these were to be found in Katanga, the easternmost province of what was then the Belgian Congo (now the Democratic Republic of the Congo), within the continent's copper belt, which the Belgians shared with neighbouring British colonies. The Belgian Congo was situated within the basin of the Congo River, which stretches from the Atlantic two-thirds of the way to the eastern side of the continent.

The Belgian government promoted and controlled investment for Belgian firms using the Société Générale, an industrial and financial conglomerate. Government and business were inextricably mixed: the Belgian royal family was a major investor in both the Société Générale and the mining company Union Minière du Haut-Katanga, while the government paid close attention to their affairs. Along with British

UMHK ore processing in Élisabethville (modern-day Lubumbashi), c. 1917 | The History Collection, Alamy

investors, the Société Générale formed UMHK to exploit the impressive mineral wealth of the Congo. Given the area's proximity to British colonies, it's not surprising the UMHK attracted British investors and employed British geologists and mining engineers to fan out across the vast river basin to find and mine minerals. Copper was the obvious objective, but other minerals were welcome. Pitchblende held some interest, but before the Belgians could exploit it, the First World War intervened.

By the end of the war, the United States was supplying 80 percent of the world radium market. The apogee of Standard Chemical's fortunes was reached in 1921, when the company funded and publicized research on radium, indulged in medical philanthropy, and financed it all from a bulging corporate treasury. It could afford to: the price of radium per gram had passed $100,000 by 1910 and $180,000 by 1916, before subsiding to $120,000 by 1921. Almost all the radium sold on world markets that year was made in the United States.[15]

Madame Curie's visit to the United States in 1921 symbolized American dominance in radium. She was rapturously received as a hero of science. When US president Warren Harding presented her with a precious gram of American-made radium – procured, of course, from Standard Chemical – the $120,000 gift was funded through public subscription. Because it was rumoured that Curie could no longer afford radium for her own laboratory, women in the United States had raised the money. It was easy to assume the enormous profits would continue.

Edgar Sengier, the Radium Executive

Brussels noticed the profits, too. UMHK, with its Congolese copper mines, had also prospered greatly during the war. With the war over and the price of copper falling, the company wondered what to do with its African mines. The board of directors decided to send out an investigator to assess the situation and make recommendations.

Its choice was Edgar Sengier, a seasoned executive who had previous experience in the Belgian Congo. Born in 1879 in Courtrai, he attended the University of Louvain, graduated as an engineer in 1903, put his training to use building railways in China, and then moved on to work for an investment bank in Brussels. He joined UMHK in 1911.

A fluent English speaker, Sengier had overseen UMHK's London office in 1914. From London, Sengier watched, horrified, as Germany invaded Belgium and a brutal war ensued. The war scarred a generation of Belgians,

Edgar Sengier listening to General Leslie Groves read the Medal of Merit citation for his contributions to the Allied war effort, c. 1946 | Courtesy Atomic Heritage Foundation

including Sengier, who worked for an international relief group to address hunger and deprivation in German-occupied Belgium. The group's head was a prominent American engineer and future president of the United States, Herbert Hoover, who called Sengier "a man of great abilities" – warm praise indeed from someone widely considered to be self-contained.[16] Sengier's wartime work also drew admiration from the Americans in Hoover's mission, and was later described as having been carried out "with remarkable conscientiousness and organizational skills," the type of work that was both "greatly appreciated and earned him cordial and lasting relations with American representatives, and especially with the future President of the United States."[17] The experience brought Sengier into the world of international negotiation and politics and almost certainly acquainted him with the American way of doing things, lessons that later proved important.

Sengier also advanced his position within UMHK to become Directeur Général Afrique, responsible for African operations. He undertook to investigate UMHK's Katanga properties and recommend what should

A postcard depicting the Shinkolobwe radium mine in Katanga (Belgian Congo), c. 1925 | Courtesy of Günter Grundmann

be done with its mines and management. The world was in a sharp postwar depression, and the issue was whether the company should cut back and await better times.

Cuts and economies were contrary to Sengier's "optimistic temperament," according to a company biography, and he recommended maintaining production, certain that demand for copper would recover, along with prices. For him, the company's supplies of copper, cobalt, tin, and silver should not be viewed as a glut but an inventory. And then there was pitchblende. UMHK's local laboratory told Sengier that tests confirmed deposits at Shinkolobwe contained radioactive ores rich beyond any hitherto discovered. "From that moment," a historian of UMHK wrote, Sengier's mind was made up.[18] UMHK should not only keep its copper mines open but also dig another, this one for radium and its by-product, uranium. He also proposed the development of a new refinery complex at Olen, just north of Antwerp.

Sengier must have drawn the board's attention to radium's fantastic price, as the board agreed and he recruited a fellow engineer and college friend to build a radium refinery.[19] It was not complicated. As far as radium was concerned, there were no new designs, no breakthroughs. The Belgians relied on the Curie process, simply enlarged and improved. Conception and direction remained in Sengier's hands, working with a tight circle of known associates. As a good engineer he was technically competent, and he understood what his subordinates were doing even if his own work had nothing to do with the production of radium or anything else that came from the mines in Africa. His career was in the business of mining, whether that involved financing or administration.[20]

The first 12 tons of ore arrived in the Belgian province of Antwerp in December 1921, and construction of the radium-processing line at Olen began in March 1922.[21] It was the second step of Sengier's radioactive enterprise.

Gustave Lechien, the Marketing Director

The first radium came off the line at Olen in December 1922, just one month after a formal announcement from the king heralding the company's achievement.[22] Several months later Madame Curie visited, also to great publicity, and made her approval known. It was recognition and sanctification all in one.

That year, Sengier created a subsidiary, Radium Belge, to serve as the marketing arm of UMHK, appointing Gustave Lechien to serve as the new company's director. Lechien, an engineer, was described as "an attractive looking man, an excellent administrator," from a well-established Belgian family of devout Catholics.[23] Once, when completing an American immigration form, he listed the Belgian ambassador to the United States, Count Robert van der Straten-Ponthoz, as a friend.[24] One of his daughters married a French marquis.

Sengier's ace was the high quality of Belgian ore, which required far less treatment than any of its competitors. High grade equalled low cost, so Olen could produce a much cheaper product than the Americans. Sengier and UMHK were determined to compete, and dropped the price of radium to $80,000. Lechien left by ship for New York, and in January 1923 arrived in Colorado.[25]

There, Lechien told Standard Chemical that the Belgians intended to market their radium at whatever price was necessary to drive it out of the market and into bankruptcy. But there was an olive branch. If the Americans agreed to stop mining and manufacturing radium, the Belgians would allow Standard Chemical to sell Radium Belge's product as its US sales agent. The benefit to Standard was relief from the very expensive cost of production: the deal might make the sale of radium as profitable for the Americans as it had been before. They accepted.

Radium Belge (and ultimately Sengier) preferred to use external sales agents instead of an in-house marketing division. They were not inclined to drive rivals to the wall, though they would use the threat of doing so. Coordination, not competition, was the trick: pooling resources and talent to produce profits for everyone involved. It also meant that after 1922, Radium Belge, through UMHK, essentially held a global monopoly on radium production. Quickly, the price stabilized at $70,000 per gram, to the benefit of both companies. Radium had a glowing future.

Boris Pregel, the Sales Agent

Working through agents in the unfamiliar North American market made sense, but Lechien extended the policy to Europe. He appointed a freelance sales agent who would be based in Paris and responsible for the continental market excluding Belgium. For the post Lechien chose not a Belgian but a thirty-year-old Russian refugee, Boris Pregel. Once again, it was Madame Curie who had the *mots justes:* To her aphorism "Anyone can make radium," she added, "but only one man can sell it: Boris Pregel." Like all good salesmen, Boris could sell his product by simultaneously selling himself. Readers should bear in mind the very unusual times he lived through, which required resilience and a talent for survival. Until the end of his life Pregel also showed a strong loyalty to his family first, and his employers second. But we are getting ahead of the story.

Boris Yulievich Pregel was born in 1893 to a very wealthy Jewish family in the prosperous port city of Odessa, then the fourth largest in the Russian empire. The family business was the production and marketing of vegetable oil and seeds from the abundant agriculture of Ukraine. The Pregels were originally Prussian, having moved to Odessa from Königsberg in the mid-nineteenth century to take advantage of the opening of Ukraine's fertile lands to large-scale agriculture. Being Jewish in Russia in the nineteenth century could be dangerous, but there were exceptions to social restrictions. Jewish millionaires flourished, and there were Jewish members of the professions. Many prominent Jews also lived in Moscow and St. Petersburg, outside the so-called Pale of Jewish settlement in the western part of the Russian empire beyond which they were not supposed to live. Anti-Semitism certainly did not prevent Jewish merchants like the Pregels from making fortunes in Odessa.[26]

At the turn of the twentieth century, the Pregel family lived in a spacious flat on Odessa's most fashionable street, where they raised four children:

Boris Pregel, c. 1940s | AIP Emilio Segrè Visual Archives, gift of Serge Korff

Boris, Sophia (Sofiya), Klara, and Alexander (Aleksandr), who was born in 1907.[27] As described by Sophia, it was a close, affectionate family that spoke Russian at home as well as German and French.[28] Sophia loved music, and later became a notable figure in Russian – not Ukrainian – literature.[29] Boris had a "Jewish teacher" who visited the house daily, probably a tutor who taught him Hebrew. He was known as an outstanding student with a marvellous memory, accomplished in every subject except handwriting and painting, in which he stood dead last in the class. Sophia describes her brother as having had a mischievous sense of humour.[30]

The Pregels were protected by their wealth and the czar's gendarmes from the anti-Semitic riots that characterized Russia in the period. For many Jews, hostility at home in Europe encouraged Zionism. Boris was no exception. In Paris in the 1930s and New York in the 1940s, he was deeply involved with Jewish charities and practice, and he developed a strong connection to Israel after the Second World War.

After finishing high school in Odessa, Boris enrolled in electrical engineering at the University of Liège in Belgium.[31] It was a crucial decision that shaped his life, but at the time it was probably just expedient. Jewish students were subject to quotas in Russian universities, and Boris's parents could well afford the cost of educating him abroad. Since he had French as an everyday language, a Belgian university was a convenient way to circumvent the quota system. When he graduated from Liège in the spring of 1914, Boris returned to Russia, destined for the family business. Events in 1914 dictated otherwise.

Boris was twenty-one when the war came, ripe for conscription into a Russian army hungry for cannon fodder. By his own account, Boris had attended the Technological Institute in Petrograd after returning from Belgium. According to his brother, Alexander, he became an engineer at the Russian Imperial Army headquarters.[32] The czarist army badly needed technical experts, and specialists had to be imported from allied countries to perform tasks that elsewhere might have seemed routine. Nonetheless, Jewish officers were extraordinarily rare.

Boris later boasted of his military experience, claiming, for example, that he had been placed in charge of Russia's only aircraft factory, with the rank of colonel. There were in fact several factories, but one did operate near Odessa, which fits his assertion.[33] In exile in France and the United States, he did not fail to mention his achievements. Exaggeration is possible, but there were plenty of Russian exiles in the West who could have contradicted his account of his life.

All this changed with the arrival of the Bolsheviks after the revolution. There was no place for the Pregels in postrevolutionary Russia, and the family – minus Boris – sailed from Odessa for Constantinople in 1920. Boris stayed behind as part of the last contingent of anti-Bolshevik White Army forces to leave Russia from the Crimea, in November that year. When the British intelligence agency MI5 evaluated his story during the Second World War, they considered it credible.[34]

Constantinople was a safe haven, occupied by British and French troops until 1923. Yet the city certainly represented adversity for many if not most Russians. Boris talked about this new experience, for the first time in his life destitute and even hungry, though ready to take advantage of opportunity. According to the later MI5 account, Boris went into business there, dealing for a time in carpets and cigarettes. Brother Alexander, who was thirteen or fourteen at the time and would have been an eyewitness, reports that he was also an agent for a Belgian firm. In January 1922, Boris appeared as a ship's agent, still in Constantinople, soliciting cargo for a ship travelling to Novorossiysk – Soviet territory.[35] The rest of the family moved to Warsaw, then Berlin, and finally Paris.[36] Alexander moved to America, where he obtained a master's degree in advanced electrical engineering from the University of Minnesota in 1929.[37] Boris, meanwhile, secured

– which is to say probably bought – a Romanian passport, which allowed him to move freely around Europe.[38]

When the British and French left Constantinople in 1923, so did Boris, arriving in Paris. Soon, he married Sofia Gruzenberg, the only daughter of a very prominent Russian-Jewish lawyer.[39] We know little of Sofia beyond her name, her parentage, her marriage, the birth in France of a daughter, Hélène, in 1925, the swift collapse of her marriage, and her death in Berlin in 1932.

How Pregel and Gustave Lechien met is unclear but meet they did. Possibly, it was Pregel's work for a Belgian firm in Constantinople that reconnected him to the country. As engineers, the two men shared a profession that was common training within management at UMHK.[40] Engineering expertise was advantageous in the mining industry generally and the radium trade more specifically. Both Lechien and Pregel could understand the scientific chatter and share that information with the customers of Radium Belge, as both suppliers and salesmen. For the next sixteen years, Lechien and Pregel worked together, promoting and selling the radium that Edgar Sengier produced.

Although he worked closely with Radium Belge, Pregel was not an actual employee of either UMHK or its subsidiary. Instead, he served as an agent paid on a commission of about 10 percent of his sales or in kind with radium. Pregel was also able to trade radium on his own account or to make side deals with customers, which he did while running a wide variety of related businesses of his own. One of his interests, at least as early as 1927, was in dental supplies.[41] How Pregel got his start in the business is unclear – he may have acted as an agent for dental manufacturers – but by the 1930s, he owned at least one company and perhaps several. With an office in Paris, Pregel was also in the ambit of Madame Curie.

Radium, the Versatile Element

Radium Belge had started off with a flourish of publicity, providing a gift of radium to Madame Curie. There was a close relationship between Curie and Radium Belge, the UMHK, its refinery outside Antwerp, and the Société Générale. The latter was UMHK's majority shareholder, Radium Belge was its subsidiary, and their management was in constant touch with Madame Curie and her laboratory. UMHK claimed it had always done everything possible to oblige her, even if there was some dispute about whether the company had been paid for its efforts.[42] In truth, the free publicity the company received from her was payment enough.

Through the 1920s, lower prices helped encourage people to find new and creative ways to use radium.[43] "With the reestablishment of trade between mainland Europe, Britain and North America, the radium consumer industry, which had stagnated rather, was able to spring into action," writes Lucy Santos, a historian of radioactive beautification. Enhancing beauty through radium-infused products and treatments, not all of them above board, was a growth industry during the period.[44] The claims made for radium treatments frequently bordered on fraud, and most of the products contained no radium. Radium in luminous paint was a far more pressing use, so significant that military applications caused a radium shortage during the First World War.[45]

One consequence of using radium overshadowed all the rest in the 1920s, however, and continues to do so today. With an almost infinite demand for radium dial watches, two million were sold in 1919 alone and demand kept growing. But in 1925, workers at watch factories began to report strange symptoms – fatigue, anemia, facial pain. Bones in the face softened, jaws broke, and in one case a hole appeared in a cheek. Death followed quickly. Dentists called the condition "radium jaw." It was an accurate description; when radium is ingested, it concentrates in the bones, killing blood cells and making the bones friable.[46] It seemed that the human body could tolerate a certain amount of exposure to radioactivity without harmful side effects, but how much was unclear. For the time being, radium producers and users agreed that precautionary measures sufficed, or seemed to: better ventilation, gloves, a prohibition against licking brushes used for luminous paint.

Major scientific conferences of the period concentrated on the theory that the atom contained neutral particles, or neutrons. Here the Curies again played a role, discovering that "alpha particles had converted normally stable atoms into radioactive ones."[47] Uranium was the element that seemed to be most promising for this transformation. What did the debate over the structure and components of the atom mean in terms of practical application for the daily life of Belgium, France, Britain, or Germany? The answer was to come sooner than expected.

While atomic theory was being debated and refined at gatherings of physicists in the 1930s, the engineers and managers at UMHK worked to keep the company solvent. Despite the commercial uses of radium, the company had placed its bets elsewhere, in engineering, science, and medicine. Engineers are applied scientists, and the business of UMHK's radium arm was the application of science to medicine. There was no doubt that this radium business succeeded, with no competition, high prices, and sales that could be supplemented by radium rentals to allow access for customers who could not afford the purchase price. Not surprisingly, by 1925 the company had more radium than it could sell, so Sengier closed the mine and waited until inventory fell to a more manageable level. It re-opened in 1928, a year after Sengier became UMHK's managing director and just in time for the Great Depression to hit, leading to the shutdown of the Shinkolobwe mine once more.[48]

From the beginning, the UMHK cultivated its public image, recognizing that noticeable acts of philanthropy might help justify the price of radium. One prominent example is its support for cancer research, which was publicized through cancer conferences held in Brussels.[49] Pregel later summed up the relationship between good works and high prices, remarking that UMHK "had an industrial and commercial interest in selling radium for the highest possible price ... But I must say very frankly that this never was to the detriment of the research or real implications of that, as they understood very well that the development of their business depended largely on research and on therapeutic use of radium."[50]

For Pregel himself, the 1920s were a time of expansion as "sole agent and distributor of Belgian radium ... except for the United States and Japan."[51] As noted above, he worked on commission to sell or rent radium but was free to conduct business on the side, and there is abundant evidence that he did so. His ties to Berlin were more than familial – more than his father-in-law's residence and his estranged wife and daughter's – as he also invested in a Berlin company, Auer Gesellschaft. By the mid- to late 1930s, his investments were organized under a shell company, Société Anonyme Demetra, located in Zurich, as was his bank.

By dealing in radium on his own account while also selling it for Radium Belge, Pregel was simultaneously a salesman and a competitor as far as UMHK was concerned. The company nonetheless tolerated the arrangement because it was not unique. Lechien probably did the same. Pregel also had an interest in a uranium mine in Cornwall, as well as a stake in the firm of J. Hodson, which marketed radium in the United Kingdom.

During his time in Paris, Boris Pregel and his second wife, Alexandra, whom he married in 1937, sat on the boards of anti-cancer societies, rubbing shoulders with the influential and the prestigious. The prestigious lent their names, and Pregel lent his talents. Their work was not confined to cancer but encompassed other ailments like tuberculosis. Alexandra was involved with the same committee as the wife of the president of France, as well as the comtesse de Chambrun, the marquise de Montesquiou-Fezensac, and numerous rich Americans residing in Paris. Boris sat on the boards of Jewish philanthropies and several pro-Zionist organizations, among other charitable entities.[52]

By the 1930s, Boris was rich, well connected, and publicly recognized. He was appointed a chevalier of the Légion d'honneur in 1930 and elevated to an officer of the order in 1939, the same year that he became a French citizen. With business interests in several European countries, Pregel had remade himself, and had the awards and wealth to prove it.[53] Pregel's political associations seem to have been with moderate republicans who connected him to government. He became a member of the elite Jockey Club, and he successfully sponsored Gustave Lechien for membership in 1937. In the late 1930s, he was an "ami de la République française" at a time when not everyone was.[54]

Whether Pregel did personal business with Germany after 1933 is unclear, but there is no doubt that UMHK (and thus presumably Pregel as an agent) did business with German firms. In the mid-1930s, Nazism did not yet pose a direct threat to France, but French democracy was under threat from a fascist right and a communist left. Pregel stood with the centrist politicians who dominated French governments of the 1930s, but there was an ominous undercurrent. The French right was strongly anti-immigrant and anti-Semitic. Pregel, a Russian-born Jew who carried a Romanian passport, would have been an obvious target.

There was a more immediate cause for concern, however. In the early 1930s came news of a pitchblende discovery in Canada. Canada was not unknown in Brussels, having sent soldiers to liberate Belgium in 1918 and sacrificed its last casualty of the Great War in that country. It was rich in minerals and had a large mining industry. The city of Toronto was a centre of mining speculation and finance. Of course, the stories of pitchblende might be exaggerations, perhaps even falsehoods. Just in case, Sengier told Lechien to investigate on one of his regular trips to oversee UMHK's radium sales subsidiary in the United States. And so, in 1932 or 1933 – the date but not the fact is uncertain – Lechien arrived in Toronto.

2
Discovering Canada's Eldorado

The key people involved in the discovery of radium and uranium in Canada were Gilbert LaBine and his brother, Charlie. Together, they formed Eldorado Gold Mines Ltd. in 1926. It turned out the gold was a mirage, so they set out to find something else, eventually discovering pitchblende near Canada's Arctic.

The LaBines' endeavours, including efforts to create a mining company from scratch, are central to this story. The birth of Eldorado, its rise to prominence in the radium trade, and the way people like Gilbert and Charlie LaBine and Marcel Pochon shaped the company's early successes in the hypercompetitive, often unscrupulous world of mining make a compelling tale.

Gilbert LaBine possessed many skills. He was a gifted prospector; he dug a mine, built a mill, and established a refinery; he raised the money to pay for it all, not once but twice. He was also a talented storyteller, especially when those stories were about himself. His audiences varied: would-be investors, small and large; Canada's Prime Minister Mackenzie King; and the governor general, Lord Tweedsmuir, who promptly incorporated LaBine's exploits and successes into his own writing and speeches. A novelist by trade, Tweedsmuir knew a good tale when he heard one, and like all good tales it was true enough – believable while allowing for embellishments here and there.

Because so much of what we know about LaBine comes from contemporaneous interviews that he did, it's often difficult to verify. What we know for certain is that LaBine was born in 1890, a farm boy from the Ottawa valley not content to stay there. According to legend, he left home for good when he was sixteen to work in the mines at Cobalt, a small mining town in Ontario that was named for the valuable mineral found in the vicinity. Drawn by the prospect of riches, LaBine arrived in the early days of a mining boom. Although mining often attracts free spirits, it is also a highly organized and hierarchical activity on a large scale. Skilled miners could be very well paid, but Gilbert preferred his independence. He quit working for a mining company after about a year to dedicate himself to something more remunerative: prospecting. By the late 1920s, he had years of experience, having spent time in the silver fields in and around Cobalt and the gold rushes at Kirkland Lake and Porcupine.[1]

Lots of miners made money but LaBine wanted wealth, and gold is the universal symbol of it. The prospector in legend scans a rocky landscape and, guided by inspiration and luck, buries his pick in just the right spot to be rewarded by a metallic glint, after which wealth and fame flow naturally into his pockets.

It was therefore unsurprising that LaBine would set out to find gold – he was, after all, a twentieth-century prospector. Although he left school after Grade 10 – probably the average school-leaving level at the time – he had not abandoned education. LaBine attended the province of Ontario's School of Mines where he was taught by an inspiring teacher.[2] He studied photographs of minerals, and the rocks that held them. He read the reports of government geologists closely. Those reports did not always lead in the right direction, but they were designed to be informative. For a young prospector, the most important qualification was time, followed by patience and perseverance. Gilbert had the time, acquired the other qualities, found the stake money, and roamed the Canadian Shield with his knowledge. It was an uninterrupted quest, Great War notwithstanding. As a miner, he was in a reserved occupation and thus not conscripted to serve, though his elder brother Charlie (born 1888) did. After 1918, the brothers pooled their talents and moved west across the Canadian Shield, first to Manitoba, and then north to Canada's Northwest Territories and the watershed of the Mackenzie River, with its attached lakes, Athabasca, Great Slave, and Great Bear.

Gilbert was not specifically looking for pitchblende, but it held a certain attraction. Thanks to Marie Curie, its promise was well known, and

LaBine's teacher at the School of Mines had shown him samples, teaching him to identify the material by its "remarkably heavy specific gravity."[3] The key to LaBine's search was Dr. James Macintosh Bell's report for the Geological Survey of Canada, prepared and printed in 1901 following a pioneering geological exploration of the Northwest in 1900 by Charles Camsell, the chief exploration geologist and later deputy minister of mines. In his report Bell, a Harvard-trained geologist, described cobalt-bloom-stained rocks on the east shore of Great Bear Lake.

There is some uncertainty about when LaBine saw the report. In one account, he claimed to have found a copy over the winter 1929–30 in a forgotten archive in the Department of the Interior, but only after he had seen the geological formations from the air. Another source suggests that LaBine read the report and then headed north for the express purpose of locating the site. The latter is more plausible, though less romantic. Any decent mining library would have had a copy of Bell's report, and it probably provided the impetus for LaBine's expedition. Like many legends, however, it hardly matters which version is true.[4]

Gilbert and Charles had visited the vast, deep Great Bear Lake in the late 1920s. They decided to return by plane in 1930, since the frozen rivers and lakes of the region would not thaw and become passable until late June. That kind of delay would mean losing the spring and part of the summer, which was the prime prospecting season. On May 15th, Gilbert went off to explore on his own and found an island. Gazing across the ice to the mainland, he noticed "a great wall ... that was stained with cobalt bloom and copper green. I walked over to this place and investigated it carefully and found all the associated ores of cobalt, including silver. Following along, I found a tiny piece of ore, probably the size of a large plum, and it was pitchblende."[5] As he would later explain, he knew instantly that "the ore was of such a grade that there was no doubt in my mind but that I had found a very rich deposit of uranium ore."

The Great Bear Lake Find

What LaBine found was extraordinary. Samples were drawn and flown out, tests were run. The results proved LaBine correct and he staked his claim. He had discovered pitchblende of a very high grade, so high that it was thought to be comparable to the Belgian find at Shinkolobwe.[6]

In March 1937, Charles Camsell explained the significance in the *Canadian Geographical Journal:*

> The radium content of the pitchblende discovered in that area (LaBine Point-Eldorado) was unusually high, being estimated at one gram per 6 ½ tons, whereas concentrates formerly treated in the United States average one gram in 128 tons, and the best grade ore from the Belgian Congo averaged one gram per 10 tons, dropping in recent years to one gram in 30 or 40 tons. The occurrence of native silver, often in large amounts, with the pitchblende from LaBine Point adds materially to its value.[7]

Camsell could not have been more encouraging, but his opinion was not entirely accurate. He was correct about the quality of the American deposits, which had led to the demise of uranium mining and radium making in the United States. But he erred where the Belgians were concerned. It was a serious mistake because the deposit in the Belgian Congo was significantly richer than the one at Great Bear Lake. We will return to that problem later.

The LaBines benefited from Canadian government support in several forms. They made use not only of its geological surveys but also of its technological capacity. The Department of Mines' laboratories – more colloquially known as the Mines Branch – were right next door to the Geological Survey in Ottawa. The department had direct jurisdiction over Great Bear Lake because it was located in a federal territory. As discovery and promotion of Canada's mineral resources were the department's raison d'être, it was delighted to receive LaBine's samples, knowing what they might contain. Where the Geological Survey explored and mapped mineral formations, the Mines Branch focused on verification, analysis, and rationalization of what had been discovered.[8]

Handling Canadian pitchblende was complicated because it comprised a different mix of minerals from the pitchblende of Katanga or Bohemia. Special treatment was needed, and scientists at the Mines Branch leapt at the chance. In the process, they developed a new, more efficient method to extract radium salts from pitchblende. Whereas UMHK took three months to produce the salts, the Canadian process produced them in just six weeks.

Testing Eldorado's ore continued over the last quarter of 1930. The Mines Branch classified samples from Number One and Number Two veins as high-grade pitchblende ore. Both contained silver, and one had a noticeable quantity of gold. One sample showed 56.91 percent uranium oxide. Another showed 63.94 percent. If these were representative of the deposit as a whole, a ton of ore from Eldorado could generate between $7,000 and $8,000 using a conservative estimate of $50,000 per gram. That, however, is the mystery. No large-scale drilling program was undertaken to see whether the deposit was consistent throughout. Nonetheless, in mid-February 1931 the Mines Branch delivered the key conclusion that the samples were very high-grade radium-bearing ore. The uranium content varied from 27.88 to 83.9 percent, which meant between 70.79 and 213 milligrams of radium per ton of ore. Multiplying these figures by a more optimistic $70,000 per gram produced a price between $4,956 and $14,910 per ton of ore. In May, Minister of Mines W.A. Gordon rose in the House of Commons to celebrate Eldorado's discovery of radium.[9]

The minister's announcement confirming that Eldorado had struck it rich – or at least had the potential to strike it rich – legitimized the company's claims and made it easier to raise the funds needed to continue. As a mining company, Eldorado also benefited from government support during the Great Depression, and the global market for minerals fared better than other parts of the economy where international trade and domestic demand came close to collapse.

Extracting radium and uranium from pitchblende required facilities and substantial logistical support, much of it funded by the state. It was an expensive endeavour. Everything required cash, and plenty of it. Equipment and materials arrived in 1931 and 1932 to dig out the Port Radium

Port Radium, a radium-mining settlement near the shores of Great Bear Lake in the Northwest Territories, 1930s | Library and Archives Canada, C-23966

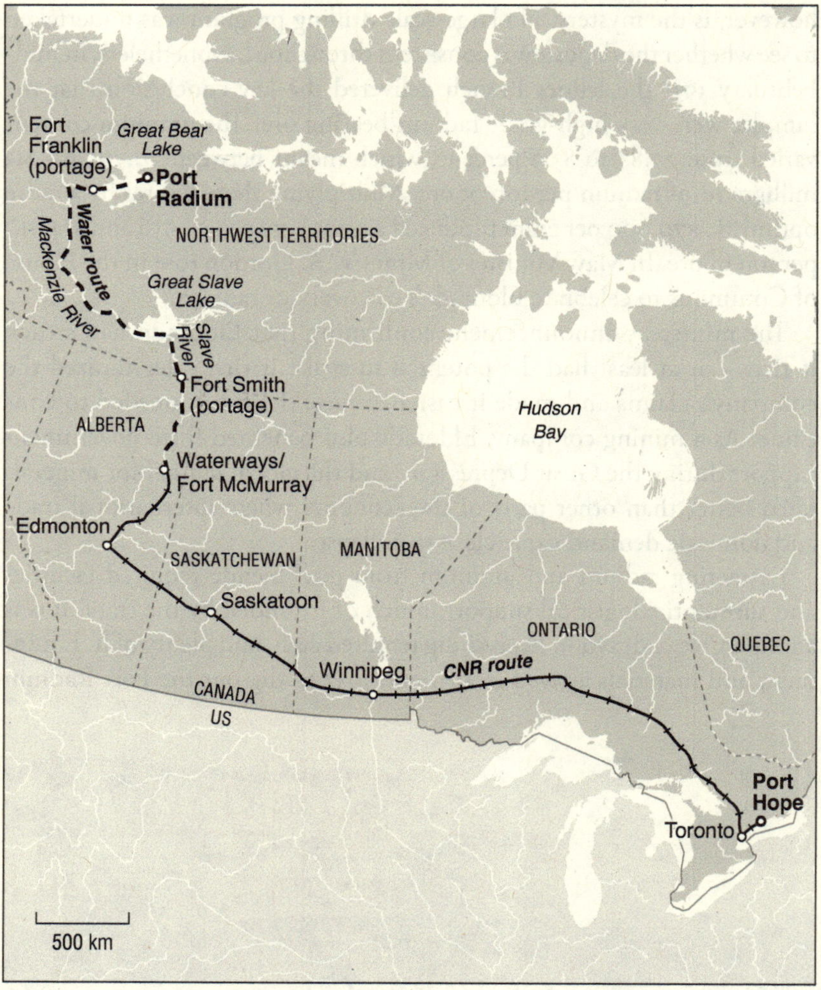

Transportation route | Cartography by Eric Leinberger

Mine, which had to be able to handle 100 tons of ore a day. Eldorado created a modern mining camp – promotionally named "Port Radium" – on Great Bear Lake in the Northwest Territories to provide amenities for more than one hundred men employed at the mine. There were bunkhouses described as "sanitary, comfortable, modern dwellings," along with a recreation hall containing "billiard tables, a library and a tobacco shop."[10]

Getting the ore out of the ground was just a small part of the equation. There was also the monumental task of shipping it south, where it would be milled and refined. From Port Radium, the pitchblende was loaded onto barges and transported across Great Bear Lake to the Mackenzie River, which moved the ore along the vast network of lakes and rivers of the Canadian North. Once the ore reached Waterways, Alberta, now better known as Fort McMurray, it was loaded onto trains using the Northern Alberta Railways line through Edmonton and the Canadian National Railway line across the Canadian Shield, covering vast distances to reach southern Ontario. Finally, the ore arrived at Port Hope, a small town on the shores of Lake Ontario between Toronto and Kingston, where it underwent milling and refining processes to extract uranium and radium. Altogether, the journey was more than 5,000 kilometres.

Show Me the Money

When a prospector had a good reputation and a powerful pitch, the money flowed. The LaBines had both and so investors flocked to help. That Toronto was the financial centre of Canada's mining industry helped, too. The Toronto Stock and Mining Exchange was founded in 1896 and joined the Toronto Stock Exchange in 1934. It did so amid the economic turmoil of the Great Depression and problems within the mining industry. The mining exchange was said to be among the most crooked in the world.[11] Toronto's *Financial Post* regularly issued warnings about the potential for fraud, warnings that were just as regularly ignored. In many respects, the modern regulation of shares and securities is built on the need to protect consumers from such sham opportunities, especially prevalent in the resource sector and particularly in mining.

Like every other mining company, Eldorado sought to raise funds. It did so at a time when two fundamentally different approaches to the regulation of securities markets were hotly debated. One approach emphasized transparency, requiring companies to disclose *all* relevant information to the public in order to give investors everything they needed to make sound investments. Companies could sell anything "provided the truth, and the whole truth, is told about it."[12] The other approach focused on the substance of company securities on offer. A regulator checked the securities and gave them a seal of approval before they were offered to the public. This "blue skies" practice developed in the United States but spread to other jurisdictions, including in Canada. Ontario's market was a hybrid between the two.

The King Edward Hotel in Toronto was the heart of the action for the mining industry. The King Eddy, as it was known, was where everyone went to "pick up tips, snag prospectors, and lure investors." Hector Charlesworth, a shrewd Toronto commentator, would recall that in 1910,

> one could not go into the King Edward Hotel at Toronto without seeing scores of crooks at work trying to separate victims from their money, flashy fellows and big spenders. This was true also of every large hotel in Canada and in every village ... [where] "strong arm" salesmen were at work endeavouring to bamboozle ignorant men and women out of their savings.[13]

News, whether true or false, could raise hopes – and cash. Without regulation, information and markets were easily manipulated. Fortunes were made and lost on mining stocks during this time. And while engineers and insiders knew that mining securities were rife with fraud, plenty of naïve investors did not.

Rampant misinformation and speculation aside, brokers also engaged in suspect stock-selling practices. A particularly common one was "bucketing," whereby a broker did not execute a client's order to buy or sell a security as instructed but instead took the opposite side of the trade for the firm's account. Rather than place the order, the firm effectively bet against the client's position. By not performing the trade immediately, a broker could profit by executing the order when the market went up, having confirmed the order to the customer at the original price. The broker pocketed the difference between the original price and the market price when the share was sold. The consumer was none the wiser.[14] Bucket shops specializing in these types of trades existed throughout North America.

Canada had developed something of a reputation for ignoring mining swindles. They were so common that *The Financial Post* started a new column, "Gold and Dross," to expose them. Between 1904 and 1933, not even one in fifty of the mining companies incorporated in Ontario actually produced anything.[15] Of course, not every mine that failed to go into production was a hustle, but many of them were. Combined with practices like bucketing, the hazards are obvious. So, when the stock market crashed in 1929, many blamed broker misconduct. What to do about it remained the challenge.

This was the environment in which Eldorado tried to raise capital. By 1931, the LaBines had raised enough to have the mine operational and begin construction of the mill. Milling the pitchblende reduced the ore to a uranium concentrate that weighed much less than pitchblende and

The Eldorado refinery in Port Hope, Ontario, where uranium from Port Radium was processed, 1930s | Library and Archives Canada, M-3375914

could be bagged for shipment. The process replicated the one UMHK had developed in the Belgian Congo, but milled ore still required refining. LaBine had to build a refinery from scratch. Like the UMHK's at Olen, the refinery required access to a range of bulky and heavy chemicals, so its location was crucial. It had to be near rail lines, and that meant southern Canada. LaBine fixed on the small Ontario town of Port Hope. He also needed someone with the expertise to build it. Marcel Pochon, a French chemist, was that person.

Marcel Pochon, the Chemist

The search for a chemist almost inevitably involved Madame Curie. Her laboratory and Radium Institute produced a steady stream of intelligent young acolytes, almost all of whom were men. Among them was a chemist named Marcel Pochon. Born in Versailles in 1889, Pochon graduated from the École supérieure de physique et de chimie industrielles de la Ville de Paris (City of Paris Industrial Physics and Chemistry Higher Educational

From left to right: Gilbert LaBine, Marcel Pochon, and Charles LaBine at a gala dinner celebrating the first ounce of radium, November, 1936 | Eldorado Nuclear Limited, Library and Archives Canada, PA-202925

Institution) in 1907, where Marie and Pierre Curie made so many discoveries. Not only did Pochon train with the Curies, but he remained close to Madame Curie following her husband's death. In 1912, he joined the Société Industrielle du Radium, which had been incorporated to refine English-owned radium in Paris. He remained at the firm, whose board of eight was divided equally between English and French members, until the outbreak of war in 1914. By then, the organization had been renamed the Société Française du Radium.

Twenty-four when the war began, Pochon was drafted into the French Army's chemical services. There is no indication that he had anything to do with radioactivity during that time, but he returned to his specialty following the war. He had some difficulty settling down. Still unmarried, he found challenging work in a mine at South Terras, Cornwall, an area of southwestern England known for its mineral deposits, particularly tin. Its importance was such that many terms still used in mining (*stopes,* for example) originated there.

Although other sources of pitchblende were found in the area, South Terras Mine was the most significant.[16] Opened in 1873, the mining operations were originally focused on iron and tin. Soon, uranium was discovered. In the nineteenth century, uranium was used by glass manufacturers, and the mine found a ready market with them.

The amount of radium extracted from South Terras pitchblende was not insignificant. The estimated 36 grams produced from 1912 to 1932 is especially impressive given that the mine was closed for the duration of the First World War. Before 1914, the pitchblende was refined in Paris, either at the Société Française du Radium or Curie's Radium Institute.[17] Once hostilities ceased and the mine reopened, the company faced a quandary: radioactive material could be recovered from the scraps, but it was too low grade to be worth shipping to France for treatment.[18] Enter – or, possibly, re-enter – Marcel Pochon.

Pochon moved to Cornwall to help build and staff a treatment facility at the mine, whether as a subsidiary of Curie's Radium Institute or the Société Française du Radium is unclear.[19] His task seems to have been to make the most of the radium scrap left over from previous efforts. Under his watch, radium was processed into radium bromide and then taken to a treatment facility in St. Austell. Pochon oversaw approximately thirty employees, with ten men working underground and three chemists in the laboratory.

An observer later noted that the refining operations were "not conducted on an amateurish basis" – a compliment, if only a backhanded one. According to another eyewitness, Pochon had "the knowledge and ability to carry out the work," but his method was "very dirty" because he was willing to take risks in handling radium "through the many elaborate processes."[20] The observation seems accurate enough. While pipetting radium, Pochon remarked to a horrified visiting uranium specialist, "It will only kill you if you're afraid of it."[21]

All was not calm at the South Terras Mine during Pochon's tenure. There is some indication of discord, possibly even fraud, though it's unclear whether he was involved. In 1928, the British and General Radium Corporation Ltd. took over the property with an eye to finding more uranium and radium. Despite its name, the company was part of a German syndicate headed by Dr. I. Straus, who was from Switzerland or Germany, depending on accounts.[22] Straus and Pochon did not appear to get along, although the French chemist later claimed to have worked closely and on friendly terms with the German to collect radium. Whatever the case, Straus disappeared in 1929, taking with him radium that MI5 believed to be worth "several thousand pounds." At the request of the Canadians, British intelligence investigated operations at the mine later, during the Second World War, but did not pursue the idea that Pochon had been involved in the incident, and no records of an additional investigation have surfaced. Although the allegations of fraud and theft are impossible to verify, they are plausible. When Straus departed, other employees were dismissed, and part of the plant was sold.[23]

Pochon then continued to refine radium from the ore that had already been brought to the surface, though no additional extraction occurred. In fact, the mine was allowed to flood in 1929 or 1930, probably because the quality of the pitchblende was not thought to be valuable enough to extract.[24] It's difficult to know for certain because the mine's records disappeared following its closure. Later, British intelligence speculated that Pochon must have taken them with him when he, too, left the company, though he could just as easily have destroyed them. Ultimately, South Terras Mine was a minuscule operation, uncompetitive with the Belgians. Nevertheless, the Belgians took an interest, as did their principal sales agent, Boris Pregel.

Pochon spent a dozen years at South Terras Mine and almost certainly met Pregel, who served as a director of British and General Radium. Later conjecture suggested that contact between mine employees and Pregel had occurred through his holding company, Société Anonyme Demetra.[25] Again, the speculation was just that, and no one inquired further. There seemed to be no need.

Throughout his time in England, Pochon kept in touch with Madame Curie and became especially close to her son-in-law, Frédéric Joliot-Curie, who was a research scientist in radioactivity and related fields. Again, we do not know the precise nature of their relationship, but they were close enough that Pochon paid a visit to Joliot-Curie in France shortly before the outbreak of war in 1939.[26] Perhaps through the Curie connection or simply via news about the closure of the South Terras Mine, Marcel Pochon came to the attention of Gilbert LaBine, who invited him to Canada at precisely the right time.[27]

A New Employee

That LaBine happened to be looking for a radium specialist in 1931 was fortuitous. Between the Great Depression and the mine's exhaustion, Pochon was seeking new employment. He later claimed that the insecurity he experienced at this stage affected his attitude to life and work. Whatever his motivation, he came to Canada in January 1932, visiting first Port Hope to talk about difficulties with refining radium ore and then Ottawa to help the Bureau of Mines – which would be renamed as the Mines Branch of the new Department of Mines and Technical Surveys in 1936 – investigate the refining process. Eldorado had much to offer the French scientist, and by March, he had signed a formal employment contract.[28] He returned to his family in England briefly, and then came back to Canada in the spring. His wife and young son joined him in Port Hope several months later.

Pochon's arrangement with Eldorado included a guaranteed annual salary of $10,000, an extraordinary sum in the depths of the Great Depression. What's more, payment would be forthcoming even if Pochon became disabled by radium poisoning. In exchange, Pochon agreed to dedicate himself exclusively to the work of Eldorado unless he received written permission to do otherwise.[29] The fact that LaBine guaranteed Pochon's salary was significant. The risk of radium sickness was real. Radium production involved progressive refinement in which the element was made purer with each turn. The final stage was dangerous, and Pochon was known for taking risks.[30]

Given the early stage of development, Pochon was surprised that the company needed him in Port Hope before 1933. Later, he suspected that he had been asked to come to Canada sooner than was necessary for the simple reason that investors needed to see progress: the company had to be *seen* constructing the facility. Eventually, Pochon was even more cynical, asserting that the refinery had probably been built "in a stock market speculation."[31]

Yet Pochon was not immune to the lure of radium, the price of which made it worth collecting even in scrap amounts. Over time, he had gathered his own collection of scraps or, as he later described it, "second hand" radium from such sources as doctors' estates, clean-ups at the refinery in South Terras, and other small-scale producers.[32] In the process, he had developed a knack for extracting radium from disparate sources. When Pochon moved to Canada, he had already accumulated about 5.5 grams of radium, worth about $302,500 in 1932 (or more than $6 million today), and he brought 2.5 grams of the concentrate with him, leaving the rest in England.[33] Of course, acquiring radium was one thing; marketing and selling it was quite another. That was a specialty practised by only a few, including Pregel. The real value of radium, however, lay in what it could do, as the *Minerals Yearbook* of the day explained: "The value of radium is largely determined not in the ordinary terms of dollars and cents but in terms of human misery saved and human knowledge acquired. From such a viewpoint radium has been invaluable."

Pochon's job involved supervising refining in all phases of production. He had the authority to sign cheques on behalf of the company, which meant he could also dispose of products from the refinery or use the company's facilities and staff for purposes other than those that were in the best interest of Eldorado. However, that is to get ahead of the story. Pochon arrived in Port Hope the same year as the pitchblende he was tasked with refining. Production, which took place in a converted seed warehouse next to the harbour, began in 1933.

As with the LaBine brothers' earlier efforts, Pochon's task was greatly supported by the Canadian government's Bureau of Mines. Branch officials estimated production at the rate of a gram of radium for every 15 tons of ore, and calculated the quantity of chemicals – tons of acid, soda ash, barium chloride, and ammonia – required.[34] At Eldorado, the Port Hope facility had two production circuits, one for uranium and one for radium. Uranium, while not precisely waste, had little use at that time except as a colouring in ceramics. Radium was where the company concentrated its efforts.

The Perils of Price

Later, Pochon claimed to have had doubts about the company's long-term viability from the earliest days. He recalled that in 1934, "It was only a question of time until Eldorado would have to give up for lack of quantity of ore and cheapness of operation." With the price of radium falling, Pochon visited Europe in 1935, believing that "the position of Eldorado was more speculative than ever before."[35] If he did indeed hold such reservations at the time, he kept them to himself, and his position within the company advanced. In August 1938, he became the formal head of refining and operations at Port Hope.

Trusted within the company, Pochon was admired outside, too. He had become one of Port Hope's leading citizens. A routine security report by the Royal Canadian Mounted Police described him as "quite conservative in both his personal life and political views, remaining fixed to the old school of politics." There was "nothing to indicate that he harbours any radical thoughts or is any way disloyal to the country. He undoubtedly comes of good parentage which is reflected in both his business and social life." According to "sources," Pochon was "of high integrity." Most important, he was "probably the only scientist in the world that has the knowledge in his particular field. In other words, he is said to be indispensable."[36]

Gilbert LaBine would have happily agreed. In November 1936, he and his brother were feted along with Pochon, who had just become a nationalized British subject, at a gala dinner in Ottawa hosted by the Department of Mines and the National Research Council to mark Eldorado's production of its first ounce of radium.[37] The three, elegant in white tie and tails, were the very picture of satisfaction and success.

Prime Minister Mackenzie King sat next to Gilbert at the dinner, and later described the event as "one of the most interesting and memorable I have attended," adding, "I felt very proud of Canada, with what our scholars and men of science are doing."[38] Gilbert would have been delighted to be in the company of his dining companions, who included Governor General Lord Tweedsmuir. Leslie Roberts of *Maclean's* waxed lyrical about the ethos surrounding Eldorado's success in the Arctic:

> Six years ago this was barren wilderness ... Now airplanes move on fast, regular schedules. Internal and external wireless communication is almost letter perfect. Mails arrive and depart with promptness and on time. Life is as comfortable and orderly as it is in [southern Canada]. The credit for all of which belongs to Great Bear Lake, the camp which set Northwestern activity in motion and spotlighted the Northwest in the eyes of the mining world.[39]

LaBine did not dwell on the price of radium that had stimulated all this activity. From 1931, when the Great Bear Lake find was made, to 1936, when the first ounce of radium was produced, the price had fallen from $70,000 per gram to just $40,000, an ominous sign of the trouble that lay ahead.[40] LaBine should also have known that UMHK would try to destroy the competitor Eldorado.

3
The Mirage of the Markets

When Eldorado began operations, it had good reason to be hopeful. In the space of three years it had dug an Arctic mine, started a mill on site, and built a radium refinery. There was a world of sales awaiting its product. But Eldorado was not operating in a void. Even before it produced its first gram of radium, word had travelled to Brussels, headquarters of the Union Minière du Haut-Katanga (UMHK), where the reaction was not friendly. Gilbert LaBine wanted to break the UMHK's monopoly in radium, and the UMHK would not relent without a fight.

Over the next six years, Eldorado's profits vanished and stock value plunged as the two companies contended for the radium market. By 1938, the Canadians and Belgians agreed that cooperation was better than competition and formed a cartel that divided the world radium market between them. The commercial war between Eldorado and the UMHK was thus not quite a binary choice, victory or defeat, profit or bankruptcy. Prosperity followed for Eldorado, but only for a year. The Belgians and UMHK had prepared for war; Eldorado had not and faltered once more.

The two companies faced and made a series of choices as war approached. This would shape Eldorado's corporate development and efforts to participate in the global radium market as it sought to compete with the Belgian juggernaut that was the UMHK.

At a luncheon with National Research Council president Dr. C.J. Mackenzie and Lesslie Thomson, special assistant to the powerful Minister of Munitions and Supply C.D. Howe, in 1943, Gilbert LaBine told the story of an ominous visit he had received from Gustave Lechien in 1932. As Mackenzie recorded in his diary after the meal, "Lechien came over to America to see LaBine and told him to keep out of the game as he would break him but LaBine would not be bluffed."[1]

C.J. Mackenzie, president of the National Research Council, 1942 | Library and Archives Canada, PA-104146 ►

◄ C.D. Howe, Canadian minister of munitions and supply, 1942 | Library and Archives Canada, Karsh Collection, Sitting 7876

Lechien must have thought he had an unbeatable argument. UMHK had cash, the world's richest uranium and radium mine, a large radium refinery, and a radium inventory to match. The high price of radium allowed the company to weather market downturns, even at the lowest point of the Great Depression. It had the market strength to be able to do something about anyone who threatened its profits.

Whether Eldorado could really compete with the UMHK depended, in part, on which company had the deeper pockets. LaBine could borrow from banks, but UMHK was in effect its own bank, with the Belgian Société Générale looming behind to support it financially if needed. The company had also been making radium for twelve years, and thus had a vault of unsold supply. That radium could be sold off, and at any price the UMHK chose.

We do not know whether Lechien offered any terms other than surrender in 1932. Dealing with the Americans a decade earlier, he had found a solution that benefited both parties. The Americans had agreed to stop mining and refining and to sell UMHK's products instead because they could make more money doing so. The Canadians, unlike the Americans, were newcomers to the game and didn't have the type of sales organization to facilitate a profitable deal with the UMHK. From Lechien's point of view, the Canadians had nothing to offer. From LaBine's perspective, he had no choice but to compete.

Tackling Competition

Initially, Eldorado did so with some success. Gilbert LaBine moved to improve his company's practices: he brought in Fraser Reid, an engineer, to supervise the construction and operation of a mill at the mine, and he put more money into improving the Port Hope refinery. These actions reassured investors and for a time shored up the company's finances. Eldorado also began to pick off UMHK customers.[2] With competition came declining prices, however, and profit margins shrank from almost unimaginable to excellent. Before long, they were simply good and then merely adequate. But UMHK could lower the price of radium to any level it wished. For LaBine, with his mine a going concern and his mill and refinery underway, surrender was inconceivable.

By 1936, LaBine had reason to think differently. Although Eldorado produced its first gram of radium in 1933, production had been painfully slow. Marcel Pochon urged him to expand the capacity of the refinery. Fraser

Reid pushed him to improve the mine and mill. All this required money, which was duly raised – and spent. But Eldorado's value plummeted as disappointed investors abandoned the company, selling their stock for whatever price it could fetch. LaBine even sold his own stock, which diluted investor holdings and drove down the share price further. From a speculative high of $8 in 1933, shares slipped to just 86 cents in 1934.

LaBine's next step was to hire a publicist, Edgar Laytha, whose task it was to promote the mine's virtues in positive, almost lyrical, terms. There were newsreels at movies, magazine articles, a visit from the governor general and, of course, that banquet in Ottawa in 1936. There were radium sales too, fetching a small profit in 1935 but not nearly enough to justify or cover the cost of the new investment. Part of the problem was the price of radium, which declined steadily.

The problem was the UMHK. The mine at Shinkolobwe produced a steady supply of ore, which was refined at Olen and translated into a growing inventory of unsold radium. The UMHK could, and did, flood the radium market, in turn lowering global prices. In Africa, the UMHK repeatedly shut down its mine, while tons of ore – more than 2,500 by 1938 – sat in storage or on the docks. Radium prices continued to fall, slowly approaching the actual cost of production. In 1934, a gram cost $50,000. By the end of 1936, it was $30,000. Two years later, it was $25,000. In the depths of the Depression, the price was still too high for many, but it was better than it had been. Alas, what was good for consumers was terrible for Eldorado. The company needed a miracle, or better still a miracle worker.

Writing in 1939, Edgar Laytha chronicled what was happening in the spring of 1936: "At this dark hour, a hand was reached out to [LaBine] from Chicago. The dynamic personality of the oil magnate Harry Snyder flung its shadow over Eldorado's mines and markets."[3] Who was Harry Snyder, and why did he take an interest in Eldorado?

Harry Snyder, the Financier

Born in 1882 to what he described as an old Virginia family, Harry Snyder enjoyed few of the advantages that background might conjure. He went to work at thirteen in a coal mine when his father's business failed.[4] His father loved hunting and the outdoors and took a hardworking approach to business. Harry absorbed that legacy in full, but also possessed an intangible quality that made him a success in business. He seems to have

Harry Snyder at Eldorado Mine, Great Bear Lake, 1937 | W. Leigh Brintnell, LAC, PA-102766

been charismatic enough to draw people to his endeavours, whether insurance sales, ranching and big game hunting, or mining and oil. Through financial ups and downs, Snyder always seemed to land on his feet – the sign of an adept speculator.[5]

He also ensured that his exploits in business, hunting, or exploration received ample publicity. Some of his stories were bizarre, some literally incredible. Contrary to the claim in his obituary, he was not a "retired Canadian army colonel."[6] He had in fact never served in war, and the military title was an honorific said to have been bestowed by the Black Watch Regiment in Montreal. Even this was not quite accurate; he was an honorary colonel of the Prince Edward Island Highlanders, who wear Black Watch tartan.[7] No one seems to have noticed, or cared.

We would now describe Harry Snyder as something of a corporate fixer, or management consultant in more restrained terms. Like Boris Pregel and Gilbert LaBine, much of the available information about Snyder comes from what he told reporters and columnists himself. The tales are plentiful, if difficult to verify; we know that he operated mainly in the American

Midwest, and that those operations made him rich. How, then, did he find his way to Canada and the radium mines of Eldorado?

Snyder developed ties to the country through his business ventures and love of the outdoors.[8] In 1932, he incorporated Champlain Oil, which was involved in all aspects of the petroleum business, from the handling of crude oil and gasoline to automotive servicing, including towing and repairs. At one time, the company operated or supplied almost five hundred service stations and outlets in Quebec and eastern Ontario. One of his associates, Joseph-Charles-Émile Trudeau, is memorable as the father of a later Canadian prime minister, Pierre Elliott Trudeau, and grandfather of another, Justin. "Charley" Trudeau sold his thirty Montreal-area gas stations to Champlain for $1 million and stayed on to run the business as part of the deal.

Snyder was a notable businessman, but he was better known for his recreational activities, especially hunting. Hunting took him to the Canadian North, with attendant publicity. He liked to describe himself as "the dean" of North American big game hunters.[9] He developed a particular interest in the musk ox: a large, hairy relative of the sheep that is native to the Canadian Arctic. Musk oxen were found in the North, Eldorado was in the North, Eldorado needed oil among other things, and Snyder knew about oil. One thing led to another.

Snyder's other specialty was raising capital. Eldorado needed capital, more than LaBine could manage. The two men negotiated terms that essentially put the financial side of Eldorado in Snyder's hands. Snyder may have had another motive. As the owner of Champlain Oil, he became the largest customer of the Imperial Oil Company, which was the Canadian subsidiary of the Standard Oil Company from New Jersey. Snyder later said that Standard Oil had asked him to invest in Eldorado because the Canadian mining company used the US oil company for its operations and the bills had not been paid.[10]

Whatever the reason, capital arrived in 1936, and so did Snyder as the company's new treasurer. It seems to have been a natural division of labour. LaBine had created Eldorado, but he found managing it tedious and the international environment baffling. He understood very well that he lacked the funds to improve the mine and the mill. He needed help and hit it off with Snyder. Snyder's interest in oil extended beyond ownership of Champlain Oil to a newly discovered oil field in the Canadian North, and Eldorado needed oil for its operations. Given the global price and purpose of radium, working with Eldorado seemed like a smart investment. LaBine had been telling investors that the recent decline in global radium prices signalled Eldorado was on to something: its entry into the market was making radium more affordable for medical treatments. The value of ore reserves was $10 million, but the price of expansion was likely to cost less than half that amount.

Shareholders at the 1936 annual meeting were asked to approve an increase in Eldorado's share capital to a total offering of four million shares. The proposal threw a lifeline to investors: 600,000 shares would be sold at 95 cents a share, and current shareholders would be allowed to buy an additional 300,000 shares at a ratio of one new share for every ten shares they already owned. Snyder, using his corporate persona, "Harry Snyder Ltd.," underwrote the latter, having agreed to purchase any outstanding shares for 95 cents. Once shareholders approved the new financing arrangement, they elected Harry Snyder to the board.

Existing shareholders may have supported the arrangement to inject new capital into Eldorado, but they did not open their wallets. In the fall of 1936, Snyder, as underwriter, purchased 247,231 shares of the 300,000 offered to existing shareholders, explaining to journalists, "I am a borrower and not a lender."[11]

Under the arrangement, the LaBine brothers retained a plurality of shares but not a majority. Gilbert remained president, but Snyder seems to have run the operation. He brought in two very well-known Detroit businessmen to sit on the board, Irving Babcock and Charles Bohn, who were prominent in the automotive and aviation industries. Sitting with Snyder around the board table, they more than likely got their way.

Carl French, Secretary to the Treasurer

When Snyder became Eldorado's treasurer, he decided he needed someone familiar and reliable to help run operations. The person he had in mind was his own secretary from Chicago, Carl B. French, who joined Eldorado's staff in early 1937. Before long, French came to dominate the way Eldorado operated as a company and thus to shape the market not just for radium but for uranium. Given his role in this story, and the eventual fraud charges arising from his negotiations to supply uranium to the Manhattan Project, we pause to consider his characteristics and his background.

The term *secretary* has shifted meaning over time. In the 1930s, private secretaries were frequently male, often well educated, sometimes professional. That was true of Carl French. Harry Snyder, who lived in Montreal, needed somebody trustworthy to sit in Eldorado's office in Toronto and keep an eye on things while he was elsewhere.[12]

A yearbook photo of Carl French from his time at Northwestern University, 1927 | Courtesy Northwestern University Archives

Born in Burlington, Michigan, in 1902 and raised in nearby Battle Creek, French told people he had been called to the bar of Illinois in 1935 and practised law for two years before arriving at Eldorado. Records of the Attorney Registration and Disciplinary Commission of the Supreme Court of Illinois indicate that in fact he never practised.[13] To the contrary, the Royal Canadian Mounted Police reported that French had worked in the auditing department of the *Chicago Daily News* for the seven years prior to coming to Canada in January 1937.[14] Since no documents support his claim, it may have been based on French's say-so. The public record is also ambiguous about where French attended law school. Although his obituary and some other accounts place his legal education at Northwestern

University School of Law, institutional records show he attended Chicago-Kent College of Law. Both are in Chicago, but the former is, and was, significantly more prestigious than the other.[15]

French's undergraduate years, however, were spent at Northwestern. When asked about his record there, university officials returned with the comment that they had seldom seen anything like it. To say that young French was involved is an understatement.[16] He seems to have participated in everything but athletics, from student government and fraternities to social clubs.[17] A deeply social person, French helped plan the junior class prom and served as the Circus Solly: the coveted role of chief organizer and grand marshal of the university's annual fundraising circus, which "brought the university's community together with socialites from Chicago and the North Shore."[18] Amid the flurry of social activities, French met his future wife, Ruth Maretta Arnold. Later, Arnold described him as "very dignified, yet relaxed," with a keen sense of humour: "He was a very gentle man, and always did everything right."[19]

How French found Snyder and what he actually did for the Chicago financier is something of a mystery. What is clear is that he arrived at Eldorado to work in a junior accounting position and rose through the ranks quickly. As the assistant treasurer to Snyder, he also received cheque-signing authority. His salary increased dramatically, especially in the context of the Great Depression, from $3,000 annually in January 1937 to $4,200 by April 1938. In mid-May 1938, he was made secretary to the board while retaining his position as assistant treasurer, becoming increasingly central to the operations of the company. That summer, the board approved the recommendation to have French "receive all correspondence addressed to the company, to distribute the same to the proper departments and to require monthly reports from all departments."[20] That is, nothing came into Eldorado without French knowing about it. LaBine later explained that he "trusted French implicitly and gave him his whole confidence."[21]

When French joined Eldorado, he also maintained an interest in the Insurance Appraisal and Rating Agency Inc. The Chicago-based company may have had ties to Snyder, who also had insurance interests in the Windy City. In any event, French set up an agency branch in Toronto, which he operated from his desk at Eldorado. It was a tidy arrangement, as Eldorado was the agency's principal source of Canadian income. From when French joined the company in 1937, he earned substantial commissions on insurance policies that Eldorado placed with Insurance Appraisal and Rating.[22] In other words, French essentially negotiated with himself to earn the fee.

A Cartel Is Born

The arrival of Carl French coincided with Eldorado's record production year. Just under 24 grams of radium was an impressive output but, as it turned out, not impressive enough.[23] By 1937, radium sold for anywhere from $22,000 to $30,000 per gram, and by 1938 the price had plunged to just $6,000–7,000.[24]

It was time to change direction. On a corporate board of no more than five members, three had extensive experience in companies already engaged in vertical integration and they would have been hardwired to look for synergies and opportunities. In early 1937, the board sent Snyder to Europe to determine whether it was possible to stabilize the price of radium and uranium. His own money, and that of his investors, was at risk.

First, Snyder visited Eldorado's British agent, J. Hodson & Company, in London. The firm, retained on the advice of Marcel Pochon, had plenty of experience marketing radium, having served as the UMHK's agent for years. Next, Snyder went to Brussels to speak with the UMHK directly. Whether the reception was cordial or not we cannot say, but the Belgians received him and gave him a tour of their facilities. The visit transformed the relationship between the two companies. It was then that Snyder must have grasped the disproportion between Eldorado and UMHK: the latter had produced 664 grams in 1937 and had 180 grams *in reserve*.[25] Eldorado's record total output of 24 grams was a drop in the global bucket.

Snyder and the rest of the Eldorado board must have concluded that competition with UMHK was futile. And so, beginning in the fall of 1937 and continuing for the next ten months, discussions between the two companies took place in Paris. The talks reportedly included some of the most senior corporate actors. At various times, Gustave Lechien and Edgar Sengier were in the same room as Gilbert LaBine, Harry Snyder, John D. Leitch, and J.H. (Jack) Greenberg. Leitch was a technical adviser to Eldorado and also its sales agent, while Greenberg was its lawyer. Lechien was undoubtedly the lead on the UMHK side, with Sengier hovering in the background. Boris Pregel was also said to be in the room, acting on behalf of UMHK.[26] Pregel later claimed the credit for making the deal happen. Like many of his stories, this may be true but there is no documentary proof. He certainly knew what was going on, and the Canadians knew of him, his accomplishments, and his legend.

When Snyder updated LaBine in spring 1938, he was forthright. Eldorado had two possible fates. First, the Belgians were willing to lowball the Canadian company in order to win business and starve Eldorado of cash. UMHK was prepared to sell radium at less than $10,000 per gram on all new business or lease it at just 4 percent of the sale price. The alternative was far more appealing: "Arrive at a convention with us on a price fixing plan" but "retain our own sales organisation and independence."[27]

The arrangement paralleled the spirit but not the form of UMHK's agreements with the Americans in the early 1920s. Now, the companies formed a uranium and radium cartel that divided the global market, setting prices and sharing the profits. Then, as now, cartels were illegal. As the clouds of war gathered in Europe, however, the attitude may have been different. In fact, the discussions may have been an open secret; there are suggestions the governments of the United Kingdom, Canada, and Belgium all knew about the cartel, which was backed by the Bank of England and La Banque Nationale de Belgique, in which Sengier was a large stockholder. King Leopold III of Belgium also had a significant financial interest in the UMHK.[28] The Belgians obviously felt no embarrassment about the cartel. Its conclusion was publicly announced in November 1938.[29]

Snyder – not LaBine – reported victory to the Eldorado board. When he presented the agreement, he attached a cover note explaining his blunt rationale:

> I am pleased to report that my negotiations with the Union Minière Du [sic] Haut Katanga extending over a period of ten months have culminated successfully. For some time I have realized the necessity for a convention which would remove all bad feelings and provide for complete co-operation in promoting uses for the company's product, increasing sales, furthering research and joint advertising, etc. The facts recently ascertained by me in England confirmed and strengthened my views of the necessity of such a convention.[30]

Subject to board confirmation, Eldorado and the Belgians had an agreement.[31] So what was the big deal?

Cartels, as the economist Adam Smith famously wrote, are conspiracies against the public. Companies collude to allocate customers, limit supply, raise prices, or some combination of the three. When competitors agree to fix prices or otherwise limit the extent to which they compete with other producers, they can charge more than in a notionally free market. For the purposes of regulating economic activity, the stockholders of several companies can transfer their shares to a single trust governed by a set of trustees.

Stockholders share the consolidated earnings of the jointly managed companies. A trust, then, is a combination of companies, an idea that has lent its name to antitrust statutes. In Canada and the United States, legislation forbade the practice as early as 1889, and the *Sherman Antitrust Act* became embedded in the American popular imagination from 1890.[32]

In Canada, by contrast, antitrust enforcement was always a challenge. The law enforcement and legal system did not have the staff or resources to investigate and prosecute anti-competitive behaviour, market manipulation, and price fixing. Additionally, federalism guaranteed decades of litigation over which level of government had the constitutional authority to regulate businesses and their profits. The Canadian antitrust regime was thus best described as weak, especially compared to the United States, and it was not until the 1930s that the courts finally settled the scope of federal authority after the introduction of legislation following the recommendations of a well-publicized royal commission on prices.[33] The Judicial Committee of the Privy Council in London, Canada's final court of appeal, made clear in late January 1937 that the federal government had the authority to prosecute cartels. The case was frontpage news, even if investigations and prosecutions were few and far between in practice.[34]

This is the context in which the directors at Eldorado contemplated forming a cartel with UMHK, an arrangement they promptly approved. Eldorado and UMHK now controlled every aspect of the production and sale of radium and uranium.[35] The agreement set quotas and minimum prices through a clearing house in Brussels. The "association," as the cartel was described, would be responsible for everything from managing accounts to coordinating research and advertising designed to promote the sale and use of both minerals. Transparency between the two companies was key, so much so that each agreed to have its accounts verified by chartered accountants and then shared with the other, along with all correspondence on the subject. The two companies pledged "not to sell any ore or raw material without the agreement of the other party."

The agreement also sought to avoid duties:

> Should any custom duties be imposed in any country, the Associates will arrange the distribution of their supplies in such particular country in such a way that they will avoid as much as possible the payment of duties for the mutual benefit of the Associates, but it is understood that as a general rule each Associate keeps the right to supply his quota in any given country if he wishes to do so.

Finally, contingency plans were made. The companies agreed to consult one another if circumstances changed for sales or even bids. More significantly, all disputes would be resolved through arbitration, which had the advantage of being private, unlike civil disputes, which would be subject to open courts – and records.[36]

Radium Sales and Loans

The agreement fixed the price of radium at $20 per milligram (in other words, $20,000 per gram) for large but unspecified quantities to be used in "bombs" (that is, for cancer treatment), and at $25, $30, and $35 per milligram for "general purposes, especially medical uses, and according to conditions." All other sale contexts would be discussed case by case. Industrial use, for example, would be "decided upon, by both parties, according to its merits and conditions that have prevailed so far." That meant radium for pharmaceutical uses would be invoiced at $20 per milligram, but radium for luminous compounds or radiography would fetch $25 per milligram.

The two former competitors thus divvied up the market for radium, with Eldorado taking 40 percent and UMHK 60 percent on the first 75 grams of radium sold annually. Any sales exceeding that threshold would be divided equally. They also set commissions for their respective agents. In the United States, the UMHK was still represented by the Radium Chemical Company (a subsidiary of Standard Chemical), which earned 7.5 percent in commissions, while the Eldorado Radium Company represented Eldorado and earned 2.5 percent. In the United Kingdom, Eldorado agent Mr. J. Hodson earned 3 percent. At the same time, Boris Pregel's company, Société Anonyme Demetra, was added to the commission structure, with payment in kind rather than cash. Both companies agreed to pay Demetra a commission in radium valued at 5 percent of UK transactions and 10 percent of business in other countries where there was an agency. In turn, Demetra agreed to use the association to sell any of the radium it could not sell on its own for the same average price that the association received.

Additionally, the agreement covered all radium loans and rentals outside Canada and Belgium. In 1938, UMHK had more than 90 grams on loan worldwide. Eldorado agreed to contribute 40 percent of that amount by the end of 1939, giving the company a 40 percent stake in this side of the business. If its contribution fell short, then Eldorado would receive a share of the rental income equivalent to the percentage of its contribution. Loans and rentals for domestic use in Canada and Belgium were outside the agreement, and each company retained the right to donate radium in its own country without having to account for it to the association, provided it was not re-leased, re-sold, or removed from the country. The carve-out for loans and rentals was a big exception; otherwise, all sales, even those in Canada or Belgium, were subject to the cartel arrangement.

The Uranium Arrangement

UMHK agreed to work with its existing English agents, the Brandhurst Company and Mr. Hodson, for uranium sales. Eldorado made similar arrangements in the United States to work with its current agent, Dupont Company, and offered to commit to the same arrangement with agents Harshaw Chemical and B.F. Drakenfeld in the future. As with radium, all sales and accounts were to pass through a clearing house in Brussels.

The two companies divided the market for uranium at 40 percent for Eldorado and 60 percent for UMHK, as they did for radium. Because UMHK already had an arrangement with the Czech government to use the clearing house to sell uranium at fixed prices in continental Europe, the agreement also included the Czechs, who received 45 percent of the UMHK share. Recognizing some uncertainty in the uranium market, the agreement also provided that "the situation will be studied to preserve the position of our mutual agents." This may be the reason for a significant difference in the duration of the radium and uranium agreements. The arrangement for radium ran for three years and was renewable annually thereafter, whereas the one governing uranium was subject to annual renewal from the outset. It was here that Pregel stood to gain the most.

Future earnings were also tied proportionately to past sales. It's tricky to parse the precise terms of the cartel agreement, but it appears to suggest that Eldorado was already producing 40 percent of the world's uranium in 1937 and agreed to contribute the same proportion to the association in 1938. If Eldorado exceeded the 1937 level, it would be entitled to 50 percent of the proceeds the following year.

The Impact of the Cartel

How much the cartel agreement influenced the price of radium is unclear. As noted, the Belgians entered the negotiations with a sizable stockpile of radium. In 1937, Eldorado was selling radium for $21,000 per gram, while Radium Belge, the marketing arm of UMHK, had reduced its price to just $7,000, which was lower than Eldorado's costs of production.[37] Without the cushion of the cartel agreement, the Canadian company would have been crushed.

For a time, the cartel appears to have done precisely what it was supposed to do: boost prices. In 1938, radium rose to $20,000–$35,000 a gram, bringing a record $338,717 in profits for Eldorado.[38] But the good times were short-lived. War in Europe interrupted the radium market, and by 1939 profits had fallen to an unsustainable $153,947.[39] The Belgians withdrew from uranium mining in Africa and suspended production in Katanga, allowing the Shinkolobwe Mine to flood. Eldorado took similar steps in June 1940, more or less abandoning its mine. Both companies still had stockpiles of radium or uranium, milled pitchblende, and raw ore, but not enough to fulfill the obligations of the cartel agreement or to reap its full benefits.

Around the same time, Jewish scientists began to flee Europe en masse. Boris Pregel also made plans. He travelled to New York on 1 May 1939, ready to set down some roots to provide a soft landing if he needed to leave the continent for good. It was a brief visit, but he found an apartment and opened a bank account before returning to Paris to see what the autumn would bring.

4
The Race to Build a Bomb

The onset of the Second World War transformed the importance of pitchblende, radium, and uranium, and with it, the significance of Eldorado and the Union Minière du Haut-Katanga (UMHK). While the latter made contingency plans for war, the former did not. Despite these different approaches, the two companies and the people related to them remained inextricably connected thanks to the global conflict, as those early days reveal.

THE PURSUIT OF the atomic bomb began with a meeting about uranium in Brussels. On 8 May 1939, Frédéric Joliot-Curie paid a visit to Edgar Sengier at his office. Joliot-Curie was Madame Curie's son-in-law. Like her, he had collected a Nobel Prize in chemistry, shared with his wife, Irène Joliot-Curie, and he had succeeded Madame Curie as director of the Radium Institute. In 1939, he was a professor at the Collège de France, working on nuclear fission. Quickly, he got to the point: a nuclear chain reaction was possible, and the energy it produced could be released in a bomb. Uranium was essential for his project: Would Sengier give him some?

Sengier would – and more: he would contribute money. According to the very well informed historians of UMHK, Sengier was keenly interested in the project because up to that point uranium was a mere by-product of radium and its market had shown little growth.[1] Nothing is known of Sengier's feelings about building a bomb, or any worries he might have expressed about the international situation, which was grim and about to become grimmer in the spring of 1939. Against that background, Joliot-Curie and Sengier reached an agreement in principle. With the uranium and the money, Joliot-Curie would build his bomb in the remote Sahara desert in Algeria, a French possession. Later in the month, the two men met once more to discuss the plan.

By coincidence, Sengier then received a summons to London via Lord Stonehaven, who was a director on the board of UMHK.[2] Sir Henry Tizard, the British government's chief scientific adviser, wanted to meet to discuss uranium. With Tizard at the meeting was General Sir Hastings Ismay, secretary of the Committee of Imperial Defence, which handled strategic military questions. In May 1939, that meant preparing for war with Germany.

With the benefit of hindsight, the meeting might seem to have been urgent. In fact, it was inconclusive. Tizard was cautious. He thought the development of an atomic bomb was more possible than before but did not believe it was imminent for either the British or the Germans. The British wanted information about UMHK's uranium stocks. Sengier told them the company had some on hand in England and some in Belgium. Most of the stocks, however, were raw, unrefined, and still in Africa. If the British wanted more, the Olen refinery would have to gear up to produce it, and it went without saying that somebody would have to pay. Sengier promised to consider shipping the company's uranium across the English Channel to the British, and he agreed to report any unusual sales of the substance – "unusual" meaning a sale to Germany. He also told Tizard about the 300 tons of "uranium residues" – probably unrefined waste left over from radium production – that he had shipped to the United States.[3]

In 1939, Sengier doubtless saw Belgium's interest and his own, as a patriotic Belgian, as symbiotic with Britain's. The German occupation of his country between 1914 and 1918 had scarred him, as it did most Belgians. A powerful Germany was always a danger to Belgium. With Adolf Hitler at the helm, it was an existential menace to any small European country. For its part, the British government also adjudged Germany as a mortal danger, remembering that German science and industry had produced the poison gas that killed so many British soldiers in Belgium during the First World War. By 1939, the Luftwaffe had more than 1,200 bomber aircraft ready to drop thousands of bombs that could devastate cities and ruin economies.

When Pierre Curie accepted his Nobel Prize in 1903, he said that radioactivity could produce unbounded energy. He knew it could be used not only for good but also for ill. As early as 1932, scientists had predicted that uranium could produce an incalculably large explosion of energy. Novelists also took up the theme, conjuring up a future atomic war. Pundits, including a then out-of-favour Winston Churchill, pronounced on the possibility in magazine articles, books, and speeches.[4] Exciting fiction was one thing, but this was real. Worse, scientists in Germany knew it, too.[5]

Sengier returned to Paris once more to meet with Joliot-Curie, this time with Gustave Lechien in tow. This conversation was more precise than their previous one in Brussels, and unlike the discussion with the British, it produced concrete results. The UMHK delivered 5 tons of black oxide (UO_2) to Joliot-Curie's laboratory in Paris.[6] Progress was slow as Joliot-Curie and his associates then considered how best to produce the chain reaction for a bomb. Before they could decide, Germany invaded Poland on 1 September. Two days later, Britain and France declared war on Germany.

Belgium remained formally neutral and hoped for the best, but not all Belgians toed this line in thought or in deed. Sengier did not act as if he thought Belgium would be neutral for very long.

A Reversal of Fortunes

The Canadian government took no interest in the possibilities of an atomic weapon. The head of the National Research Council, Dr. C.J. Mackenzie, kept abreast of revelations about atomic fission, and authorized one of his scientists to work in the area. The limitations of budget and personnel hobbled his work, but at least there was no shortage of uranium. Eldorado, like the UMHK, was happy to dispose of it to anyone who would buy it.

Having stabilized production, the cartel seemed to promise a happy and predictable future. It was business as usual in Eldorado's offices, and thus its focus remained radium. In October 1938, shortly after Eldorado had approved the cartel agreement, the smallest of the three companies involved, the St. Joachimsthal mine in Czechoslovakia, fell under German control, but its production was so low that it made little difference. Despite the war, the cartel continued to function through its clearinghouse in Brussels. Belgium was neutral and could trade with any country on either side; Canada was not, but Gilbert LaBine issued no special instructions.

It didn't take long for radium sales to hit the radar of the British Ministry of Economic Warfare (MEW). One of the UMHK's customers was of particular interest: Germany. The Germans duly paid, the money went to the clearing house in Brussels, and Eldorado received 40 percent of the profits. Eldorado had thus profited from trading with the enemy even if it had not made the sale itself. The British soon learned of it, but the sum was small, Eldorado was clearly not the driving force in the trade, and the UMHK was more important to the UK government as a friend in the business of supplying copper than as a blacklisted enemy supplier. During an investigation into the matter, the name Boris Pregel came up. The investigation went no further but his name remained on file with the MEW.[7]

The Gathering Storm

Boris Pregel could read the international situation as well as anyone. Hitler moved from one triumph to the next, facing down the British and French at Munich in September 1938, dissolving democratic Czechoslovakia, and establishing the German-occupied Protectorate of Bohemia and Moravia in March 1939 from what was left. Spirits in France plunged as doubts that the country could hold out against German aggression were openly and widely expressed. At some point in the winter of 1939, Pregel and his wife, Alexandra, called at the American embassy in Paris and applied to immigrate to the United States. With visas in hand, the Pregels arrived in New York aboard the SS *Normandie* on 1 May 1939, seeking residence and, eventually, citizenship.

Boris brought with him a letter of credit from his Zurich bankers that produced a startled and warm reception from the local bank. There is good reason to believe that the letter was for a million dollars, and conceivably more. The New York bankers later admitted they had never seen such a letter before, and it guaranteed generous treatment. Pregel could be a player in whatever business he chose.[8]

He had every reason to leave France. Despite his many years of residence there, his charitable activities, his membership in elite clubs, his admittance to the Légion d'honneur, and his lucrative business activities, he struggled to gain acceptance. It took until 1939 for him to secure citizenship, for example, the same year he was promoted to a higher grade in the Légion. In the polarized world of French politics, he may have been on the wrong side or offended influential people. Anti-Semitism may also have been a factor. French intelligence seems to have viewed Pregel sceptically, claiming that he had communist connections, but that ludicrous charge – surely evidence of partisanship or bigotry – reflects badly on the officials who made it.[9]

When Boris set out for New York, he had no intention of leaving France permanently, nor, it would seem, until he had to. The 1939 trip was to prepare for a soft landing when the time came. As well as opening a bank account, he rented an apartment across from Central Park. Arrangements made, the Pregels returned to France for the summer. In September, war broke out. By the beginning of 1940, Boris was serving as the director of radioactive matters for national defence under the supervision of Minister of Armaments Raoul Dautry, a position he held until France fell in June 1940.[10] An engineer by training, Dautry was interested in radioactivity – luminous dials were an important piece of military equipment – but he was also knowledgeable about and interested in the explosive experiments that Joliot-Curie and his scientists were proposing.[11]

With Pregel back in France, Sengier and Lechien meanwhile were sailing to New York from Genoa in still-neutral Italy, arriving separately in New York in October 1939. They returned briefly to Belgium in the fall – again on separate itineraries – but by January 1940 they were back in New York, along with several of UMHK's senior officials. (Although Sengier remained in the United States until the autumn of 1944, Lechien stayed only until December 1941, when he moved to Central America.) Together, they were in the United States to look after the interests of the UMHK, which had shipped its entire 120-gram stock of radium from Belgium, some of it going to England and the rest to New York along with what Sengier called "certaines quantités" of uranium ore. He was referring to 600 tons of ore containing a high grade of uranium oxide (U_3O_8).[12] The stocks were a bet on the future.

Sengier and Lechien already had a corporate home waiting for them in the United States. African Metals Corporation, also known as Afrimet, had been incorporated in New York in 1926. The company was a fully owned subsidiary of UMHK and handled all non-radium sales in the United States for the Belgian parent.[13] For years, Lechien had visited the United States annually to supervise radium sales. They also established a new company, Central Trading Corporation, said to be responsible for handling marketing. In fact, by spring 1940, Central Trading had the 600 tons of ore sitting in a warehouse in Staten Island.

Flight from Paris

Time was up for Boris on 10 May 1940, when the Germans attacked Belgium, Luxembourg, the Netherlands, and France.[14] Within a week,

German tanks broke through the French lines, reaching the English Channel on May 20th and cutting the main Allied armies off from Paris. It was a stunning defeat for the Allies, and it proved to be decisive. The German Army marched into Paris on June 14th.

Thousands fled Paris before the Germans arrived, travelling by train, by car, and on foot. Boris and Alexandra Pregel travelled in one car, while his mother, Rachel, and two sisters, Klara and Sophia, went in another. His fifteen-year-old daughter, Hélène, went to live with her maternal grandfather, Jules, in the south of France. Later, she found refuge in Switzerland, perhaps helped by her father's Swiss business connections.[15]

A leader in Jewish philanthropy and active in Zionist causes, Boris Pregel's activities had been recorded in Jewish newspapers and other media. His activities were noticeable, and foreign-born Jews were particularly vulnerable to persecution. Boris and Hélène were both eventually denaturalized, and it is almost certain that the whole family would have been deported to the German concentration camps in Poland had they stayed.

What property the Pregels left behind was confiscated. The Nazis took a particular interest in Alexandra's work. A notable painter, she had maintained a studio in Paris, and its contents were seized. More than three hundred of her paintings were automatically destroyed as the products of a Jewish artist.[16]

Getting out of Paris was one thing. Returning to North America was another. As France collapsed around them, Boris and Alexandra drove south from Brittany to Bordeaux, where the French government had relocated and had been replaced on June 17th by a group of far-right politicians led by Marshal Philippe Pétain, who led the French surrender to the Germans on June 22nd.

The Pregels chose the most obvious alternative route for escape: across the frontier to Spain and into Portugal. Spain's government was sympathetic to Germany but did not expressly support Hitler against Britain and the United States.[17] Those with Spanish visas could cross the border and proceed onward. Eventually, Boris and Alexandra reached Lisbon, where they secured passage on the Pan American *Yankee Clipper,* a luxurious small airplane that took them across the Atlantic, flying from Lisbon to the Azores and then on to Bermuda before landing in New York on July 29th. They were promptly detained at an immigration holding tank on Ellis Island, on suspicion of irregular visas, but were released the next day because the visas they had been issued in 1939 were still valid.[18] They returned to their apartment at 1 West 67th Street in Manhattan, overlooking Central Park. In their luggage was more than half a gram of radium.[19]

After the Fall of France

The fall of France in the spring of 1940 raised the serious possibility that Nazi Germany was unstoppable. Even the English Channel might not halt the onslaught, thanks to the Luftwaffe and regular air raids on London and other British cities, while U-boats cut British supply lines in the Atlantic. No one doubted that the Germans would win if they succeeded in landing their army in Britain. And lurking in the background was the military application of German science and technology. Experiments in Berlin in 1938 demonstrated that nuclear fission was possible using uranium. As we have seen previously, experiments in Paris showed the same thing.

By 1938, Italy's fascist government under Benito Mussolini had rallied to the German cause. Enrico Fermi, an Italian and the 1938 Nobel Prize–winner in physics, was married to a Jew. Having seen the enactment of anti-Semitic laws in Italy, he moved his family to the United States after collecting his prize in Stockholm. Arriving in January 1939, Fermi soon joined Columbia University, where he continued to experiment with fission using 200 kilograms of ceramic-grade uranium (U_3O_8) from Eldorado.[20] In fact, there was even more uranium close by. Sengier had already sent 450 of the 600 tons stored in New York to Port Hope to be refined. The quantity was entered in Eldorado's books, but nobody seems to have noticed or drawn any conclusions.[21]

Unlike the UMHK, Eldorado was not a deliberate or knowing participant in the atomic age. Nor were the governments of Canada and Belgium the wiser. The Canadian government thought of Eldorado as a radium company. Belgian government officials thought the same about the UMHK.

The US government was better informed but neutral, at least formally. In October 1939, President Franklin Delano Roosevelt received a letter from Leo Szilard, a German-born physicist newly arrived from England, and other physicists including Albert Einstein, then the world's most famous scientist. They warned that Germany might build a fission bomb out of uranium and urged the United States to beat it to the punch, noting Canada's uranium deposits.

The plea was ignored until France collapsed. Then, the US administration took steps to prop up the British and mobilize American resources for a war Roosevelt was almost certain would soon involve Americans. In June 1940, the National Defense Research Committee was created, which then established the Uranium Committee. In the committee's mandate, much thought was given to what would become known as atomic science. Much less thought was given to uranium itself, where to find it, where to get it, or how much to pay for it.

Eldorado took no part in any of this. Unlike Sengier, Gilbert LaBine was not interested in science or high politics. If a physics laboratory at New York University wanted to buy his uranium, that was just desperately needed business, for in 1940 his company was in financial trouble.

The UMHK did not face the same hardship, thanks to Sengier's strong management style and his decisive move to transfer its centre of operations to New York in the fall of 1939. The company was also buoyed by its supply of multiple minerals, especially copper. As far as radium and uranium were concerned, Sengier continued to rely on Lechien, his trusted associate. It was Lechien who met with the Americans on 21 June 1940.

These supposed representatives of the US government were not civil servants or military personnel but university physicists working part time for the administration. With that status came a very limited mandate. But they were motivated, worried the surrender of Belgium and France would extend German control to Africa, the Belgian Congo, and the Shinkolobwe Mine. The American physicists had already bought limited quantities of uranium ore from the UMHK, which Sengier had sent to Eldorado's Port Hope facility to refine. Now, they wanted more as insurance in case the Germans took over the mine, cut off supplies, or worse, took it for themselves.

Lechien had what they needed and was willing to ship it from the Congo to New York if the Americans paid for both the ore and the cost of transporting it. The final price tag was uncertain because Lechien reserved the right to increase the price if the value of the ore rose above its current low levels.[22] This purely commercial transaction reflects Sengier's position, for only he had the authority to direct the UMHK's administration in the Congo to ship the ore. It was also Sengier who realized the Americans might need more than the 30 short tons of ore they had ordered if they were working with uranium, and directed 1,100 metric tons be brought to New York. Over the course of several weeks in November and December 1940, roughly 1,200 short tons of ore arrived in New York Harbor by the shipload and was duly transferred to a warehouse on Staten Island. This cache became immensely important for the future of the UMHK,

Eldorado, and the eventual atomic project. For the time being, however, the hoard simply sat, its vast potential unrecognized and unrealized.

Pregel's Return to New York

Pregel was not met with a hero's return when he reunited with Sengier and Lechien at the UMHK. We can only speculate about the details of the meeting, but no job was waiting for him. In Pregel's later account, Sengier and Lechien "brutally" dismissed him as the company's sales agent, advising him that his services would not be needed. UMHK already had an established sales organization in the United States in Standard Chemical subsidiary Radium Chemical, and Pregel had never dealt in the American market, so he had no credentials or connections upon which to draw.[23]

It's plausible that Pregel had cut corners with his radium dealings over the winter of 1939–40, once Lechien was in New York. Pregel later asserted that Sengier and Lechien had accused him of irregularities in his handling of sales, perhaps something to do with radium that he had acquired from the official left in charge of the UMHK radium department on the departure of the two men, and that the official could not account for in a later audit.[24] But the dismissal felt more personal than that. Why?

Pregel was never one of Sengier's intimates, but his relationship with Lechien was different. The two had been very close, and Pregel later bitterly claimed Lechien had engineered his downfall. British intelligence accounts in New York reported that Pregel had a "blackmail" hold over Lechien, but if so it was insufficient to preserve his direct connection to UMHK in the short run. How could Pregel blackmail Lechien? Again, British intelligence records suggest a credible explanation. Lechien had been skimming and selling radium for personal gain, and falsifying the accounting records of Radium Belge to cover it. Pregel discovered the scheme and blackmailed him. We don't know what sort of explanation was offered, or to whom – perhaps Lechien blamed Pregel – but whatever the reason, Sengier supported Lechien, who stayed. Pregel was out.[25]

Pregel did not wallow. The split with UMHK was simply an opportunity. Now, he turned his attention north, deploying his ingenuity and charm to cultivate a link with Eldorado. Recall his claim to have been involved in negotiating the radium cartel with Eldorado. Possibly. He certainly would have known about the company.[26] By the fall of 1940, Harry Snyder was gone as Eldorado's treasurer and Carl French now filled the role.[27] Pregel knew Snyder and Jack Greenberg from the cartel negotiations and probably knew French for the same reason. He also knew Marcel Pochon from the South Terras Mine in Cornwall, where he had been a major investor.

The Contract with Eldorado

On 7 November 1940, Boris Pregel formally joined the Eldorado team, signing a sales agency agreement with Gilbert LaBine in Toronto. Pregel was not an employee but had fiduciary duties to act in Eldorado's best interests. The terms and implications of that arrangement would be of fundamental importance for the events that followed.

Under the agreement, Pregel became Eldorado's sole universal sales agent. On the surface, LaBine hired a salesman, and Pregel seems to have replicated his arrangements with UMHK in Europe. He earned a commission of 10 percent on uranium sales and 12.5 percent on radium sales. If he sold more than 5 grams of radium, the commission increased to 15 percent. That was not all. Pregel would earn a commission even when he did not participate in sales negotiations. It was a form of insurance: if Eldorado sold any product without going through Pregel, he would still be paid. Payment took the form of either US dollars or in kind – radium – which he was free to trade on his own account. The agreement was to last four years, expiring on 31 December 1944, unless either party gave eighteen months' notice of intent to terminate. What's more, the contract would renew automatically until 31 December 1947 unless Eldorado gave notice by 30 June 1943.[28] Pregel could also buy radium at a concessionary rate from the company and market it however he wished – including, potentially, in competition with Eldorado. This made it possible for him to capture the most lucrative sales for himself by selling directly, while channelling the less profitable sales through Eldorado, thereby maximizing any potential commissions.

It's unclear whether LaBine realized the upside he had given to Pregel, but it may not have mattered. By autumn 1940, Eldorado teetered on the verge of bankruptcy. It had a surplus of radium and far too much uranium, refined or unrefined. The LaBine brothers closed the mine and reduced refinery operations to the barest minimum, but no bank would lend the company money, and Gilbert had to fund Eldorado from his own resources.[29] That meant there was a limit. If the company had to file for bankruptcy, decisions would no longer be in the hands of the LaBines. Pregel understood this. Hope is not a strategy; Eldorado needed a plan, and Pregel had one. As a skilled salesman with twenty years of experience, he offered a life preserver to a drowning company.

The Canadian Radium and Uranium Corporation

Contract in hand, Pregel returned to New York. At the end of November, he incorporated a new company, the Canadian Radium and Uranium Corporation (CRUC), telling LaBine it was a marketing vehicle for Eldorado's products. That was at least partly true but the venture had another purpose. Later records show that Pregel on some occasions referred to Eldorado and its refinery as "his." Of course, it was not, but American customers probably believed either that Eldorado was subordinate to CRUC or that CRUC actually owned the Canadian mine. Certainly, CRUC made it appear to American purchasers that Pregel was marketing his own uranium and radium, whether supplied by Eldorado or through other means. Those who were better informed – Sengier, for example – knew the difference but quickly came to understand that access to Eldorado's Port Hope refinery passed through Pregel's office, which was prominently and stylishly located in the new and impressive Rockefeller Center on Fifth Avenue. Sengier needed Eldorado's facilities if he wanted to refine any ore in North America, and that meant his connection to Pregel resumed, even if the latter no longer worked for UMHK.

It's significant that "radium" came first in CRUC's corporate name. Pregel was, after all, a radium salesman and the product had reliable medical, industrial, and military purposes and markets. There was more than enough radium to go around, and Pregel's efforts to drum up sales in the United States bore fruit. Within the year he had shored up Eldorado's radium sales. Better still, the company's radium now dominated the market, perhaps not a difficult thing to achieve given the war. The principal competition remained the UMHK, and Pregel and Sengier saw each other from time to time as business warranted. They were, after all, in the same city, and their respective offices were just a mile or two apart.

One way or another, Pregel knew about the 1,200 tons of ore sitting in the Staten Island warehouse.[30] He also knew how it could be used and who could use it. Through 1940 and 1941, his door was open to scientific refugees from Europe. He knew about the experiments and research at Columbia University, and must have known the project was hampered by inadequate funding and a lack of official encouragement.[31] He understood little about the US government's scientific apparatus, but that did not prevent him from trying to tie Eldorado's uranium to its rudimentary atomic program. He did not, however, make any attempt to connect with Canada's war programs, which may explain why he approached an American agency to fund the reopening of Eldorado's mine at Great Bear Lake in January 1942.[32]

Building the Bomb

Canada had already been at war for fourteen months when LaBine and Pregel signed their sales contract in November 1940. Eldorado was subject to stringent government controls to ensure that industrial materials went where they would be most beneficial: manufacturing war supplies. Fortuitously for Eldorado, exports to the United States brought vital American dollars to be plowed back into the Canadian war effort, so the company could continue to buy chemicals for its refinery. The refinery had a shrunken workforce but had kept its longest-term employees, overage men or those with wives and children to support, who were in a lower draft category.

When the United States joined the war in December 1941, its government had to consider more urgently the possibility of a German atomic bomb. In this atmosphere, the British and the Americans began to weigh what to do about atomic energy. Even if the Germans and the Japanese could be stopped, the extent of their territorial gains guaranteed a long slog to push them back: years, probably. Though the economies of Britain and its empire had reached full wartime capacity by the end of 1941, the United States was only halfway along in mobilizing its wartime economy. At this time, the British were ahead of the Americans when it came to atomic energy. They understood a bomb was possible, though just how long it would take to produce remained unknown. The British hypothesis suggested three or four years once serious work began.

The British government decided in August 1941 to take steps toward an atomic weapon. The decision came after the circulation in February 1940 of an essay in England by two scientists, Otto Frisch and Rudolf Peierls, both refugees from Germany. The Frisch-Peierls Memorandum revealed a breakthrough that made an atomic weapon more than a theoretical possibility. Its first paragraph, explaining the possibility of a "super-bomb," was elegant and concise in summarizing their conclusions:

> The attached detailed report concerns the possibility of constructing a "super-bomb" which utilises the energy stored in atomic nuclei as a source of energy. The energy liberated in the explosion of such a super-bomb is about the same as that produced by the explosion of 1,000 tons of dynamite. This energy is liberated in a small volume, in which it will, for an instant, produce a temperature comparable to that in the interior of the sun. The blast from such an explosion would destroy life in a wide area. The size of this area is difficult to estimate, but it will probably cover the centre of a big city.[33]

Frisch and Peierls made clear that German atomic science was well advanced and had the capacity to develop such a weapon, particularly given access to uranium from Czechoslovakia and perhaps elsewhere.

Slowly, the Frisch-Peierls document had moved through the British government's scientific establishment. A committee of the country's most prominent physicists prepared its own report in July 1941. In the interim, the United Kingdom purchased modest amounts of uranium oxide from the Brandhurst Company, a specialized enterprise that was in all probability owned or controlled by Pregel through his shell company, Société Anonyme Demetra.

In August 1941, having decided to build an atomic bomb, the British shared their views with Vannevar Bush, the head of the Office of Scientific Research and Development (OSRD), who then spoke to President Roosevelt, who in turn agreed that research should continue. Until now, preliminary atomic research had been confined to university laboratories, with a budget limited to six figures and scientific personnel numbering in the low hundreds.

Limited contact had already been made between scientists in the two governments. In the late summer of 1940, Sir Henry Tizard, who headed a British mission that included notable physicist John Cockcroft, had arrived in Washington. Tizard knew the British had developed the theory to support advanced weaponry, but the Americans had the all-important means of production. The objective was to meld the two, and the best way to secure American cooperation was to open up to them. As in his discussions with the Belgians, Tizard remained skeptical that an atomic bomb could be produced by the end of the current war, a view Cockcroft shared. Conversations in this Anglo-American atomic group quickly moved on to more immediately important technologies.

Buying Uranium

Although not yet embarked on a formal project, the group decided to buy more uranium to expand their efforts. Separately, each approached Eldorado to make the purchase. In the days around Japan's attack on Pearl Harbor, the British asked for a ton or two of unrefined uranium oxide, and placed the order through the Canadian National Research Council, which meant Eldorado had no idea it had come from the UK. Replying for the company, Carl French, who had replaced Harry Snyder as treasurer and now sat on the company's board,[34] quoted them $3 a pound – lower than what was charged to Canadian ceramic companies for comparable 98 percent pure uranium oxide – with thirty days for delivery. Despite grumbling that the price was still too high, the British accepted.[35]

The British acted properly by placing their order through an appropriate Canadian authority. The Americans, however, approached Eldorado directly. The fact that US government representatives ignored the Canadian government and dealt directly with Eldorado would lead to much later mischief. Indeed, it took more than a year for the Canadian and US governments to act as one to handle radium and uranium. Instead, the Americans left it to the most knowledgeable man in the field – Boris Pregel.

In late December 1941, the directors of the early American atomic program were largely unfamiliar with Pregel. Lyman Briggs, the head of the US atomic group, wrote to Gilbert LaBine as the president of Eldorado to advise him that an emissary would visit his office in Toronto on December 29th. That person, Briggs wrote, would be authorized to discuss with LaBine "any of your work pertaining to national defense." Whose national defence? Evidently not Canada's.

That emissary was Eger V. Murphree, in civilian life a chemist whose usual task was figuring out how to convert the theoretical physics around uranium into industrial production.[36] His business in Toronto was limited to buying uranium – *more* uranium. The Americans had in fact already bought 5 or 6 tons of ore via Boris Pregel back in the spring, an arrangement implying that at least some of them knew he was the company's universal sales agent.[37] Murphree's order for 15 tons, which came on top of the earlier one, nonetheless bypassed him. Pregel thrived by knowing what was going on behind the security wall, but Murphree swore the Eldorado executives to secrecy, not just about his meeting in Toronto but about a subsequent visit by LaBine to New York.[38]

When Pregel found out, he contacted Murphree, who was puzzled by the encounter. "I am not clear as to what the connection is between you and Pregel," Murphree wrote to LaBine on 4 February 1942, "although I understand he has been acting as your representative in this country." He wanted to deal directly with LaBine and Eldorado; there was simply no need for Pregel's services. Nevertheless, in separate correspondence, Murphree told Pregel that his organization had another 45 tons in mind. Pregel replied before LaBine did, promising to have Eldorado work on the order even before finalizing a contract for a now combined 60 tons.[39]

Finalizing the contract should have been simple enough. It was not. For one thing, who were the proper parties to the agreement? Here, Pregel and LaBine were at odds. Pregel wanted to use his corporate persona Canadian Radium and Uranium Corporation as the seller. LaBine wanted Eldorado to be a party to the contract, thereby establishing the company as a war supplier and allowing it to claim wartime priorities in accessing supplies and labour.

That LaBine wanted to re-open his mine in the summer of 1942 was no secret in Toronto's mining community.[40] If he could show reason to do so, in the form of a firm order by March 1st, LaBine would be able to ask the Canadian government for permission to recruit miners, buy supplies and tools, and fly them to Great Bear Lake. Pregel, for his part, urged Eldorado to keep the refinery producing U_3O_8 oxide even before the contract was signed. Yet soon, LaBine was urging Murphree and the OSRD to use Pregel's services.[41] What had happened? Murphree was confused by this turn of events. In his experience, Pregel's contribution had been negligible.

How Pregel came to find out about the talks between Murphree and LaBine is unclear. The answer may lie in his links to some of the scientists in the OSRD project, particularly at the University of Chicago and especially Leo Szilard, the brilliant physicist whose calculations had helped focus attention on uranium as a source of incalculable energy in 1934.[42] Szilard worked at Chicago's Metallurgical Laboratory (almost always called the Met Lab during the war) under the Nobel Prize–winning physicist Arthur Compton.[43] A channel to Szilard would be slightly surreptitious but understandable.

There is an alternative explanation. Pregel knew Marcel Pochon, Eldorado's refinery director, and Carl French, the company's secretary-treasurer. Indeed, with LaBine's permission, French had joined the CRUC board shortly after the company was formed. The assumption was that it would be for a short period of time, but he would not serve as an officer of the company, nor would he receive a salary. The two firms shared an interest, and French would be a valuable link between them. In effect, the arrangement made him the servant of two masters. Meanwhile Pochon, while not a member of the CRUC board, was on Pregel's payroll as a technical adviser, and thus he too had divided loyalties. It is conceivable though not provable that French passed information to Pregel, especially if he had accompanied LaBine to New York to meet with Murphree.

Pregel wrote to LaBine at the beginning of March 1942. He talked up his connection to the scientists and referred to two different sources who had told him about Murphree's talks with Eldorado. He reminded LaBine that he was the company's universal sales agent, and it pained him to learn that Eldorado had been talking to the Americans behind his back. He went so far as to warn that these independent discussions might well upset delicate negotiations he was already having with the Americans (discussions he had neglected to tell the company about before, and precisely with whom he did not say).

There was, in fact, a valid reason for Pregel's indignation. There was a lot at stake. At one point, the Americans had considered placing an order for 200 tons before deciding that 60 tons would suffice for the time being.[44]

Pregel implied that Murphree and any associates working with him were merely purchasing agents shopping around for the best deal. It was a preposterous suggestion. Where else they could have gone, given the few uranium companies in existence, was left to the imagination. The implication was obvious: the policy that created the need for uranium in the first place was not made at Murphree's level.

Pregel cut to the chase. He told LaBine that Eldorado's negotiations with the OSRD had endangered his livelihood and must stop. "I am very much concerned about the future," he wrote, "not only of your own company, but of my own, in case we lose the ground which we have acquired with so much difficulty in such a short time." How this applied to the fact that Murphree had arrived unsolicited in Toronto with an order for uranium and why subsequent orders should be different went unaddressed. Pregel demanded that LaBine promise to cease any independent discussions between "Canadian officials and bodies" and to have all future contacts go through Pregel, including any meetings.[45] By Canadian officials Pregel probably meant officers of the Eldorado company rather than agents of the Canadian government, but by bodies he definitely meant anyone representing the American government.

Pregel followed up with another firecracker of a letter two days later, telling LaBine, "We have learned that other institutions have been working and experimenting with uranium ores, both domestic and of other sources." In the face of this dangerous competition, Pregel had shored up the 45-ton order for the Americans, which was now on track for completion and signature.[46] LaBine passed along the letters to French, who seems to have been in New York, with the comment that Pregel had "in all probability discussed this matter with you." He, LaBine, would refrain from replying until French came back to Toronto.

French returned that same day, March 6th, and no doubt helped LaBine draft his reply to Pregel, which would have left in the evening post to New York. On the other side of the coin, it's possible that French also helped Pregel draft his letters to LaBine, though their phrasing and language point to Pregel as the author. The Eldorado president conceded all points to Pregel, asserting that he had mistakenly acceded to Murphree's request for secrecy without realizing that Murphree had another, possibly disadvantageous, agenda.

Pregel's access to what would have been a carefully guarded state secret in March 1942 is noteworthy, but it is unclear if anybody had the job of taking notes on him or anybody else on the fringes of the bomb project. Operating on a level of confidence with Szilard, Pregel could have grasped or been told that the Americans intended to create a nuclear bomb. He used concerns about security to discredit Murphree in LaBine's eyes and cement his own position as the person entitled to be informed of any sales to the American government. The 60-ton contract secured Eldorado's future, one that was bound to Pregel to his immense benefit. Now, there was no question that the Americans had to work through him, as did anybody else wanting to buy the company's products or use its facilities.

Port Radium Reopens

Up to this point nobody had seemed to recognize that Eldorado was a private Canadian company located in Canada. It was a separate legal entity, with a distinct identity apart from CRUC and Pregel. It had its own board of directors. It operated under Canadian law and was subject to Canadian jurisdiction in a closely regulated war economy. That was certainly what was supposed to happen.

In Canada, however, some things were tightly controlled while others operated on an honour system. By showing government authorities in spring 1942 that it had an American contract, Eldorado was allowed to procure a scarce aircraft to bring in the miners and supplies needed to reopen its mine. Miners themselves were also a scarce commodity. Many had enlisted in the armed forces, and those who remained were needed to mine copper, cobalt, or nickel. Some had to be coerced out of the army to do so. All this required permission and support from the Canadian government.

LaBine began sending crews north by his new plane to clear the mine of ice and water and repair its deteriorated infrastructure.[47] By the autumn of 1942, Port Radium began to produce ore once more. With the winter freeze coming to Great Bear Lake and the Mackenzie River in early October, the shipping season was short. LaBine was hopeful the caches of ore from 1940, scattered in burlap sacks and metal drums along the river and railway shipping route, could keep the refinery producing the uranium oxide necessary for the work envisaged at the University of Chicago and to supply the vast expansion of atomic facilities anticipated in the United States.

Events were beginning to move in Eldorado's direction, and LaBine excitedly began to call his contacts for miners, supplies, and the vital permission from Ottawa to make use of all these scarce commodities. Eldorado's future seemed bright at the end of winter 1942.

5
Allies and Rivals in the North Atlantic Triangle

The pivotal events of 1942 occurred in a crucial year for the development of the atomic bomb in the United Kingdom and the United States. Canada was also involved, thanks to Eldorado and its supply of uranium and capacity to refine even more from Belgian ore. Any discussion of these events necessarily deals with growing tensions among these three allied countries, fuelled by misunderstanding amid a rivalry to determine who would – who *could* – lead the effort to build the bomb.

ON 15 JUNE 1942, three representatives of the British government arrived at Canadian prime minister Mackenzie King's office for a discussion. Malcolm MacDonald, the British high commissioner in Ottawa, led the group. He was a particular favourite of King's, a feeling the high commissioner reciprocated.

MacDonald knew well that King was strongly pro-British. Under his direction, Canada had already sent more than 500,000 soldiers, sailors, and airmen and women to Britain. Most recently, King had held a divisive referendum on conscription as a sign of Canada's commitment to total war.

Helping the UK meant increasing taxes, building factories, and constructing a military that by 1945 numbered 1 million in uniform out of a Canadian population of 12 million. In January 1942, King's government handed the British a "billion-dollar gift," equivalent to 10 percent of Canada's gross domestic product in 1942. When the gift ran out at the end of that year, billions more were made available in grants, war supplies, and loans. It was an enormous show of support but also a measure of pragmatism because the British could not afford to pay for it. Everything destined for the UK was financed in and by Canada, something MacDonald understood.

Malcolm MacDonald also understood politics. The son of a prime minister, he had enjoyed an elite education, served as a member of Parliament from 1931 to 1945, and spent more than five years in the cabinet in various portfolios: colonial secretary, dominions secretary, and minister of health. When Winston Churchill formed a coalition government in 1940, he removed MacDonald from cabinet, considering him "rat-poison." Churchill smoothed a quick departure by offering him the high commissionership in Ottawa, a not unimportant post given Canada's contribution to Britain's defence.[1] Canada was next to the United States in offering tangible support to the British war effort and, unlike the United States, also took part in the war. London's information on Canada and Mackenzie King was sparse and often deficient, but the prime minister was flattered to have a British politician of such stature arrive in Ottawa. The new high commissioner had a winning personality and was embraced by a strongly anglophile society that nonetheless had little contact with senior British politicians, especially ones who were handsome, intelligent bachelors.[2]

The second member of the British delegation was as notable in his field as MacDonald was in his. George Paget "G.P." Thomson, a Nobel Prize–winner in physics, arrived in Ottawa in 1942 as a liaison officer with Canada's National Research Council.[3] Last was Michael Perrin, a chemist by profession. In 1942, he was part of the early British atomic program, code-named Tube Alloys. An intelligent and persuasive man, Perrin was often sent on missions in which more senior scientists, diplomats, and administrators might put their feet wrong – his superior in Tube Alloys, Wallace Akers, to name one. It was Perrin who could put scientific thought into plain words, and as such he was invaluable for talking to Mackenzie King.

The subject of the meeting was uranium, and thus, Eldorado. The British explained the strategic importance of uranium to the prime minister, along with their desire to ensure steady access to Canadian supplies. To accomplish this, they suggested, the government could expropriate the company and run it as a joint enterprise with the British. They knew King would need a rationale, and they had one ready: an atomic bomb was feasible, and to make one required uranium. Canada – Eldorado – had that uranium.

MacDonald led off with a mild request, telling King that the British were interested in "the acquisition of some property" in order to "prevent competition in price on a material much needed in the manufacture of explosives." That was one way of putting it, and Perrin thought it best to clarify. "A military weapon of immense destructive force" was closer to the mark. As Perrin proceeded, King understood clearly what he was being told. As the scientist later recalled, "a look of absolute horror and panic" came over the prime minister's face.[4]

King did not question what the British said and considered what to do next. What he had been told made uranium a war supply, and thus under the remit of the Department of Munitions and Supply. Its minister was C.D. Howe, who happened to be in his ramshackle office that day, a mere block away. The British delegation made it their next stop.

It was much easier to learn about Eldorado than one might think. The British would have done well to read *The Northern Miner,* the bible of the Canadian mining business, which would have told them in March 1942 that Eldorado was reopening its mine. Gilbert LaBine had boasted about it because the move had improved the price of his shares. If they had known, the British might have realized there was already demand for what Eldorado was able to produce.

That spring, as Eldorado's stock increased in value, the British had become uneasy. By May, they were preoccupied with the question of how to control the company and ensure a steady supply of uranium. They also worried that Eldorado might increase the price if they knew uranium was now in high demand, a disaster-in-waiting for the cash-starved British. Determined to control the company, they urged the Canadians to consider using wartime emergency powers to dictate sale prices.

Finally, there was the question of national security or, as the British defined it, "secrecy." It was a fair concern given the task at hand, but it was widely known in the press that Eldorado had supplies of uranium. Indeed, how else would the British have known?

C.D. Howe, the Minister

C.D. Howe, the person who would have to manage Eldorado's future, was an experienced administrator, businessman, and engineer, with plenty of international experience. Born in Massachusetts in 1886, he had attended the Massachusetts Institute of Technology before taking a job as a professor at Dalhousie University in Halifax, Nova Scotia. He abandoned academic life to move west in 1913 to help supervise Canada's grain trade as a civil servant. Two years later, he founded his own engineering firm, the C.D. Howe Company. In the process, he became the world's leading constructor of grain elevators, from Liverpool to Buenos Aires. Howe's work had excited the French architectural theorist Le Corbusier, who saw the stark geometric form of the elevators as a harbinger of a new age of design. Howe was more pragmatic, moved by neither aesthetics nor theory. He saw the structures as merely efficient.

An engineer who worked in Howe's company left a perceptive description. Howe wasn't a brilliant engineer but a brilliant organizer: "He could see the big picture of many things, but ... a [details] person, as far as I can see, he was not. He was not a technical engineer in that sense. He was ... more of an organizer and a developer."[5] He was, in short, one of the great success stories of King's government.

Elected to Parliament first in 1935, Howe represented the riding of Port Arthur in northwestern Ontario, and came to be known for his administrative talent. In the 1930s, he had supervised the creation of the new Department of Transport and the establishment of Crown corporations to run the national airline and the national broadcasting service, the Canadian Broadcasting Corporation. When war broke out Mackenzie King gave him the newly created Department of Munitions and Supply, which by the middle of the war had engulfed half the Canadian economy.

Helpfully, Howe was a multitasker. His staff were awed by his ability to switch from one subject to another on a daily docket that might include ten or more appointments on subjects that ranged from aircraft to shipbuilding. J.P. Moffat, the US envoy in wartime Ottawa, compared Howe to a ringmaster "not of a three-ring circus, but a thirty-ring circus ... playing a vital role in each ring."[6] Leaping from one ring to another could be stressful, but Howe was not intimidated by the corporate lions and tigers and bears who populated his department. Moffat continued that Howe was "at home with, and consequently able to deal, without a sense of inferiority, with the representatives of 'money.'"[7] This factor alone made Howe almost unique in the King cabinet.

He was also loyal to his businessmen-turned-executives and shouldered the blame for his subordinates' faults and errors. Howe said that anyone could make a mistake. It was natural and inevitable. But a second mistake would catch his eye, and he would ease the inadequate and inconsequential out of their jobs. "Howe was soft, you know, he never really fired anybody," an old associate commented.[8] No one was humiliated under Howe.

His administrative style worked in part because of remarkable luck, only some of which he created: his subordinates were competent and, in almost every case, loyal. He usually had the perception and confidence to make the right choice. He was also canny and willing to go for the jugular, the latter rarely deployed because circumstances almost never called for it.[9]

Although some parts of Canada's wartime economy were built and owned directly by government, most were merely regulated and subjected to orders from above. When a private company did not exist, Howe created a Crown corporation that was wholly government owned but run by CEOs and boards of directors, as in private industry, but all appointed by their single shareholder: the government of Canada. In practical terms, that meant Howe. Crown corporations were not new to Canada, a country that already had a government-owned airline, a government-owned radio service, and a government-owned transcontinental railway. They were a powerful tool when nobody else could – or would – do the job.

Howe's Helpers

Howe's own department was loosely organized. It had a normal departmental structure on paper, with a deputy minister, accountants, and file clerks whose job it was to record what had already been done by others, especially the minister. But governing in wartime was adventurous, exciting, and not always orderly. Ordinary controls and examinations were sporadic, sometimes missing altogether. Because the usual departmental hierarchy was lacking in practice, everything depended on the minister. There was no associate minister, and Howe deliberately confined his deputy minister to mere administrative tasks. But the minister could not be everywhere. The sheer number of activities that he had to supervise was daunting, and it could also be crippling. At several points during the war Howe went on forced vacations to recover from exhaustion.[10]

As a result, when – not if – something went wrong, the minister did not and could not ask his deputy what to do. Instead, Howe relied on a small circle of friends and aides. Dr. Chalmers James (C.J.) Mackenzie, the president of the National Research Council, was one of those people. Just two years younger than Howe, he had been the minister's student before the First World War, and the two men had kept up contact since. In 1939, Mackenzie moved from his job as dean of engineering at the University of Saskatchewan to Ottawa to become president of the National Research Council. Though not a scientist himself, Mackenzie was well informed about scientific developments. In the circumstances, he knew enough to know about nuclear fission, and he had physicists on his staff to keep him up to date.[11] Mackenzie's position was prestigious, and Howe used him as an emissary to Washington and London, where title or position could open doors.

Lesslie Thomson | Library and Archives Canada, EP Taylor Fonds, DAP Accession 1994-258

Inside Canada, Howe relied on Lesslie Thomson, a confidential aide who was also an engineer by training but not employed as such. The same age as Howe, Thomson had a strong record in civilian life, having taught at McGill University in Montreal and written a book about transportation. He was upright, experienced, and had good judgment. Howe brought him into his office with a roving assignment as a confidant and problem solver. Thomson was not given to rash decisions, preferring to rely on evidence gathered over time. Some thought him old-fashioned, fussy, and slow; McElhone, for one, complained later that he was "not impressive."[12] But when Thomson acted it was efficiently and honestly. Thomson made it clear that he not only spoke *for* the minister but could speak *to* the minister, as quickly and frequently as he needed to.

Responding to the British

When the British trio met Howe and Mackenzie on 15 June 1942, the Canadians were not completely surprised. By then, G.P. Thomson had been in Ottawa for six months, and he and Mackenzie had discussed the British atomic project as early as February.[13] In March, Howe had authorized assistance for Gilbert LaBine to reopen his mine, but those efforts were meant to help the Americans, not the British.

An early and well-informed chronicler of Canada's atomic history with first-hand knowledge of the events and personalities involved succinctly summed up what Howe had done and what he already knew: "Mr. Howe was not disposed to interfere with Eldorado's chances of supplying the U.S. government with uranium oxide and ore ... The Canadian government, Mr. Howe said, was prepared to assist Eldorado by granting priorities for obtaining the necessary machinery and supplies." Insofar as it was possible, "The whole transaction, on the insistence of both the U.S. and Canadian governments, was to be conducted with the greatest secrecy."[14] With the benefit of hindsight, it becomes evident that secrecy hampered coordination among the various parties involved, including the governments of the United Kingdom and the United States.

The decision to help LaBine was not made casually, but it was informal and based on second-hand information about Eldorado's contacts with the Americans. The US government did not approach Howe directly, nor any other part of the Canadian government. The minister learned of its desire for uranium, and as a good ally he did what he was asked. The fact that the Americans supplied a scarce aircraft to LaBine for flights in and out of Port Radium was a clear sign that their interest was serious, but J.P. Moffat knew nothing of the matter, and there was no reference to cabinet or authorization from Mackenzie King.

Howe decided that atomic matters – which in Canada in 1942 meant only Eldorado – should be separate from the existing directorates and divisions within his department. He justified the arrangement for security purposes, and security meant secrecy, keeping those in the know to the smallest possible number. At Eldorado, that resulted in "continuity of operational management" in practice and in principle.[15] Even if Howe had wanted to, the government couldn't supplant management because it had neither the resources nor the expertise. During the war, most companies worked as normal, with war production remaining by and large in private hands. Howe expected to use the same matrix for managing atomic affairs. It may have worked if Eldorado had been a company like any other.

Nationalizing Eldorado

The scientific background was disposed of quickly at the meeting with the British. For Howe, the context was familiar: it was a matter of supply, which was his specialty. But the British proposal to nationalize Eldorado was unusual. They further recommended that the company be subject to joint Anglo-Canadian ownership to allow British control and access to the supply of uranium. Usually protective of Canadian sovereignty, Howe did not object this time. Nevertheless, he said that formal arrangements would have to wait because the British demanded secrecy.

Nationalizing Eldorado secretly was challenging because it was a publicly traded company. Howe suggested the government quietly buy out the company's shareholders. After checking market conditions, he was advised that $1.25 per share would be a proper price, higher than the current market dictated and therefore tempting to shareholders, but not so high that anyone would question the offer. The purchase would be done in secret. Only a handful of key shareholders knew the government's price: Gilbert and Charlie LaBine, Carl French, and Marcel Pochon. Almost certainly, other members of the board of directors knew as well. To get the ball rolling, Howe told the British he would talk to Gilbert LaBine, whom the minister described as "a personal friend of mine." Contact would be informal, friend to friend.

On 7 July 1942, duly summoned, LaBine arrived in Ottawa to talk with Howe. LaBine's reaction to the government offer proved that $1.25 was a good price; he accepted for himself and on behalf of his brother, selling Howe the brothers' stake of just over a million shares. Keeping management was essential to maintain appearances. It was business as usual, with Gilbert LaBine remaining the president of Eldorado as part of the deal.

The Share Purchase Agreement

In truth, Howe and LaBine were hardly intimates. More accurately, Howe knew LaBine by reputation – by word of mouth, newspaper reports, and associated publicity. They might have called each other by their first names, Gilbert and C.D., as most of Howe's wartime subordinates and associates did. It was a privilege but not an uncommon one because Howe liked to feel that important businessmen were "his" boys.

Howe may have thought that LaBine's conception of being a company president was like his own as a minister: eliding or sometimes evading customary practices because he wanted to get things done. LaBine also favoured trusting his subordinates but differed from Howe in that he did not seem to have an overarching vision of how to do so, nor did he seem to understand the implications of running his company that way. Mostly, he wanted someone who could relieve him of the burden of details, and he found one in Carl French. The few secretaries, accountants, and minor employees around the Eldorado office worked for French, not LaBine.

Lesslie Thomson, who became a frequent visitor to the company in 1943–44, later described the result. An instinctive organizer who believed in documentation and hierarchy as the rational method of taking responsibility – more formally than Howe did – Thomson later observed that LaBine appeared to have no idea of the necessary organizational methods and techniques, "Nor, in my judgment, did he have any appreciation of the importance of internal organization." There was worse. LaBine had "an extraordinarily trusting disposition. If he has confidence in anyone he appears to be willing to sign any document which that person may put before him."[16] It was a noble quality in a friend but a potentially disastrous one in a corporate president.

After mid-1942, LaBine's principal responsibility became buying up outstanding company shares to help the federal government nationalize his company. Although the LaBine brothers had sold their shares, they amounted to only a quarter of the total issued. That meant tracking down the other shareholders. The process was simple and informal, even a bit bizarre.

LaBine acted as the government's agent, travelling around Canada and the United States with John Proctor, a banker, who carried a suitcase filled with Canadian and American dollars. LaBine approached shareholders individually and offered to buy them out without explaining why or identifying who was behind the offer – secrecy again. He thus did not tell them the reserve price or even that one existed. He paid whatever price he could negotiate, and on returning home turned over the shares and the proceeds to the government. In some cases, LaBine offered and shareholders accepted less than what the government was willing to pay. While it's unclear if this ad hoc takeover of a publicly traded company was contrary to the comparatively rudimentary stock exchange rules of the time, it's notable that LaBine did not use the opportunity to enrich himself by pocketing the difference between what shareholders accepted and the government's reserve price. Because the funds were supplied by the Department of Finance, they were audited by the Canadian auditor general.[17]

The most obvious feature of the secret share purchase arrangement was that it was slow. Although it was not exactly public, how well was secrecy maintained? The evidence is mixed. In 1943, Carl French wrote to Pregel that something secret was going on, noting that in some respects the company was now being directed out of Ottawa instead of from the corporate offices in Toronto.[18] The two corresponded regularly and met frequently in Pregel's office in New York. Nothing explicit made it into their correspondence. Given their candour and relationship, one would have expected it would if they knew about it. And if French didn't know about the share purchase, then the process was truly secret.

Eldorado Business Laid Bare

It was more difficult to maintain secrecy in a general sense. The specific interest in uranium shared by the three governments – the United States, the UK, and now Canada – was easier to keep quiet, though not altogether secret, but little about Eldorado and its business was private. *The Northern Miner* told you all you needed to know.

Eldorado frequently appeared in its columns. For example, on 6 November 1941, the *Miner* reported that radium was in considerable demand for military purposes. On 9 April 1942, the magazine gave its readers further good news about the company, which had "secured some very favorable contracts on uranium by-products, particularly in the United States." In June of that year, the *Miner*'s annual supplement on the state of Canadian mining covered Eldorado with such accuracy that it might have served as a governmental briefing note. Ministers would have been better served if it had. For example, the supplement reported that the radium refinery had "been put to increased use on military production" and shareholders had recently been told that "90 percent of the work now being done is for various branches of the military forces of the British Empire and the United States." The source of the uranium and radium was well known, too: "The available market still continues to be largely supplied, however, by radium and uranium from the Belgian Congo," and much of that had been "shipped to the United States, which, in 1939, imported 2,400,200 pounds of Belgian Congo uranium ore and semi-processed compounds, valued at $2,100,297."[19]

The Northern Miner seemed to know more about UMHK's 1,200 tons (the 2,400,200 pounds) than the British, Canadian, and American governments combined. Where had it got its information? Carl French was the most likely immediate source, repeating what Boris Pregel had told him. In that sense, the *Miner* serves as a guide to Pregel's own level of information. How could he know how much uranium was on Staten Island? In summer 1942, he was trying to buy all of it.

What about the possibility of German spies? After all, the Germans were the primary reason for concern and secrecy. The answer is twofold: first, the Germans did not have an espionage network in Canada; second, Hitler's atomic program floundered in a state of contradiction, confusion, and ignorance. Perhaps more significantly, the Germans had all the uranium they could want or need from the UMHK's stocks in Belgium.

Boris Pregel evidently knew more about the Eldorado's business than its board of directors did. Thanks to wartime secrecy, the board was not an especially effective one and after the spring of 1942 played only a minor role in guiding the company. According to board members who spoke later about the company's wartime activities, any queries were met with French or LaBine invoking secrecy. Soon, they learned not to ask questions. It's probable directors knew something about the company's nationalization, but there is nothing about it in the minutes. Howe left such matters to LaBine.

Throughout the period, Eldorado still operated as LaBine's company, even after Howe bought his shares. Over the course of 1942 and 1943, the arrangement seemed to be nothing to worry about. Sales of uranium were guaranteed by the American contracts and Boris Pregel had worked miracles in selling radium. The company functioned smoothly because Carl French handled the office work and took the details of the business off the president's shoulders. LaBine appreciated him all the more for that and, as more than one observer saw, trusted him implicitly. LaBine was a busy man, with other interests, other companies, other mines, even other government work as a member of the board of directors of another of Howe's Crown corporations. If there was paperwork to sign, French handed it to him in good order, having digested the details, another burden removed from Eldorado's president.[20] But nobody looked over French's shoulder to see what *he* was doing.[21] They should have.

Tripartite Control of Uranium

A gap clearly existed between what governments were saying and what private actors were doing. In many respects, Eldorado conducted a version of its own foreign policy up until the summer of 1942. The Canadian government eased the path by helping to reopen the mine at Port Radium, but it gave the company no direction, political, economic, or otherwise.

Initially, and logically enough, the British saw uranium supply as a resource to be shared among the Canadians, the Americans, and themselves.

Canada was a loyal part of the British empire, so there was really no thought that the dominion would refuse. Howe accepted the British proposition and promptly dispatched C.J. Mackenzie to Washington to announce and secure the new arrangement.

This was more easily done in form than in substance. Mackenzie gravitated to Vannevar Bush and James Bryant Conant – all three were experienced university administrators with PhDs, and thus entitled to be called "doctor." They concluded that a tripartite agreement overseeing Eldorado's resources was a good idea: Bush took it to President Roosevelt, who also thought it was a good idea, and figuratively waved his hand in consent.

There the matter stood. Howe decided to wait until all the shares were in hand. Months passed. Then, a year. After a while, the idea of tripartite control was overtaken by events, and the assignment of shares to the governments of the United States and the United Kingdom became obsolete. In the United States, Roosevelt had a lot on his plate in the summer of 1942: a succession of Allied defeats in Asia and Africa, a visit from Winston Churchill, and strategic decisions about how best to deploy Allied power to defeat Germany and Japan. Uranium was a minor item, soon forgotten.

For their part, Bush and Conant turned the atomic project over to the administration of the US Army as the only organization that could handle its size and complexity. But the US Army did not know about the Canadian offer to divide ownership of Eldorado among the three nations. The Canadians had effectively decided against it but did not tell the Americans, who did not care, nor the British, who continued in a state of delusion. In fact, tripartite ownership was a dead letter.[22]

Pregel the Émigré

By fall 1941, Boris Pregel had reason to be satisfied – and relieved. His fortunes were on the upswing. He and Alexandra had escaped from Europe, followed by his mother and two sisters. All had faced almost certain death as Jews in wartime France. In New York, they lived comfortably. Alexandra continued painting, using their fashionable apartment in Hotel des Artistes as her studio.[23] Boris's sister Sophia, already a poet of note, became an important literary figure. We know little of his sister Klara except that she lived in New York and was married. His mother died in 1944.

Pregel continued the philanthropic patterns he had established in Paris. He supported the cause of la France libre, Free France, which pursued the liberation of the *patrie* under the leadership of General Charles de Gaulle. In 1942, he supported the foundation of the École libre des hautes études, in association with the New School.[24] He supported Jewish causes and provided succour for refugee scientists when they arrived penniless and disoriented in the United States.[25] As in Paris, Pregel established himself in New York as a man of culture and an authority on atomic matters.

At some point, Pregel's advocacy for the use of radioactivity in everything from electricity to growing crops caught the attention of the vice-president of the United States, Henry Wallace. An agronomist by profession, Wallace was excited by the possible application of radiation to agriculture to increase food production, and Pregel basked in the resulting publicity. Not all his dealings brought such a positive response. By late 1941, Pregel's activities brought him under J. Edgar Hoover's growing umbrella of surveillance, conducted by the Federal Bureau of Investigation. When Pregel began to develop a warm relationship with Henry Wallace in late 1943, the FBI took note, having had Wallace under surveillance for some time.[26] There was quite a lot to see. Pregel presented himself as an anti-Bolshevik veteran of the White Army, and his prophetic vision of an atomic future won him an audience among the future minded, as it had with the vice-president.

Pregel also replicated his business personality from Europe, believing that what had worked in Paris, Berlin, and Zurich would surely work in New York. He was courtly, sophisticated, and multilingual, fluent in French, German, and – of course – Russian. Although he was a quick study, his grammatically perfect English was accented, as he had not lived in an English-speaking milieu until he moved to New York. Judging from his correspondence, his style was correct but formal, unlike that of his brother, Alexander, who had moved to the United States at a much younger age to attend school. Where Alexander was a thoroughly assimilated American, Boris never was. And as Alexander later commented, his brother's European airs did him no good with the Anglo-Saxons in New York.

Nevertheless, early on, Pregel and Eldorado seemed to be a perfect fit. Pregel offered the company his sales ability and knowledge of markets. Through his scientific friends, Pregel offered the company an entrée into the burgeoning atomic bomb project in the United States. Without him, Eldorado had no such connection, nor did the government of Canada. By 1942, however, Eger Murphree's independent contact with Gilbert LaBine suggests that Pregel's indispensability was beginning to wane.

Reconstructing Pregel's entire web of business ventures is next to impossible. He understood the power of information, thrived on the uncertainty of others, and manoeuvred for advantage at a time when nothing was quite certain. Radium was the foundation of his business, and with it the more broadly radioactive substances and the many uses to which they could be put, or to which he said they could be put. Canadian Radium and Uranium Corporation was the core of that enterprise, but Pregel's other businesses included International Rare Metals, which had its own small refinery at Mount Kisco, about 100 kilometres north of Manhattan. There Pregel's technicians, many of whom were refugees, handled radium, polonium, and whatever other rare metals he could process for marketing.[27]

International Rare Metals functioned as one of the benefits available to Pregel through his rather one-sided agreement with Eldorado. Because he could choose to receive part of his commission fee in radium, he did. He then marketed that radium on his own account, and along the way created the impression among American buyers that his companies were the dominant businesses in the field. Some even believed Pregel owned Eldorado.

Pregel may have liked the idea, but it's doubtful that was ever his primary goal. Appearances were enough. Most likely, he wanted prestige, to be valued as a patriot, a scientific statesman, a person of importance. He wanted to be seen as not only eminent but pre-eminent. Soon, he would get his wish.

6
Opening Eldorado for Business Again

The Roosevelt administration's decision to pursue the development of the atomic bomb was directed by the US Army Corps of Engineers within what came to be known colloquially as the Manhattan Project. The effort involved complicated interactions between the governments of the United States, the United Kingdom, and Canada and was solely responsible for saving Eldorado from bankruptcy. Eldorado's role in the effort to provide the uranium needed was crucial, although not all the uranium originated in Canada. Much of it was owned by the Union Minière du Haut-Katanga (UMHK). What mattered was the refining process, and here lay the indispensable role of Eldorado. Without the Port Hope refinery, uranium for the Manhattan Project would not have been available.

Although uranium came to overshadow radium in the history of Eldorado and the war, radium is the key element in this story. Through 1942 and 1943, contracts to refine uranium at Eldorado turned into a windfall of radium for three key figures at the company: Carl French, Boris Pregel, and Marcel Pochon.

During the Second World War, enough uranium was found, refined, and employed to fuel the research efforts of three nations: the United States, the United Kingdom, and Canada. American demand was by far the largest of the three. It was met by Canadian supply – if not Canadian ore. At this point the reader might find useful a description of the various stages of production of radium and uranium as it happened in the 1940s.

All the initial stages remained the same, probably since Madame Curie had first devised them. The ore excavated from the mine was milled to remove as much extraneous material as possible. This was essential as otherwise the bulk would have been impossible to move. The ratio was 500 tons of raw ore to 10 tons of "concentrate." The concentrate had between 35 and 50 percent uranium content. It was then shipped to Port Hope, where it was treated with chemicals, as Madame Curie had done. The radium was separated out for further treatment by precipitation, as we have described. Some uranium was further processed into "ceramic grade," but most was dumped as a slurry into the lake.

In 1942, the process changed. Most obviously, the formerly waste uranium was retained and then further processed in chemicals, starting with sulphuric acid, then caustic soda and ammonium hydroxide. After roasting, it became U_3O_8 – "triuranium octoxide," a tangle of vowels and consonants that for obvious reasons is seldom used. Today, it bears the name yellowcake – strangely, because it is blackish green in colour. Between 1941 and 1945, Eldorado's Port Hope refinery produced approximately 2,000 tons of U_3O_8. The atomic bomb project, run by the US Army Corps of Engineers, was Eldorado's most important customer but not its only one, just as uranium was not the company's only product. Although radium soon took a backseat to uranium in the company's bottom line, it remained significant. If only people had noticed.

In many respects, location was the key to Eldorado's ultimate success. After Germany occupied Belgium, Eldorado became the only uranium refinery under Allied control that could produce large quantities of U_3O_8. For this reason, it was an essential part of the infrastructure that supported the atomic bomb project. Like other crucial utilities (sewers or electric power grids, for example), its existence was largely taken for granted.

Eldorado's primary wartime concern was matching supply with demand. Reports in the media, even the well-informed *Northern Miner*, assumed that supply and demand were in balance. But the demand came from more than one source, a point not easily grasped even inside the atomic project.

When C.D. Howe and Gilbert LaBine met on 7 July 1942 to arrange the purchase of Eldorado shares, LaBine must have mentioned the contract with the Americans for 60 tons as something that assured the company's future. At the time, it was the only offer for Eldorado's ore. The British had not yet made any requests because they assumed their joint ownership entailed control, and control meant access to uranium on demand because the mine had reopened four months earlier.[1] Ordinarily, that would have been more than enough. But these were not ordinary times.

Reopening the mine was more complicated than just turning on the lights. When the facility shut down in 1940, the electric pumps that kept the water out of the underground shafts had shut down too. Water flooded in and then froze. The first task of the miners who arrived in the spring of 1942 was to repair damage so extensive that mining operations proper could not resume until summer's end, and shipments of ore were thus delayed until the lake thawed in spring 1943. As before, piles of uranium ore bagged in sacks had been stored along the transportation route from Great Bear to Port Hope, along with a quantity of ore at the refinery, but that was not enough for Eldorado to meet its contractual obligations.

It Depends What You Know

Gilbert LaBine was slow to appreciate the problem, as were the Canadian government and its customers, both actual (the Americans) and potential (the British). Eldorado's management team, however, did. Armed with information provided by Carl French and Marcel Pochon, Boris Pregel knew exactly where the company stood in late spring 1942.

Where others saw only obstacles, he saw opportunity. Although Pregel continued to sell radium, in 1942, he was focused on uranium because he knew from his connections with scientists working on the atomic bomb project that there were big sales to be had. By the summer, as a reader of *The Northern Miner,* he would also have known exactly how much uranium was available, where it was located, and how long it would take to process it. Of course Edgar Sengier definitely knew about the ore stored in Staten Island, because he was the one who had put it there. And over the previous two years, he had tried without success to sell it to the American government. No one in the administration would return his calls.

But Pregel did not have all the facts. He knew that American demand would almost certainly exceed their own expectations, but he did not know the Canadian government was secretly nationalizing Eldorado and would thus eventually make the company's fate a matter of public policy. He was also probably unaware that the Americans were reorganizing the management of the atomic bomb program. There was only so much he could learn.

The highest atomic policy was the purview of others. In the United States, that level was occupied by James Conant and Vannevar Bush, and only rarely the president, who had a thousand and one urgent items to claim his attention. On the British side, the Tube Alloys project reported to the prime minister, Winston Churchill, but he was also a busy man, and he delegated day-to-day supervision to Chancellor of the Exchequer Sir John Anderson and his principal scientific adviser, Lord Cherwell, who intervened as needed. Wallace Akers, a former executive with British chemicals conglomerate Imperial Chemical Industries, served as the liaison with the Americans and Canadians. He was a man of considerable culture and charm, forthright and decisive, but that did not mean his actions were always well advised or well informed. This was particularly true in his dealings with the North Americans. A man of certainty in uncertain times, he was especially ill suited to grasping the question of uranium supply in the summer of 1942.

In June, Akers had lunch with Pregel in New York. It was a business lunch, though the cultured and music-loving Akers had more in common with Pregel than he knew. Akers was aware that officials involved with the National Radium Trust, the British quasi-governmental organization created in 1929 to acquire radium for medical use in that country, distrusted – even detested – Pregel. The latter was unlikely to have known just how tentative British policy was – the key decisions about the direction and requirements of both the British and American atomic projects had yet to be made – but he understood the need for uranium and offered to help. Akers took a non-committal attitude that was both unlucky and ill timed.

Pregel had already taken steps to secure the Belgian ore, having suggested a deal to Sengier in April whereby Eldorado and UMHK participated in a fifty-fifty joint venture to sell uranium to the Americans. The two met again in May, but Sengier was not interested because he wanted to deal directly with the Americans despite the futility of his recent efforts.[2] Why would Pregel try to deal with the British when he knew the Americans were also in the market? Probably, he thought a firm order from Akers would improve his own chances of buying the 1,200 tons of Belgian ore sitting in Staten Island. Combined with Eldorado's tonnage, Pregel would then hold a monopoly on all known stocks of uranium.

Pregel was determined, and he held a clear advantage over Sengier. Thanks to the secrecy of the project, one branch of the US government had no idea what others were doing. Sengier had been trying to broker a deal through the State Department, as had worked well enough for the cobalt, copper, and tin he had to sell. His main contact at State showed interest but did not know enough to make a connection to the requirements of the atomic bomb project. Pregel, however, knew who wanted uranium and how much – a figure that moved steadily upward during the summer. Eldorado had begun 1942 with an order for 60 tons, which was soon folded into a new contract for 350 tons, negotiated by Pregel. By July, the Americans were beginning to talk about 500 tons.

Here was the hitch. Pregel needed access to the Belgian uranium ore if Eldorado were to have any hope of refining 350 tons, let alone 500. Once again, he approached Sengier, who was increasingly discouraged that his repeated overtures to the US government had borne no fruit. In July, Pregel told Sengier that the Americans – he didn't specify precisely who – were talking about 500 tons. At the end of August, he proposed a joint venture with profits shared equally. Soon, the figure became 700 tons.

Now Carl French joined the discussions in his role as a Canadian Radium and Uranium Corporation (CRUC) director, not as Eldorado's secretary-treasurer. In a meeting with Sengier on 14 September 1942, he and Pregel tried another tactic. This time, they offered to buy the Belgian uranium directly for $1.615 per pound. Sengier again delayed, assuming correctly that they must have a buyer but without knowing what price they would charge and thus their possible profit.[3] While he stalled, he asked the State Department, which controlled the export trade in strategic commodities, to allow him to ship 1,200 tons to Canada for processing and refining. The move implies that he was now prepared to sell.

Even at this point, the exact terms of the proposed deal were murky. Despite making his proposals to Sengier wearing his CRUC hat, Pregel does not appear to have intended to use his own funds to acquire the Staten Island ore. That money was almost certainly going to come from Eldorado, effectively controlled by Carl French.

For his part, Sengier would surely have realized that Eldorado could not hope to make up the necessary tonnage by itself. How did Pregel justify the offer of shared profits? The proposal must have involved monetizing Eldorado's refining capacity. What's more, although the published history of UMHK does not mention it, the deal could have produced a substantial commission for Pregel under his agreement with Eldorado. If he made a separate agreement with UMHK, the commission would be higher still.[4] A potential obstacle – as became evident later – was the question of whether Pregel was entitled to a commission under his Eldorado sales agreement if the company refined someone else's uranium.

Hopes Postponed

By this point, Pregel believed he had outwitted Sengier and was within days of securing ownership and control of all the existing stocks of uranium in North America: whatever Eldorado had, plus whatever belonged to

UMHK. He was wrong. When Sengier approached the State Department, Pregel hit a wall. State objected, and the deal fell apart. Finally, somehow, Washington had begun to connect the dots, and for the first time there was a mechanism to do it.

In June 1942, the Roosevelt administration had transferred responsibility for atomic development to the US Army, specifically charging the Corps of Engineers with the task. The army created an entity they called the Manhattan Engineering District (MED), a natural enough name given that the engineers divided their organization into geographical units and the atomic project was run by the group located in Manhattan. Over the summer, Sengier's contacts at the State Department realized something was going on with the army and talked to the MED, which revealed that it had been engaged in its own discussions about acquiring uranium, but with Pregel. The Manhattan Project was the mystery customer that Eldorado's salesman had hinted at. That customer now connected with the original seller, Sengier, and cut out the middleman, Pregel.

What does the 1,200-ton affair tell us about Boris Pregel? In retrospect it is easy to dismiss his manoeuvres as a grand folly. Yet it is remarkable how close he got to cornering the market in uranium, with nobody to stop him. Once they grasped what was happening, the British labelled Pregel the Uranium King, which seems fitting for his combination of boldness and ambition.

Pregel did not place all his eggs in one or even two baskets. In addition to dealing with UMHK and Eldorado, he used Ventures Ltd., a Toronto speculative mining firm, to stake claims at Great Bear Lake. He also had an interest in another entity, International Uranium Mining Company Ltd., which he shared with Carl French. Although ethically dubious, investing in two separate uranium companies was not strictly forbidden by his contract with Eldorado, as lawyers in Toronto probably advised him.[5] It suggests an intention to get into the actual mining of uranium, perhaps with an eye toward folding Eldorado into a larger mining company that he would control.

Having assembled the building blocks for his uranium kingdom, he was starting to move them into place, negotiating with the MED for the sale and processing of more than 1,000 tons of uranium. Had he been working with the usual supervisors and civilian administrators, Pregel's experience and savoir faire might have seen him through. But this time his mixture of careful planning and luck forsook him.

The Manhattan Project Grows Up

By the summer of 1942, the US atomic project had outgrown the informal administration that surrounded its creation in late 1941 and early 1942. Perched atop the new administration run by the US Army was a superstructure of civilians, headed by former university presidents James Conant and Vannevar Bush. Roosevelt also tasked Vice-President Henry Wallace, the only political member of the administration who was also a scientist, with the project. He was knowledgeable but had no executive authority, stayed on the sidelines, and was generally ignored. That summer, British involvement was still a possibility though hopes of a partnership faded rapidly in the autumn.

In mid-September, American civilian and military officials met at the Bohemian Grove resort, just outside San Francisco, to sketch out the dimensions of the Manhattan Project. The agreement to pursue a bomb had implications for the British Tube Alloys nuclear project, but the British weren't invited. Because the Americans did not yet know how they would create an atomic bomb, they decided to pursue several lines of attack at full cost for each, sums it was assumed would be astronomical. Whatever they were, the British couldn't afford them, and thus the project went forward on American terms, shifting the balance of power between the two countries.[6]

With so much uncertainty, the Americans needed every pound of uranium available, but it was only after the Bohemian Grove meeting that it became apparent how significant the requirements would be. The army sent Lieutenant Colonel Kenneth Nichols to see Sengier. On September 18th, Nichols bought all 1,200 tons of Belgian ore on behalf of the MED. The two parties had agreed, in principle, that an intermediary was unnecessary.

But the Belgian ore still had to be refined, so Eldorado had to be part of any transaction. Negotiating with the Canadian company was the logical next step, made complicated by concerns about secrecy. The army engineers could not consult the usual range of American diplomats, bureaucrats, and army personnel about the arrangement. Information was spotty and context was missing. The situation encouraged a certain tunnel vision.

The British were not involved, and nor were the Canadians, at least not directly. Although Gilbert LaBine was effectively working for C.D. Howe, he seems to have told the minister nothing.

General Leslie Groves, 1948 | US Army Corps of Engineers

Confusion was exacerbated by the transfer of personnel from the original civilian atomic project to the MED. On September 17th, Brigadier General Leslie Groves became the head of the project.[7] Ambitious, egotistical, and bloody minded, Groves was summed up as a "son of a bitch" by his deputy, Lieutenant Colonel Kenneth Nichols, who added that he profoundly respected his boss. Groves could be difficult, rude, and inconsiderate, but he was also an excellent executive who was not impervious to effective argument, facts, and reason. He was cautious about foreigners but worked easily with those he liked and respected.[8]

Groves maintained a suite of executive officers around him at his headquarters in Washington. Nichols was more sophisticated, better educated, and better travelled. Sometimes impatient with his superior's views and actions, he concluded that they often arose from a lack of familiarity with the subject. Nichols had travelled to Canada in connection with the production of heavy water in Trail, British Columbia, and knew well that dealing with Canadian officials involved an international border and a responsible minister.

John Lansdale and Lieutenant Colonel William A. Consodine handled legal and security matters. Consodine managed intelligence, in particular surveillance. To ensure secrecy and preserve national security, the Manhattan Project had its own dedicated security staff, some of whom, like Consodine, enlisted for the war. Many had experience in various police departments and even the Secret Service.

There were also geologists, based in the Murray Hill unit of the MED, including Major Phillip Merritt, who knew Canada and its mines. With his specialized knowledge, he was able to brief Groves and Nichols about the condition of the Eldorado mine and refinery. In 1943, he travelled north to see the mine at Great Bear Lake, so he knew about its production limitations and transportation problems. That same year, he also met Boris Pregel, whose Russian-Romanian-French background had already aroused suspicions.

The Seats at the Table

Although the Manhattan Project was not formally a tripartite affair, Canada and the United Kingdom had to be involved in some way. For so many Americans, Canadians were not foreigners. Canadian scientists often trained in the United States and were indistinguishable by accent and habits from their American colleagues. More troubling was the existence of a border. Groves treated it as invisible, even non-existent, and was utterly unaware of the Canadian government. He had no connection with C.D. Howe, and did not know of his existence, though to be fair, Howe knew nothing about Groves, having relied on Gilbert LaBine to keep him abreast of what was going on with the Americans.

Bush and Conant, now directors of the Manhattan Project, made the decision early on to exclude the British from most atomic research, and Groves – who agreed – merely implemented that decision. There was no reason to include them because they could not contribute to expenses. This came as a nasty surprise to the British. They had wanted to work out their own problems with Tube Alloys before approaching the Americans but waited too long, having failed to understand how quickly the Americans now moved in mid-1942.

Without talking to the US administration, the British decided to transfer their most significant research and development to the safety of a laboratory in Montreal, Canada – far from German bombers and close to the United States but still within the British empire. The benefit was not just safety but funding; the Canadians knew well the British could not afford to pay for the atomic laboratory, so they did. Howe, having been consulted, approved the arrangement almost immediately on August 17th.

More detailed arrangements were made in October 1942, when Howe was in London to discuss war supply. The British would staff and direct the lab in Montreal; the Canadians would pay for it. Howe agreed, and assigned Lesslie Thomson, his special assistant, to make it happen. By 1942, Thomson had been elevated from "assistant to the minister" to "special liaison officer" in recognition of his indispensability.

And make it happen Thomson did. Over the winter of 1942–43, British scientists arrived in Montreal, ready to continue their atomic research. Waiting for them was a laboratory with better equipment than what they left back in England. The only thing they lacked was uranium. When he returned to Ottawa from London, Howe had directed his staff to restrict trade in uranium and radium. Having conferred with the most knowledgeable people on the subject, LaBine and French, his staff produced a regulation at the end of January 1943 that required formal permission to trade in those substances.[9] Regulations of this sort had proved sufficient for dealing in other scarce and valuable commodities, and there was no reason to expect a different result this time. The task was even more straightforward because Eldorado was the only producer of either uranium or radium in Canada, and the government owned most of its shares. No one stopped to consider whether ownership meant control.

The Uranium Contracts

Wallace Akers's refusal to commit the British to buying Boris Pregel's uranium in the summer of 1942 was a mistake. By autumn, it became clear why. Rather than deal through Pregel, Akers had preferred to follow proper channels and deal with the Canadian government. The government in turn asked Dr. C.J. Mackenzie to order the uranium through the National Research Council, which would preserve secrecy and security. Both were illusory, as already noted.

The Northern Miner had already made it clear that the Americans were buying Eldorado's uranium, though there was a certain complexity to the deal. A series of contracts folded one agreement into the next and involved two sources of ore from two separate companies in two different countries. Every arrangement committed production and sale of U_3O_8 to the US Army. But that was not all: the contracts included by-products such as irradiated lead, radioactive residues and, most importantly, radium. While the US Army took all the uranium, the other substances were supposed to be returned to their original owner, either UMHK or Eldorado. The British weren't mentioned anywhere. The only questions were how quickly Eldorado could satisfy the demand and how pure the product was going to be. The answers were problematic.

The earliest contracts involved Eldorado and Stone & Webster, a contractor for the American program while it was still under civilian management. The first negotiation between Eldorado and the US Army followed almost immediately on the sale of the Belgian ore to the army in autumn 1942. That ore had been owned by African Metals (Afrimet), the North American subsidiary of UMHK. Carl French led Eldorado's negotiations, with Marcel Pochon in reserve, while Lieutenant Colonel Nichols represented the Americans. The Pregel brothers – Boris, who was now joined by the younger Alexander – did not participate, though it hardly mattered. They were amply represented by French, who sat on the board of their company CRUC, and Pochon, who was a salaried CRUC employee.

The contract should have been simple. French and Pochon admitted that Eldorado could not fulfill the 350-ton order from its own ores, but the Americans already knew this and proposed a new contract, this time between the MED and Eldorado, to use the Port Hope facility to refine the 1,200 tons of Belgian ore now owned by the US Army. Someone – probably French or Pochon – suggested that CRUC and Pregel be included as parties. Nichols rejected the idea. No other parties needed to be involved, particularly not CRUC, which he referred to specifically.

Eldorado agreed to stop refining its Canadian ore, only 150 tons of which had been processed, and to turn to the Belgian material first. The remaining 200 tons of the previous 350-ton contract was rolled into a new one, becoming 500 tons in December 1942 and then 700 tons. The 700-ton contract, concluded on 22 June 1943, would become central to the legal proceedings that would eventually follow.

French pushed back on the arrangement. He insisted there could be no direct contract between Eldorado and the US Army, claiming that the company did not want to be responsible for housing US government property at the refinery because the Americans might use their ownership to interfere with the facility. Instead, French told Nichols the Belgian ore would have to be kept separate from the Canadian product, a peculiar argument because the Canadians would soon run out of ore to process.

French told the Americans they would lose nothing in the exchange: the price would be the same, but Eldorado would have peace of mind that the Americans would not interfere with the company. That argument seems to have made the difference. In September 1942, the MED agreed to a contract in which it would sell the uranium content of the Belgian ore to Eldorado and buy it back when refining was complete.

At no point did French mention that Eldorado was no longer a private company or that the Canadian government was its majority shareholder. Had he done so, it might have occurred to the Americans that they could deal directly with C.D. Howe and the Canadian government. For obvious reasons, French wanted to avoid that. Nor do MED officers appear to have considered whether to include the Canadian government in the atomic secret, or to cooperate with it.

The Persistence of Pregel

Unspoken were the terms of Pregel's 1940 contract with Eldorado, which covered the sale of the company's radium, uranium, and ancillary items. It did not, however, refer to refining. That meant Pregel did not benefit unless there was a sale, which French's proposed transfer of ownership supplied.

The Canadian government knew nothing about the September 1942 contract or any of what followed. Gilbert LaBine knew but did not tell Howe. In the version of events that French gave LaBine, the Americans had insisted on Pregel's involvement. They wanted to deal with and through an American company, and CRUC was definitely that.[10]

In fact, it was French who insisted to the Americans that CRUC become part of the contract, as "co-adventurer" with Eldorado. Had French explained it accurately to LaBine, the Eldorado president might not have been charmed. CRUC invested no funds and expended no effort but pocketed the proceeds. The arrangement cost Eldorado a lot: Pregel's commission on the transaction.

The devil was in the details. One obvious detail involved the mathematics of the arrangement. Eldorado had committed itself to refining 1,200 tons of Belgian ore plus 700 tons of Canadian ore at the rate of a ton a day, or 1,900 days. Even allowing for improvements in the plant – greater efficiencies and greater capacity were required – this would keep Eldorado producing ore for the Americans into 1947 or 1948.

With this production schedule, Eldorado would also keep producing radium and other radioactive substances, such as lead. As far as the Americans were concerned, radium was merely a by-product of the uranium they wanted. They knew it had some uses, but most of those were unconnected to the atomic project. Eldorado and the UMHK knew that radium was worth considerably more than the cost of production, even if it commanded a lower price than it once did. Under the arrangements with the MED, the tonnage of pitchblende that would pass through Eldorado was unprecedented, creating not just economies of scale but actual savings because the sale of the by-products covered the cost of separating uranium from radium.

For Pregel and Sengier, the real market involved radium, and uranium provided the opportunity to make more of it at a reduced cost. The Americans handed back all the radium to Afrimet (for UMHK), replacing what had been lost when the Germans occupied Olen in 1940. And the same benefit was replicated for Eldorado. It was like old times: Sengier profited from the MED deals, and Pregel took his cut, though this time from Eldorado.

Years afterward, Nichols stated that he neither liked nor trusted Boris Pregel.[11] When they met in the summer of 1942, Pregel had not told him of the pile of uranium ore stored in Staten Island and gave no sense of a common purpose in the atomic project. Nichols was concerned enough to ask Sengier if he could build a refinery of his own in the United States. Presumably the MED could have met the cost, or UMHK could have recouped it through its sales to the army. Sengier, however, demurred. When the Germans seized Olen, they had taken over not just the plant but the technicians who knew how to run it. Sengier could not replicate their skills in North America, and thus Port Hope was the only option. Sengier warned Nichols that Pregel could not be trusted to keep his hands off radium that properly belonged to UMHK. Not all was forgotten. Pregel's dismissal and Lechien's flight to Central America had not happened by accident.

Nichols realized he could not get around Pregel or his contract. He was not willing to ignore legal forms by invoking emergency powers. He and his colleagues respected what they regarded as a valid contract between Pregel and Eldorado. It was the same in Canada, where legal forms similarly insulated Pregel's activities unless or until his sales agreement was terminated.

Pregel was thus a party to all the American contracts from March 1942 until the summer of 1943. There were no disagreements over the price of uranium, and the economics of radium were still favourable. It could be produced for $6,000 a gram in Port Hope and sold for anything from $12,000 to $20,000 per gram, far less than the prices commanded in the

1920s but still far more than any other mineral. And the market was active: between 1940 and 1945 Afrimet sold 266 grams of radium, worth 116,242,000 Belgian francs (US$3.91 million at the time). Pregel continued to work with radium and to come up with new, imaginative ways to turn a profit.[12]

Corporate Adventures in Radium

Pregel had participated in and promoted all manner of uses of radium in Europe before the war, and had not stopped once he got to North America. Throughout the conflict, Eldorado continued its radium production because it was easy to do; every ton of uranium ore that arrived at the refinery carried with it a small harvest of radium. By the 1940s, the production cost was a few thousand dollars per gram, depending on the quality of ore fed into the radium circuit. During this period, the price of radium fluctuated, but even at the low range, there was a profit because there was demand.

There was a serious military use for radium. Thousands of airplanes rolled off North American production lines, each with dials made luminous with radioactive paint. Radiation could also reveal defects in steel. Vice-President Henry Wallace was one of many who believed that radium could benefit crops. By 1942, Pregel had established a variety of companies to promote these uses, maintaining either direct control or control through family members such as his wife and sister-in-law as officers or directors. His brother, Alexander, continued an involvement that had started in 1930, but his role was more of an adjutant, with some executive responsibility. There was no doubt who called the shots.

Pregel and Carl French became partners in a number of these companies dealing in radium, the most prominent of which was French's Radium Luminous Industries, established in Toronto in 1942. There was nothing surreptitious about this, either. French asked for and received Gilbert LaBine's permission to run the company's affairs out of Eldorado's office until he rented quarters a few blocks away at 103 Church Street in downtown Toronto. In fairness, it was not unusual for mining speculators to divide their attention among various companies and interests. Even LaBine had another company, Gunnar Gold Mine, and easily drew an analogy to French as the head of Radium Luminous Industries.

Pregel and French were also involved together in CRUC. Here, however, Pregel ran the show and French served on the board and received a salary.

More than his other companies, CRUC served as Pregel's alter ego when it came to negotiating contracts. With Gustave Lechien now out of the way, Pregel and French dealt directly with Sengier, not as agents of Eldorado but as representatives of CRUC. Whether LaBine knew fully about French's involvement with CRUC is unclear, but he certainly knew about Pregel's, since the CRUC name was party to contracts with Eldorado.[13] Perhaps more significant was that to the outside world, Pregel represented Eldorado as a useful asset rather than his principal client.

Pregel needed French's administrative skills for his private business ventures. From Marcel Pochon, he needed know-how to set up a factory to refine radium. This he did in Mount Kisco, New York, under the name International Rare Metals Refinery Inc. The company was a miniature replica of Olen or Port Hope but designed and equipped to process only the later stages of radium manufacture. By 1942, Pochon and Pregel had known one another for almost twenty years, since they worked together at South Terras Mine in Cornwall, and had only grown closer once Pregel became involved with Eldorado in 1940. Whether Pochon offered his services in June 1942 or Pregel requested them is unknown. Whatever the arrangement, Pregel paid Pochon as a salaried employee and board member (though whether of CRUC or of International Rare Metals is not altogether clear), all the while urging the French chemist to remain in the same position at Eldorado until "we feel that you would be much more useful by joining the organization here, or until we require your full time services."[14] Whereas French and Pregel operated on equal footing, Pochon's relationship to Pregel was as a subordinate, albeit a necessary one.

A Spat between Allies

During this period, the British secured the 20 tons of uranium they needed through Canada's National Research Council, thanks to C.D. Howe's visit to London in October 1942. The British had something else to discuss. Michael Perrin handed Howe a memorandum on Boris Pregel, drawn from sources that included British intelligence and materials from British High Commissioner Malcolm MacDonald in Ottawa. Not everything in the memo was well founded, but it was highly uncomplimentary and presented Pregel as an unsavoury operator, with the implicit suggestion that he was a swindler. It focused on his very complicated business structures, his holding company Société Anonyme Demetra, and his ambitious nature, along with speculation that Eldorado's salesman might try to corner the market on postwar atomic power, having acquired patents that might help him to do it. Pregel was too well informed and operated outside the security system.[15] The British worried that something was wrong at Eldorado, though they mistakenly thought that UMHK controlled the company.[16] In reality, Carl French ran the day-to-day operations.

Howe trusted his subordinates. Knowing nothing about Pregel and his operations, he sent Gilbert LaBine a copy of the British memorandum for his opinion – standard procedure for Howe. LaBine, too, knew little of Pregel's background, so he turned to Carl French, who lost no time passing the memo on to Pregel. Together, French and Pregel composed a response, passed it to LaBine, who signed and sent it on to Howe.[17]

As French explained through LaBine, the British memo mischaracterized Pregel. Dwelling on the various inaccuracies in the memo, including the year and place of Pregel's birth, the response tried to set the record straight. Pregel was an upright, honest, and efficient citizen. Numerous Americans could – and did – attest to his loyal service to the Allied cause. What's more, the memo stated, "His knowledge of the uranium field is of vital importance." The hostile comments from the British were just jealousy and spite, probably emanating from Gustave Lechien and UMHK.

Howe bought the explanation and forwarded the company's response to MacDonald, who was horrified. A secret assessment drawn from intelligence sources had been shared with its subject for comment. It shook British confidence in Howe. There was more to come from someone who knew Pregel.

Bertrand Goldschmidt, a young Jewish chemist who had trained at the Curie laboratory, fled France in 1941. When he arrived penniless in New York, he sought help from Madame Curie's salesman. Pregel got him a job in the refinery at Port Hope, where he was delighted to meet a fellow Frenchman, Marcel Pochon. The two became friends and kept in touch when Goldschmidt moved on to work in the British lab in Montreal.

In Montreal in 1942, the British were trying to develop a plutonium-producing reactor called "piles." They assumed they had the necessary uranium because of the 20 tons that Wallace Akers had secured. Of that, 5 tons had been sent to England, while the remaining 15 had been sent to an American facility for further purification, to be ready for the new lab early in 1943. But the Americans needed all the uranium they could get in autumn 1942, and begged to borrow what the British sent. The British agreed on the understanding the Americans would provide them with uranium when they were ready for it.

There matters stood in January 1943. Relations between the parties deteriorated as the Americans were no longer interested in an equal partnership. They limited cooperation and exchanges of information to what would be useful to the American project and refused to return the promised 15 tons of uranium.

The news reached the Montreal lab casually, almost accidentally. Goldschmidt stopped in to see his friend Pochon in Port Hope en route from Montreal to the Met Lab in Chicago. Pochon mentioned how busy the refinery was, describing how the contract with the Americans to refine Belgian ore had pre-empted Eldorado's capacity for the next several years. Goldschmidt was shocked and quickly understood the implications. The British had established their atomic laboratory in Montreal on the assumption that uranium would be forthcoming from the Americans. Now, the very basis of the lab was in jeopardy. Howe, the British discovered, knew nothing of the arrangements with the Americans, nor did any of his staff.

The first eight months of 1943 were spent trying to find a way to patch up the atomic dissonance between the British and the Americans. The British wanted and needed an arrangement and were dismayed when the Americans no longer agreed. Soon, Churchill and Roosevelt were involved. But the uranium contracts were a symptom, not the cause, of British nuclear discontent. As junior partners, the Canadians refused to take sides. This irritated the British, who blamed Howe and Mackenzie for undermining their position. Churchill fulminated that Howe had "sold the British Empire down the river," words that were repeated by British officials in Ottawa. Howe was not amused.

As a result, the British never stopped regarding Pregel with suspicion. In May 1943, they undermined Pregel's reputation with the Canadians by sharing the news with Howe that he was busy staking his own claims around Great Bear Lake. Outraged, Howe wrote to LaBine on May 26th, observing with a touch of incredulity that Pregel would be competing directly with Eldorado if he were to find uranium. The minister could not tolerate that and said so. In such a situation, he wrote, "the Government must intervene as we can only have one company in the radium [and uranium] business."

LaBine acknowledged that the International Uranium Mining Company Ltd. had staked claims near Port Radium, and in mid-1942 Pregel had acquired an interest in them. But Eldorado's president said they were good for nothing but a bit of silver, which he had already told Pregel. LaBine was correct. There were no other viable uranium deposits within hundreds of miles of Port Radium. Nevertheless, in the unlikely event that Pregel did make a radioactive find, "government machinery" could take care of it.[18]

Howe was not satisfied. On June 12th, he wrote to LaBine with a clear admonition: "I hope that Mr. Pregel can be taken out of the mining field in Canada. As you suggest, we must keep this as an Eldorado monopoly." By mid-1943, any notion that Eldorado might become a venture shared with the British and Americans had disappeared. Howe was making decisions about the company on his own.

By August, the spat was resolved. At a highly secret military conference held in Quebec City and codenamed Quadrant, British prime minister Winston Churchill and US president Franklin Roosevelt settled the direction of the Manhattan Project, along with the division of uranium supplies. Now, the Montreal laboratory would get the uranium it needed, which turned out to be very little compared to the many tons travelling south from Eldorado's refinery.

Eldorado had played a prominent and embarrassing role in the affair by failing to report its sales to the government. Howe was the responsible minister but had been completely unaware of the contracts or their meaning. Yet Howe appears not to have reproached the man who headed a company in which the Canadian government held a majority of the shares. The British had been told that Eldorado was a Crown company, but that was not yet true. It was still a private entity, with publicly traded stocks. Here, secrecy led the governments of Canada and Great Britain into a dead end.

After the Quebec Conference, the conflict among the three atomic allies, which focused almost exclusively on uranium, was resolved. Now, the position and importance of uranium and radium had been reversed, but Eldorado still had a production line that was turning out grams of radium – and that radium had value.

Americans in the Dark

By summer 1943, the directors of the Manhattan Project believed they understood the British only too well: their touchiness, their assertiveness, and their determination to have their way. They did not, however, understand the Canadians. There was no means by which they could have done so, officially. The atomic project was too secret for the American legation in Ottawa to be told. Other American war production agencies, which had multiple contacts with the Canadians, knew nothing either. Canadian and American war production was closely integrated, and exchanges of supplies were routine, all managed by Howe's Department of Munitions and Supply. So close was the relationship that the Canadian metals controller, who was responsible for directing minerals from mines to factories, was the brother of the American metals controller. The two even shared a house in Washington at one point during the war.

The depth of American ignorance about Canada and the Canadian government was remarkable. Contacts between Ottawa and Washington on atomic matters began in June 1942 but were confined to Vannevar Bush and James Conant, who reported directly to the president. When administration of the atomic project was transferred to the MED, the army was not briefed about relations with Canada. Carl French and Marcel Pochon could thus present a distorted view of Canadian government policy to the Americans, ostensibly representing Eldorado but serving only themselves during the contract negotiations of September 1942. The Americans had no reason to look behind their presentation or question their motivations, and resigned themselves to having Pregel serve as intermediary.

When Kenneth Nichols led the contract negotiations and the creation of MED's transcontinental facilities in 1942–43, his contact with Eldorado was French. Their discussions coincided with some of the fiercest exchanges between the British and the Americans over uranium supply, while the Canadian government scrambled to find out what was going on. It was only in June 1943 that Nichols discovered there was a problem with the Canadian government. Only then did French suggest he contact Howe in Ottawa. From staff, Nichols learned of scattered references to Howe throughout the MED files, and asked his secretary to call him. When the two finally spoke, Howe confirmed that he did indeed have questions about MED's Canadian contracts and "in a pleasant voice" suggested a meeting in Ottawa to discuss it. Nichols took an overnight train from New York to Ottawa and arrived at the address provided. Only then did he realize that Howe was Canada's minister of munitions and supply.[19]

Howe handled Nichols with aplomb, as the American's later account makes plain:

> Howe turned out to be a most friendly person and I soon realized that he knew what we were doing in the Manhattan Project. He confirmed that the Canadian government had purchased Eldorado and had turned it into a Crown company. He laughed and chided me about how long it had taken us to contact him. Now that we had acknowledged that the Canadian

Colonel Kenneth Nichols, 1945 | Photo by Ed Westcott, US Department of Energy

> government existed, he said that he would designate Leslie Thompson [sic] as a liaison with us and I could expect no further opposition to the contracts.[20]

The two also discussed prospecting in Canada's North. Howe remarked that he knew the Americans were looking for uranium, and observed that it was a matter better left to the Canadian government. Nichols readily agreed. On July 21st, Lesslie Thomson accompanied Nichols to Port Hope, where they met Pochon to discuss the possibility of increasing the rate of production. Pochon also took the opportunity to show Nichols the radium production circuit, where a batch had just been completed. He showed off the luminous properties of the radium by holding a vial of the substance under his jacket so the American could see the glow.

It was around this time that Groves also learned of Howe's existence. In response to the general's musings about how one might get in touch with Howe, Nichols suggested he simply pick up the telephone. This Groves did, with the result that he and Nichols met with Howe and C.J. Mackenzie in late July. Mackenzie was already familiar, and Howe and Groves discovered that they shared a common bond as MIT alumni. Most important, Howe and Groves established friendly and confidential contact. As Nichols had learned, Howe was already on the right side of the security wall, so conversations could proceed without concern.[21]

Within weeks, Roosevelt and Churchill resolved the atomic quarrel during the Quebec Conference. Along with Mackenzie King, they created the Combined Policy Committee (CPC), the guiding body consisting of the United States, United Kingdom, and Canada. Howe was designated the Canadian member, and for the next two years, he travelled back and forth to Washington for its meetings. When he could not attend in person, Mackenzie was his substitute. Membership on the CPC was an acknowledgment that Howe, his associates, and his agents were all people the Americans could trust.

The Pregel Problem

Boris Pregel was among the problems that Howe and Groves discussed. He was everywhere. His name was on contracts and yet he seemed to serve no purpose. He had established his own factory to process radioactive substances. He marketed his own radium. He talked freely to scientists working for Groves. His very existence seemed to negate the security and secrecy that surrounded the Manhattan Project. From Howe's perspective, Pregel's relationship with Eldorado presented a conflict of interest that could harm the company. On Pregel the governments' views were aligned. After attending the July meeting, C.J. Mackenzie recorded in his diary that "Groves would like to get Pregel out of the picture and would like a direct contract between the U.S. Army and the Department of Munitions and Supply."[22]

Groves acted first. He simply rewrote the contracts to exclude Pregel as far as uranium was concerned. Pregel seems to have accepted this development as inevitable, and acquiesced, painting his concession in vivid, patriotic colours. Yet he remained a factor in the sale of radium and other products, such as radioactive lead. Those were marketed separately and belonged to Eldorado and UMHK, respectively. The Manhattan Project had nothing to do with them.

Howe acted next to exclude Pregel from staking claims in the Arctic. Great Bear Lake is in the Northwest Territories and thus under the direct control of the federal government.[23] On 15 September 1943, with no provincial governments to obstruct Ottawa's will, an order in council declared all radioactive substances found in the Northwest Territories were to be reserved to the Crown.[24] At a stroke, the International Uranium Mining Company Ltd. was out of business.

Pregel was furious. He complained to Thomson in what appears to have been his first personal contact with the Canadian government.[25] The gist of that conversation was reproduced for the benefit of the US Army Corps of Engineers in a memorandum the following month, when Pregel related what he had told Howe's aide. His claim that the new regulation was "anti-constitutional" was very much a misinterpretation of Canadian law, and his question to Thomson – "What have you paid for this order?" – might have better fitted czarist Russia than wartime Canada. "Until now, nobody was interested in radio-active materials and everybody worked there and now you won't have anybody," Pregel avowed. Neither Thomson nor the Americans were impressed by Pregel's intimation of corruption.[26]

Interestingly, Pregel might have considered approaching the Canadians about his exclusion from the uranium contracts, but he did not. Instead, he decided to speak to Groves directly on October 25th. The general prepared by securing a telephone in the middle of a table where he sat across from Pregel, which was in fact a microphone, wired to a speaker in an outer office. In that office sat geologist Major Phillip Merritt, who was interpreting Pregel's accented English for the stenographer transcribing the conversation.

Pregel asked Groves to get the Canadians to withdraw the order in council. As he told Groves, he was acting as an American patriot, while the Canadian intervention was, by definition, anti-American. "Everybody knows you are interested in radioactive material – everyone," he told Groves, "and [the Canadian action] is against the interests of the United States." Soon after, Groves ended the interview, owing to his busy schedule.[27]

The order in council remained in place. The US Army had not and did not complain about Howe's designation of "radioactive substances." It was far better to place uranium procurement on a government-to-government basis, better still to get Pregel out of the way. On this the Canadians and Americans firmly agreed.

The Question of Secrecy

There remained the elusive question of secrecy. As Pregel had observed to Groves, "Everybody knows you are interested in radioactive materials – everyone." It was true enough. Mining stocks continued to be traded on the Toronto Stock Exchange, with rumours propelling investors to buy up so-called radioactive securities. Howe decided to act. On 28 January 1944, he rose in the House of Commons to announce that Eldorado had been nationalized. Its stock had been selling for $1.31, but the government would pay $1.35 for any outstanding shares. Investors would have no choice but to sell.

Although the move was intended to implement government control, the government did not seek any changes at the company, which operated with the same executives after June 1942 as before. The quarrel between the British and the Americans in the winter and spring of 1943 did not include Eldorado, despite its sales contracts being the most pertinent feature of the confrontation. Even the formal announcement in January 1944 changed nothing.

That Eldorado was somewhat furtively nationalized was of no obvious benefit to the company or the various governments involved in the atomic project. Depending on one's perspective, it was either pointless or farcical. Although uranium was the reason behind nationalization, the company was still a significant producer of radium. Authorities either missed or ignored the inextricable connection between the two. It was not overlooked by the three men at the centre of this story: Boris Pregel, Carl French, and Marcel Pochon.

7
From State Secrets to Corporate Fraud

When he finally announced the nationalization of Eldorado Mining and Refining on 28 January 1944, C.D. Howe told the House of Commons that he hoped "no questions will be asked until the necessity for withholding information no longer applies."[1] Most of Howe's listeners would have thought the minister was referring to matters of national security and the necessity of keeping strategic information from the enemy. But wartime secrecy was a double-edged sword. While it protected, it also obscured; the sense of safety it created was often illusory. One thing was undoubtedly true: there was no transparency.

Nobody had any idea what was going on at Eldorado, including the minister. The problems at Eldorado surfaced only after the company was nationalized, and led Howe to order a formal investigation of its financial management and transactions during the war. Investigators J. Grant Glassco and John Robinette were awarded sweeping powers under an order in council.

To many within Canada's mining industry, Eldorado's recent business activities were not news. Anyone reading not only *The Northern Miner* but the *Toronto Daily Star* or *The Globe and Mail* already knew that Eldorado had been supplying uranium to the Americans since 1942 for a secret project. Investors bought and sold the company's shares on the information, wondering whether they had made a good deal. Readers also knew from popular science articles that splitting the atom could release a huge amount of energy.

The war brought widespread concern about enemy agents planted within existing communities of immigrants across Canada and the United States and ready to send secrets back to Berlin or Tokyo or Rome.[2] That Canadians and their government took precautions made sense – we do not mean that there were no spies in Canada or in the atomic project – but the state of atomic affairs was not nearly as secret as those with security clearance wanted the population to believe, and still isn't.

When the war began in 1939, the Canadian government had one agency and one statute to guard the country's secrets: the Royal Canadian Mounted Police (RCMP) and the *Official Secrets Act, 1939*.[3] Many have questioned if Canada had secrets worth keeping, and many more remembered efforts during the First World War to prosecute those alleged to be disloyal. The result was a general disinclination to do the same during the Second World War, which meant there was no pre-censorship of information although some details about military movements and Atlantic convoys were obviously sensitive and dangerous. "Loose lips sink ships" was an effective and necessary general admonition on the news. Other information could be restricted or protected. The explosive RDX was believed likely to attract espionage, and so the RCMP kept an eye on it to ensure that facts that could assist a hostile power were not disclosed.[4]

The RCMP – the Mounties in common parlance and popular culture – was charged with overseeing national security issues in Canada. Organized along paramilitary lines in thirteen divisions spread coast to coast, the force numbered just under five thousand by 1943, only ninety-eight of whom were commissioned officers. As in other police forces, officers were promoted from the non-commissioned ranks, though most enlisted Mounties would never make it to commissioned status. The RCMP had the usual police authority and mandate that could command attention, but it was not an extravagantly funded organization. The Mounties enjoyed none of the extra resources and specialized training that had become commonplace in the United States within its counterpart, the Federal Bureau of Investigation, which was housed within the Department of Justice and under the watchful eye of J. Edgar Hoover.[5]

During the 1920s and '30s, the RCMP were regularly deployed to monitor radicals, real and imagined, including communists and fascists. In 1939–40, officers rounded up individuals considered disloyal or detrimental to the war effort. Most, but not all, were foreign nationals or foreign born, especially Germans, Italians, and Japanese. Some were Canadian citizens, especially those of Japanese ancestry. Because Canadian communists followed the lead of Soviet dictator Joseph Stalin in resisting the war between

1939 and 1941, many were also rounded up, only to be released when Germany invaded the Soviet Union.

While the RCMP took a primary role in the protection of federal agencies and wartime industries, the Canadian government was slow to implement security screening to protect the civil service and sensitive war work from those who were actively or potentially disloyal. RCMP officers were nonetheless assigned to assess individuals in particularly sensitive posts, a process based not just on evidence of disloyalty but on character flaws or circumstances that might make someone vulnerable to blackmail. It was a wide, subjective category, and its definition was left to a select group of individual agents, most of them in the junior ranks.

At Eldorado, secrecy had been an aspect of the American uranium purchases in 1942, and few employees knew the particulars of the contracts or how they were carried out, not even board members. From 1942 forward, the information that came before the board was severely limited. Some were curious, but they were routinely stonewalled when they asked for details of operations.[6] Once the company formally became a Crown corporation, regulations required security reviews of key employees who were privy to classified material, broadly defined. Corporal Terrence Guernsey was assigned the task.

Terrence Guernsey, the Police Officer

Terrence Guernsey's background was unexceptional for a police officer in Canada in the 1940s. Born in Penticton, British Columbia, in 1913, Terry came of age in the Great Depression, and the economic turmoil of the time led him to the Mounties. University education was uncommon in the 1930s; for many, finishing high school was a challenge despite high ability. It is not clear that he managed it. Without the credentials that would be considered commonplace today, Guernsey's options were few. The Mounties offered "three squares, clothes, and a warm place to sleep," he later recalled. It was a job that took him across the country, from basic training in Regina to postings in Winnipeg and Ottawa. He was assigned to the Preventive Service, whose task it was to chase bootleggers in New Brunswick, and then moved into general criminal investigations in Alberta before landing back on the East Coast in Prince Edward Island, where he was stationed in 1939. It was then that he found a job that allowed him to shine: industrial security in Toronto.[7]

Terrence Guernsey, 1930s | Royal Canadian Mounted Police, Library and Archives Canada, PA-202110

As Guernsey described it, "industrial security was seeing that the plants which had war contracts were protecting their own interests in relation to the Department of Munitions and Supply contracts, and also I was on suspected sabotage investigations within that area and the armed services."[8] When it came to the Manhattan Project, his primary objective was to keep ongoing research away from current and potential enemies.[9] The enemies he expected to find were external, foreign agents or enemy sympathizers who might betray the country. German agents were scarce, but Soviet sympathizers were plentiful. Even though the Soviet Union was an ally, its government engaged in espionage.

Meanwhile, more run-of-the-mill communists were working for Eldorado. Among the immigrant hard rock miners at Great Bear Lake were "Red Finns," who had fled Finland when a communist revolution failed. The postmaster at Port Radium was amused by the appearance of their mail: magazines in Finnish, with the hammer and sickle on the covers. But the Soviet embassy in Ottawa did not know about the Red Finns, and the Red Finns did not know about the embassy – it would have been difficult to run a spy ring across thousands of miles of rock, muskeg, and mosquitoes. At Port Radium, the work of the local RCMP constable consisted largely of breaking up brawls and keeping an eye on illicit liquor. Toronto was different.

Security work was a challenge, tedious but potentially important.[10] According to one of his colleagues, Guernsey "had a completely analytical mind, and had a genius for cutting through to the heart of any matter ... He was so inquisitive and incisive you had to be awfully sure of yourself."[11] Conducting security clearances during the war was a routine, even monotonous job, but it did not take long before Guernsey's life became much more exciting.

In the fall of 1944, he was assigned to report on Eldorado's key employees. Gilbert LaBine was above scrutiny, but Carl French, Marcel Pochon, and French's secretary, Germaine Vermandere, were not. It was a routine assignment, perfunctory even.

Guernsey had no qualms about Marcel Pochon. No one had reported anything that caused concern, and the company's chief chemist and refinery manager passed with a glowing report in November. Recall that Guernsey had already described Pochon as "quite conservative in both his personal life and political views, remaining fixed to the old school of politics."[12] He exhibited no signs of radicalism or disloyalty to Canada – Guernsey attributed his unimpeachable character to "good parentage" – and also seemed to be irreplaceable: "My sources of information describe Pochon as being of high integrity and probably the only scientist in the world that has the knowledge in his particular field. In other words, he is said to be indispensable."[13]

Carl French, the Secretary-Treasurer

Carl French was a different story. What was it about Eldorado's secretary-treasurer that concerned Guernsey? His influence and role within the company had grown over the course of the war as LaBine's attention wandered to other fields. In January 1944, the board recognized French for his efforts by increasing his annual salary to $7,500. Yet in January 1945, he resigned abruptly.[14]

Despite his training as a lawyer and accountant, French was an entrepreneur at heart. Unbeknownst to his fellow directors, French's outside business interests had blossomed during the war, touching everything from insurance to the radium and uranium industry.[15] The most significant of his business activities during the war was Radium Luminous Industries, which carried out the bulk of its business at 103 Church Street in Toronto, where it manufactured luminous paints and dials. The company also had an office in Chicago, Radium Luminous Industries Inc., not to be confused with French's other Chicago-based company, Industrial Radium Corporation, which had been founded by Boris Pregel. French also served on the boards of two of Pregel's companies: Canadian Radium and Uranium Corporation (CRUC), and International Rare Metals Refinery in Mount Kisco. Additionally, French was involved with CRUC subsidiaries American Radium Industries Inc. and American Luminous Industries Inc., and finally, he created the latecomer Radium Industries in 1945.[16]

Any of these companies could have raised suspicions, but it was French's involvement with possible stock manipulation that troubled Guernsey when he undertook his security review in 1944, especially French's involvement with a securities firm by the name of Bay Securities Ltd. LaBine had experienced his own troubles in this area, too, having been investigated for stock manipulation regarding his company Gunnar Gold Mine in the mid-1930s.[17] Such market manipulation was not uncommon in the mining sector, and the executives at Eldorado were no strangers to it.

This background of competing and conflicting interests, commonplace in the mining sector, was but one piece of the puzzle Guernsey confronted while looking into French. He also suspected that French was involved with International Uranium Mining Company Ltd., about which Howe had complained in 1943. The company, which Guernsey correctly surmised was nothing more than a stock promotion scheme, shared office space with French's other ventures at 103 Church Street. Well-known shady operators were involved, including Charles L. Hershman, who had ties to Bay Securities, which had taken a chunk of share options in International Uranium. Those connections made Guernsey wary, and he refused to approve French's clearance until he had received more information from the Americans, who were also concerned and investigating International Uranium.[18]

It took some time, but the Americans had information that reinforced Guernsey's suspicions. As Guernsey learned, Boris Pregel was also involved with both Bay Securities and International Uranium. In February 1945, the New York US Attorney subpoenaed Maurice Holt, a director of International Uranium. In talking to the Federal Bureau of Investigation, Holt detailed how he had helped arrange the sale of 200,000 shares to the Toronto firm Yam Securities. Pregel had talked up the stock, saying that uranium and radium were surefire postwar investments given their peace- and wartime uses.[19] Holt told investigators he was worried that he had helped to boost the value of the stock artificially, thus benefiting Carl French and the Pregel brothers, each of whom owned sizable blocs of shares. For the time being, the FBI and RCMP had a much narrower concern: Where had the transactions occurred? It mattered because a Canadian company could not lawfully offer its stock for sale, or consummate a sale, in the United States. The proper procedure would have been for a customer to give an order to an American broker to buy the shares on the Toronto Exchange.[20] This had not occurred.

While the police were sniffing around French's business activities, Howe's office was scrutinizing how Eldorado was run, which meant, of course, how French was directing it. By the end of 1943, having been tasked by the minister to monitor Eldorado, Lesslie Thomson also had qualms about the company's management. Though he did not use the word, he came close to saying that Gilbert LaBine was a puppet in French's hands. Thomson could not have known the extent to which French had what was later described as "complete control over the refining operations and financial management of that company" once Harry Snyder left the company in 1940. He ran operations in a way that "permitted no one to question in any way the purpose or motive behind any proceedings instituted under his instructions." Germaine Vermandere, his Belgian-born secretary, "maintained a constant guard over all incoming mail and over all Carl French's records and correspondence files and no one was allowed access to them." The arrangement, an official report later concluded, put French "in the unique situation of being able to manipulate the affairs of Eldorado if he so desired."[21] French did indeed so desire.

As a member of the Eldorado board of directors, French owed a fiduciary duty to the company to act in its best interest. That meant putting Eldorado's needs ahead of his own, whether as an individual or in his many corporate interests. As a matter of contract law, French's terms of employment with Eldorado also obligated him to report outside business ventures, at least any that might compete with Eldorado or that arose from information gleaned through his work with the company. French claimed he had been careful to secure Gilbert LaBine's permission for his involvement with Pregel and his companies, including CRUC, but his other business interests were fair game for investigation.

No evidence suggests that French told anyone about his outside ventures and quite a bit indicates the contrary. Nothing in the Eldorado minute books shows any disclosure by French to the board of his interest in the companies Eldorado was dealing with, nor did he refrain from voting on questions involving transactions with them. Later, when asked, directors confirmed that they knew nothing about his activities. The claim is unprovable but plausible; none of the directors was willing to come to his defence. LaBine was especially upset. He had trusted French so much that he had given him responsibility for much of the company's finances. He had – or at least claimed to have – no idea that French, Pochon, and Pregel were working on outside ventures at the expense of Eldorado.[22]

It was quite a record, much more than Guernsey might have anticipated, and made it easier for him to conclude that French was disreputable. In January 1945, he recommended that Eldorado's secretary-treasurer be denied security clearance. French *was* loyal – but only to himself, his family, and Boris Pregel.

The Net around Pregel

On 30 March 1945, Lieutenant Colonel William A. Consodine and Lieutenant A.E. Whitaker arrived in the Washington office of George Bateman, Canada's metals controller and its representative on the Combined Development Trust (CDT). The CDT was established specifically to coordinate uranium supply for the Manhattan Project. It paralleled the Combined Policy Committee (CPC), which governed British–American relations within the atomic project and made the ultimate decisions on the manufacture and use of the atomic bomb.

Both the trust and the committee arose from the discussions at the Quebec Conference in August 1943, and the Canadians were members of both. C.D. Howe served as their representative on the CPC. He also sat on the CDT, which was chaired by General Leslie Groves. When Howe could not attend, Bateman served in his position.

In an investigation that was wholly separate from Terry Guernsey's probe into Eldorado, the American officers had come to discuss Boris Pregel. Did Bateman know about Pregel's activities in connection with Eldorado? He did not. As the Americans talked it became clear that they knew a great deal more about Pregel than Bateman or any other Canadian official did. When they left, Bateman telephoned C.D. Howe in Ottawa. There was, he told the minister, a problem. Why was Boris Pregel such a source of concern for the Americans?

The Manhattan Project was a security conundrum. How could an organization with thousands of employees spread across a continent keep from being noticed or talked about? What could be done with the hundreds of

George Bateman, 6 June 1941 | Yousuf Karsh, Library and Archives Canada

experts devising the bomb when those experts were professionally wired to chatter among themselves and to anyone else who might be knowledgeable or helpful?

Security policy in the American atomic project had been haphazard before Groves took command. Because of the extreme secrecy that applied to the Manhattan Project, he developed his own intelligence service, which was effectively autonomous from the rest of the army.[23] At first, the Manhattan Engineering District (MED) used officers recruited from army intelligence, but it expanded to take in army volunteers who had served in security in their prewar civilian life. Lieutenant Whitaker, for example, had been a member of the Secret Service for sixteen years before the war.[24] Groves also imposed a policy that was consistent, simple, and easy to understand. Each employee was allowed to know only enough information to do their job properly. Only a very few at the top saw the entire project.

By the time Groves took over the MED, the mining horse was nonetheless well out of the secrecy barn, as we have seen. Nor was his approach entirely effective in suppressing or diverting news reportage. Groves's staff knew that sometimes overt censorship would only draw attention to stories that would otherwise be suppressed. Gossip inside the Manhattan Project, especially among scientists, was naturally a problem, and surveillance could not be everywhere. For example, in 1943, scientists at the Met Lab in Chicago not only allowed British government scientist Bertrand Goldschmidt into the lab but gave him a sample of plutonium to take back to the British lab in Montreal. The British needed it, they reasoned, and Goldschmidt was a friend and trusted ally. There was no spy around, they assumed – erroneously, as it turned out, but that is another story – the gift was not reported to Groves, and as relations improved with the British, so did the communication of information. All this was well and good, but it directly violated the policy set out by Groves. There might well have been unpleasant consequences for the Chicago scientists and for Goldschmidt had Groves found out.

If Groves could not control people working within the Manhattan Project, he certainly could not control the civilians outside the program. Boris Pregel was the prime illustration of this uncomfortable fact. He knew several of the principal scientists involved: Enrico Fermi, Leo Szilard, Jean Perrin,[25] and Arthur Compton. He also knew something about the British Tube Alloys project. There was no point in pretending he didn't know what the uranium was for. The Americans might complain about Pregel's participation in the Eldorado contracts, but they had gullibly accepted his demands, conveyed through Carl French.

There is no doubt that the MED, and especially Groves, resented and mistrusted Pregel. It was not merely that he knew so much but that he was so clearly also talking about it beyond the Manhattan Project.[26] Indeed, it seems to have been the British who set off the chain of events that caused Pregel to attract as much if not more surveillance than almost any of the people usually cited as intelligence targets in histories of the atomic bomb. Pregel was on the Allies' radar even before his efforts to gain Groves's confidence in October 1943 struck precisely the wrong note. As his brother Alexander later commented, Boris Pregel's mannerisms, his assumptions, were simply "off" as far as people like Wallace Akers and Groves were concerned.[27]

The intelligence file on Pregel's activities grew throughout 1943 and 1944 because of the extraordinary effort Groves ordered his staff to take. The MED intelligence unit was not subject to the kind of budgetary constraints that governed the RCMP, and from at least 1943 it deployed considerable resources to shadow Pregel. At one point no fewer than twenty agents were keeping an eye – and an ear – on him, which is why there is a transcript of the conversation he had with Groves in October that year. There were other surveillance operations. The army had rented an office in the Rockefeller Center to house the very large, heavy surveillance machines of the day.[28] That meant the conversations with French and Pochon, who were frequent visitors to Pregel's office in the same building, were also captured.

The MED was not alone in its suspicions. The Secret Service, in its role as Treasury investigators, expressed concerns about Eldorado in relation to foreign exchange matters as early as 1943. The Treasury knew exactly who to speak to in Canada: the part of the RCMP that dealt with commercial crime, in this case Corporal William McElhone, who was based in Toronto.[29] McElhone worked with the Foreign Exchange Control Board (FECB), which regulated transfers of money between Canada and the rest of the world. The Canadian government employed a large staff to keep track of money flows, especially when, as in the case of Eldorado, it involved hundreds of thousands of dollars. On a more modest level, the FECB rationed the foreign exchange Canadian travellers could take abroad. McElhone developed a speciality in financial crimes.

The relationship between the Canadians and Americans on these financial matters was both close and personal. In 1943, Whitaker, who had worked with McElhone before, learned that the Canadian officer would be in New York on FECB business and invited him to stop by the MED offices. It was then that Whitaker shared his concerns about Pregel, hoping McElhone might have information to share. He did not but agreed to be on guard.

Thus, by the time Bateman called Howe on Easter weekend in 1945, Pregel's name had already come up in certain law enforcement circles within Canada. Now, Guernsey and McElhone began to work together. They were different types: Guernsey more forceful, McElhone quieter but more experienced. The RCMP recognized white collar crime as important, but they had few resources and fewer specialists in the area. It was an excellent partnership.

Suspicions Converge

The Americans had confidence in their Canadian contacts, and they knew in early 1945 that matters were starting to move north of the border.

Nevertheless, we do not know what led Groves to decide it was time to bring the Canadians fully into the picture. It was neighbourly, the kind of thing that allies do, but above all it was a decision to use the Canadians as an instrument – *the* instrument – to get rid of Boris Pregel. Whether that was the best way to proceed, or even wise, is a matter of debate, but there is no question it was an American decision to blow the lid off what was going on at Eldorado and drag down Pregel, his associate French, and Marcel Pochon as co-conspirator.

Whitaker told Bateman a lot, all supported by evidence. As Bateman related to C.D. Howe, "Apparently, there is no telephone message sent or received, no telegram sent or received, and no conversations carried on of which they do not have verbatim reports, and I am not sure but what their investigations may be carried still further."[30]

With this sort of coverage, what could Whitaker and Consodine possibly need from the Canadians? Permission. The US Army had no jurisdiction in Canada, and wanted to work with the RCMP to make sure that the surveillance web was complete. "They are very anxious to cover the Canadian end and I expect to phone tomorrow to suggest that you might ask Inspector [W.H.] Williams of the RCMP in Ottawa to cooperate with them," Bateman explained to his minister. The Americans didn't yet have enough information to prove that Pregel was committing a crime. The raw surveillance is no longer accessible, but the summaries and memoranda it generated suggests the contents of the original full record: lots of discussions but few documents detailing the execution of those plans. The MED almost certainly suspected fraud, and almost as certainly wanted to do more than prove a mere conspiracy.

Bateman urged Howe to pursue a broader inquiry, explaining that the American reports contained plenty of material to justify one. The Americans were particularly concerned because they knew that Pregel was in the process of negotiating a new sales agreement with Eldorado, something many at the MED opposed: "They feel that under the terms of this agreement the Canadian Government itself is assuring Pregel of a living and thus maintaining him in a position where he can carry on the activities which Groves's office considers to be of a very dangerous nature."

The matter was pressing enough that Lieutenant Whitaker planned to meet Lesslie Thomson in Ottawa on Easter Monday, 2 April 1945, to provide more detailed information about the investigation of Pregel and how the Canadians could help. In fact, Whitaker had been in Toronto two weeks earlier to discuss matters with the RCMP. Within the day, he had made the necessary arrangements to put Pregel under RCMP surveillance.

Over the next two days, colleagues from the US Army Corps of Engineers also arrived in Toronto by train. One even took the same train as Pregel on March 21st.[31]

When Pregel visited Toronto for two days in March 1945, he stayed at his preferred hotel, the Royal York, directly across from the train station. While there he spent a lot of time in his suite talking with J.H. Greenberg, Eldorado's lawyer, and Carl French, focusing on just two things: renewing his contract with Eldorado, and business involving International Uranium Mining Company Ltd. He returned to New York on March 22nd. Unbeknownst to Pregel, the authorities had heard every word.

Pregel was back in the Royal York on April 2nd, the same day that Whitaker was in town to see Thomson. No one seems to have known that Pregel would be in Toronto until that afternoon, when he was actually in the city. He again focused on renewing his contract with Eldorado and was planning on attending the shareholder meeting of International Uranium, which was being held at the Royal York the next morning. No one seems to have contacted the RCMP about the visit.

The Church Street Raid

By pure coincidence, the RCMP was busy planning and executing a document raid at 103 Church Street on behalf of the Foreign Exchange Control Board while Pregel was in Toronto for the International Uranium meeting.[32] Carl French was present when officers removed materials from the offices but said very little as the day wore on. Investigators were shocked by the sheer quantity of documents and their origins; in addition to papers relating to Radium Luminous Industries and Dial and Instrument Finishers Ltd., they found files belonging to International Uranium Mining Company Ltd. It was too much of a coincidence. The RCMP took everything.

As investigators reviewed the materials, they discovered a treasure trove of documents related to Eldorado, Canadian Radium and Uranium Corporation, Radium Luminous Industries Inc. of Chicago, Port Radium Mines Ltd., Yam Securities Ltd., and Bay Securities Ltd. There were also countless records referring to Boris and Alex Pregel, along with Alexander's wife, Anna. The existence of these records was not surprising since 103 Church was also the home of International Uranium and other companies in which these individuals had interests, even if they were unknown to Gilbert LaBine and the board of Eldorado. The cache of documents detailed the extensive personal and financial relationships between French, Pochon, Radium Luminous Industries, and International Uranium, heretofore unknown. They went back years.

The Mounties quickly realized that the US Army Corps of Engineers would want to look at the papers. Lieutenant Winston H. Pickett of the US Army Corps of Engineers had been in Toronto in March, and at that time he had asked the RCMP for any information about Port Radium, International Uranium, and a bloc of claims in Yellowknife near Contact Lake Mine at the southeastern corner of Great Bear Lake. Presumably, the Manhattan Project wanted to know who owned the uranium they were purchasing. The RCMP had no information at that time. Now, they had more than they knew what to do with.

The materials taken from 103 Church Street were so voluminous that Guernsey's supervisor, Superintendent F.A. Blake, felt the need to issue a caution. It would "take some time before the full facts are known," given the "elaborate but confusing business system" of Boris Pregel.[33] But Guernsey's initial review of the documents bore fruit immediately. Although International Uranium's claims were in the name of Doris Stewart and staked by people named Bryson and Bode (each of whom received $500), the documents made clear that the principal shareholders were Pregel, French, and Pochon. Charles Hershman, the operator behind Bay Securities Ltd., was also involved.[34]

It was easy to run afoul of the FECB regulations; many Canadians carried too much currency with them when travelling to the United States. Was the contravention of foreign exchange regulations a mere pretext to investigate Carl French? Perhaps, but RCMP investigators really seemed to be looking for information about Pregel. They were also focused primarily on stock manipulation and tax evasion, and they got more than they bargained for. The documents provided evidence of a complex web of cleverly concealed theft and fraud.

By the end of April, the RCMP understood many of the key facts. The stash of documents confirmed what the Americans had already learned from surveillance. Pregel, French, and Pochon had extensive hidden financial interests outside Eldorado that put them in conflict with their obligations to the new Crown corporation. Guernsey and McElhone had untangled a collection of corporate ownership structures and detailed evidence that many of the transactions involved sham corporations either owned or controlled by French and Pregel. It was a shell game of sorts, designed in some instances to hide profits in order to evade taxes and exchange controls and in others to increase profits artificially. Evidence of corporate malfeasance was abundant, and the centrepiece was radium stolen from Eldorado's refining operations in Port Hope.

The Church Street raid was a turning point. The mining business was filled with cozy relationships, but efforts to conceal those relationships rang alarm bells for investigators. Quickly, it became clear that the companies Eldorado was doing business with were independent from one another in name only. None of the significant financial interests that French, Pochon, and Pregel held in these companies had been disclosed to Eldorado's board or to Gilbert LaBine. More troubling was French's involvement in the contractual negotiations that bound Eldorado to the companies. In many transactions, he was basically negotiating with himself and benefiting financially from the process. Investigators began to suspect that the trio had been defrauding Eldorado for years.[35]

Radium Luminous Industries soon became the focus of the inquiry. Initially, investigators believed that the two companies – Inc. in Chicago and Ltd. in Toronto – were shams to evade FECB regulations. Soon, it became apparent more was amiss; Radium Luminous Industries was central to the web of fraud at Eldorado.[36] We can take French's word for it because he described the arrangement precisely in correspondence with Pregel.[37] The scheme was so clever that it took months to unravel – and to find the supporting documentation.

A Family Affair

Carl French had created Radium Luminous Industries Ltd. in 1941, incorporating the company a year later in Toronto. He was the company's president and a director alongside his wife, Ruth Arnold (who served as secretary-treasurer), and friend Charles Scarr (who was general manager). On paper, French's mother-in-law held the balance of outstanding shares. French used the company to buy radium from Eldorado while also negotiating the purchase agreements on behalf of Eldorado. Small wonder he got a good deal. Radium Luminous Industries also used Eldorado's key personnel, including Marcel Pochon, along with other resources.

As RCMP investigators reviewed the documents from Church Street, they noticed information about Industrial Radium Corporation of Chicago. Soon, they discovered that Boris Pregel had founded this company in late 1943 for one purpose: to buy a large quantity of radium from himself. Specifically, 22 grams at a cost of $6,000 per gram. It was a lot of radium, and the transaction was especially magical because the company had no obvious source of funds. Nor did anyone seem to know the provenance of the radium. Investigators guessed it originally came from Eldorado, having found records from a series of transactions, approved in stages by the Department of Munitions and Supply, that allowed radium to be moved to the United States, but they had no idea why Eldorado would be selling the radium to Pregel or CRUC in the first place.[38]

Superficially, the transactions seemed legitimate, but inconsistencies suggested something else. Banking and trading accounts in Toronto made no sense for a Chicago-based company like Industrial Radium. Investigators could find no corporate accounts or funds. That naturally raised a question: How could Industrial Radium afford to purchase, or even lease, that much radium?[39]

Guernsey saw red flags when he learned that the company's board was filled with family and friends: Alexander Pregel, French's wife and mother-in-law, and his friends or close associates, Richmond Corbett and Paul Collins. To be clear, there was nothing wrong with involving friends and family members on a private company's board, but Industrial Radium went to great lengths to disguise their involvement. The identity of the seller changed, too. Originally, the company agreed to purchase radium from Boris Pregel, but when the board finalized the purchase, the seller was listed as CRUC.[40] What had previously been Pregel's personal radium was now CRUC's corporate property. Was this a difference without distinction or a means by which to evade taxes and export controls? The RCMP suspected the latter.

The pieces began to fall into place when Guernsey and McElhone realized what happened next. In late 1944, Carl French's Radium Luminous Industries bought Industrial Radium. Originally, the total share value of Pregel's company was $150,000. Radium Luminous Industries paid $445,000 for it. With the transaction complete, Industrial Radium was dissolved.[41] The dissolution of the purchased company was not uncommon; paying a premium for its shares was something different. It seemed to be a way to disguise the provenance of the radium when, down the road, French and Pregel wanted to sell or lease it.

That CRUC was involved in the sale of radium to Industrial Radium also raised eyebrows. As they pieced together the Church Street documents, investigators were surprised to learn that French also had ties to Pregel's principal company. Remember that Pregel was the president of CRUC, while his brother, Alexander, served as vice-president and secretary. CRUC also had subsidiaries: American Radium Industries Inc. and American Luminous Industries Inc. It was only when they assembled a chronology and disentangled the web of corporate entities that investigators realized French had been deeply involved with CRUC for a long time, having joined the board in September 1941 while he was serving as secretary-treasurer at Eldorado.[42] French could have told Eldorado's board he was doing this. He could have told Gilbert LaBine. Instead, he told no one. Failing to do so looked like he was hiding something.

The RCMP was in a predicament. Most of the so-called objectionable transactions seemed to have occurred before Eldorado became a Crown corporation. The force believed it had no role to play in policing the activities of a company in the private sector, albeit one that was publicly traded. The hook was the impact of French and Pregel's activities; they had chipped away at Eldorado's profits, hurting the company's bottom line and its overall value. That was something for the minister. And so at the end of April, it was time to talk to C.D. Howe.[43]

In late April 1945, Inspector W.H. Williams of the RCMP met with Lesslie Thomson. Thomson could not have been surprised about what he heard. He had just returned from Toronto, where he had met the FECB investigators to discuss the same matter.[44] Thomson had already gone so far as to write a memorandum in November 1944 detailing his questions and concerns about the various contracts, companies, and financial interests associated with Boris Pregel and Carl French.[45]

Having been apprised of the RCMP's findings and realizing this was no ordinary matter, the FECB retained a special prosecutor: John J. Robinette, KC.

John J. Robinette, the Prosecutor

Appointed King's Counsel in 1944, the thirty-eight-year-old Robinette was a young lawyer of promise who would eventually develop a legendary reputation. Robinette was a good lawyer and a politically well-connected one, but at that time he remained on the cusp of greatness. His known Liberal sympathies had a hand in (or at least had not hurt) his selection, starting in 1940, for war work for the federal government.[46] Some of his hallmark techniques were already well established: "painstaking preparation, encyclopedic knowledge of the law, a rare ability to hammer at opponents' weak points while forcefully forwarding his own." The advance work was key; in his view, "Few cases are won on courtroom facility, but the bulk of cases are won or lost on preparation."[47]

John J. Robinette, 1934 | L. Lyonde, Library and Archives Canada, PA-053721

Robinette had begun prosecuting cases for the FECB in 1940, working alongside William McElhone. The first one involved a Toronto mattress manufacturer who was tried and convicted of defrauding the government. Robinette and McElhone developed an excellent working relationship, so much so that Robinette agreed to work on the Eldorado case only with McElhone's participation. If there were any chance the investigation would turn into a prosecution, he wanted McElhone along. Guernsey had already proven himself to be a top-notch investigator, but he had no experience of trial preparation. Preparing complex financial cases for trial was McElhone's specialty, however, and this one looked like a doozy.[48]

Robinette had already been retained by the FECB when Williams met with Thomson on the morning of April 30th to review Guernsey's preliminary report, which encompassed his initial findings on Eldorado and broader conclusions drawn from the documents taken from Church Street. The RCMP inspector was confident that Pregel and French had come into a "considerable quantity of radium from sources yet undetermined, which was used to operate Radium Luminous Industries Ltd., Toronto, finance International Uranium Mining Co. Ltd., and probably including some enterprises in the U.S.A." After several weeks reviewing documents, investigators understood the basics of the story but thought more revelations were almost certain, given its "international scope."

Thomson promised to get back to Williams with a detailed response after talking to the minister. The implication was that Howe and his department might wait to see what else the FECB uncovered before getting involved. There was also the possibility of checking with the Department of Justice, and its experienced deputy minister, F.P. Varcoe.[49]

Thomson's response turned out to be swift. By that afternoon, he had read the report and shared it not only with the minister but also with lawyers in the Department of Munitions and Supply, probably Guy M. Jarvis, who served as counsel at the department. Howe knew Jarvis and trusted him. So did McElhone, who later called him "astute."[50] It's likely Thomson also shared Guernsey's report with Robinette and Varcoe.

In short order, Robinette moved into high gear and quickly scheduled an interview with Carl French for May 7th to discuss the documents that had been found at his offices. Robinette and Glassco expected a lengthy process to follow, with an initial round of examinations, followed by a break for concerned parties to compare the information provided on examination with what had been found in the documents. Even in late April, everyone expected that French's interview, then just one week away, would be the start of a broader investigation. In a note to Inspector Williams, Thomson explained that the Department of Munitions and Supply would almost certainly get involved directly after that first round of interviews because Eldorado was now a Crown corporation.

Events moved rapidly, however. LaBine secured Pochon's resignation from the Eldorado board following an off-the-record conversation just before a board meeting on May 5th, while French retained a team of lawyers that included John Joseph (Joe) Bench (a young Liberal senator from St. Catharines), Herman Rogers, and Arthur Slaght, a powerhouse defence counsel and former Liberal MP.[51]

Robinette's interview with French did not take place as planned.[52] Not only did May 7th mark the end of the war in Europe but, more importantly for the purposes of the investigation, it was the day C.D. Howe ordered an expansive investigation into every facet of Eldorado's operations. The secret order in council that authorized it was broad, but it was enacted under the *Department of Munitions and Supply Act,* not the *War Measures Act.*[53] It was an important distinction because the *War Measures Act* was a general statute that conferred comprehensive powers to deal with every facet of the war effort while the *Department of Munitions and Supply Act* granted more limited authority.

J. Grant Glassco, the Investigator

The question was no longer whether there had been fraud at Eldorado but to what extent. Howe was especially keen to learn more about the company's various contracts to sell or otherwise dispose of uranium and radium, and to determine just how much money the company had lost because of them. In this, as in other matters, Howe no doubt leaned heavily on the advice of John Robinette and Guy Jarvis. Formal records have long since disappeared, but Howe was well known for relying on the expertise of a trusted cadre.

Based on Glassco's discovery of "anomalies" and "irregularities" in Eldorado's financial records, the order in council granted sweeping authority to an investigator to keep digging. Under the *Department of Munitions and Supply Act,* the minister could investigate anything related to a munitions

J. Grant Glassco, 1962 | *Toronto Star* Photograph Archive

contract.[54] Howe thought the Eldorado contracts fit the bill, and the investigation of the company's financial affairs was to include activities that pre-dated nationalization.[55] Although the *Department of Munitions and Supply Act* was not as open-ended as the *War Measures Act,* it did provide a depth of authority to the minister to investigate anything related to a munitions contract. By acting under the *Department of Munitions and Supply Act,* the chosen investigator would have all the powers of someone appointed under the *Inquiries Act,* but those under investigation had none of the protection that act conferred.[56]

The *Department of Munitions and Supply Act* empowered the minister to order investigations of precisely the type involving Eldorado but importantly also gave the investigator the power to act without limiting his ability to compel witnesses to give self-incriminating evidence.[57] This disregard for protection against self-incrimination deviated dramatically from the standard set by the *Inquiries Act.* Under that legislation, testimony could be compelled but not used against a witness for the purposes of criminal prosecution. Although the prohibition against compelled self-incrimination existed at common law, it could be overruled by statute and there was no guarantee the government would observe it in wartime. Indeed, in the current case, it would defeat the purpose of the investigation if the information could not be used to prosecute French, Pregel, and Pochon.

Given the stakes, the person appointed to lead the investigation would be even more powerful than one typically leading an inquiry. Howe had just the man: J. Grant Glassco, a chartered accountant from Toronto. With the help of a coterie of accountants, along with Robinette, McElhone, and Guernsey, Glassco was tasked with uncovering the full extent of chicanery at Eldorado.[58]

Like Robinette, Glassco would come to be known as a giant in his field, and it was his work investigating fraud at Eldorado that solidified his reputation within government circles as smart, indefatigable, and reliable. He was able to tackle large, complex cases and make sense of them in a way that was understandable to non-tax specialists – people like John Robinette. His education was privileged: private school followed by McGill University and then the Sorbonne. Becoming a chartered accountant in 1931, he joined the elite firm of Clarkson Gordon in Toronto. During the war, Howe appointed him as government controller overseeing an important aircraft factory, a difficult and sometimes unwelcome assignment.[59] With Howe's confidence, Glassco was a natural choice to lead the investigation.

With a team in place and broad powers, Glassco got to work.

8
Follow the Money, Find the Radium

The Glassco investigation did not remain entirely secret for long. On 10 July 1945, the *Ottawa Citizen* published a small article noting the existence of a high-level investigation into "the affairs and operations of Eldorado and the sale and disposition of its products." To add spice to the story, the report noted that J. Grant Glassco would lead the inquiry held under the authority of a "secret" order in council issued two months earlier, on May 7th.[1] The rest of the brief story recounted the details of the company's recent nationalization, though it misstated the number of shares outstanding at the time of C.D. Howe's announcement in Parliament the previous January.

By July, Glassco and John Robinette understood they had a first-class scandal on their hands: an elaborate scheme to defraud Eldorado, a Crown corporation, and thus the government and people of Canada.

THERE WERE, IN fact, three investigations. The original was the American effort to keep Boris Pregel under surveillance, mostly through wiretaps, for three years. That investigation morphed into a Canadian concern when William A. Consodine met with Canada's metals controller, George Bateman, in Washington. The second investigation was initiated by the Canadian Foreign Exchange Control Board (FECB), which monitored currency flows and transactions between Canada and the United States, and was conducted by the Royal Canadian Mounted Police (RCMP) on the FECB's behalf. The third investigation, also conducted by the RCMP under the guidance of Terry Guernsey, involved the RCMP's scrutiny of personnel at Eldorado. That line of inquiry registered concerns about Carl French, denied him security clearance, and probably precipitated his resignation from the company.

After the raid at 103 Church Street in early April, 1945, the RCMP continued to monitor Pregel's activities when he came to Toronto. As a result, they knew that Pregel was desperate to renew his sales agreement with Eldorado now that the war in Europe was over. Whether his determination was despite or because of the FECB investigation no one could tell, but he was worried enough about that investigation that he retained counsel.[2] So did French. The same counsel.

With the full powers of the order in council effectively consolidating both Canadian investigations, Glassco and his crew of accountants carefully picked their way through the mess of papers, trying to make sense of them. The records from Radium Luminous Industries and various related companies did not represent bookkeeping at its finest. Not even close. Soon, however, a clearer picture began to form. The ingenious scheme took advantage of the fact that, after 1942, radium became a secondary product for Eldorado. The trio of French, Pregel, and Marcel Pochon counted on the fact that no one would miss what was now viewed as the less important by-product of the refining process to steal large quantities of it.

On May 29th, Lesslie Thomson met the group of investigators from Canada and the United States in Ottawa. Terry Guernsey was there, along with Inspector W.H. Williams, who was the RCMP's coordinating security officer on the nuclear project. From the US Army Corps of Engineers were Consodine and Lieutenant Winston Pickett. Hugh Jones represented the FECB; Guy M. Jarvis was the counsel from the Department of Munitions and Supply; and accountant J.E. Beckett was working with Glassco. The FECB was still formally responsible for conducting the day-to-day operations of the investigation, but behind the scenes, C.D. Howe's department was increasingly responsible for the strategic decisions that arose as it unfolded.

Getting the Band Together

They were an agreeable bunch, and decided to meet every two weeks with Thomson serving as the liaison. Neither government would act without coordinating first with the other, and they would work together unless a matter was unique to one government.[3] Glassco and Robinette should and would be left to make key decisions. They had the freedom to go where the investigation led them and to make recommendations. Implicitly,

C.D. Howe would not interfere, nor would Groves or anyone else from the Manhattan Project.

By late May, French, Pregel, and Pochon knew they were under investigation but thought their liability was limited to Canada, whether for contravention of FECB regulations or of the *Income Tax Act*. They knew nothing about the broader investigation or American involvement. It was best to keep it that way, even as the investigation began to expand to determine whether anyone had violated Bateman's February 1943 order that required permits from the metals controller to acquire or dispose of radium or uranium.[4] Three companies and two individuals were the initial focus of inquiry: Radium Luminous Industries Ltd., Dial and Instrument Finishers Ltd., International Uranium Mining Company Ltd., Ruth French, and Marcel Pochon.

Perhaps the most pressing concern was the radium that seemed to have been stolen. Documents from 103 Church Street suggested that French had been collecting a lot of "radium scrap." Where was it? The FECB, which continued to be the public face of the investigation, agreed to spearhead the search, with Leslie Cook, a chemist at the National Research Council, taking the lead.[5]

There was a remarkable degree of agreement within the group, except when it came to one subject: whether there was enough information to issue arrest warrants immediately. Munitions and Supply was willing to support them, but only if Consodine, Pickett, Glassco, and Robinette made the recommendation unanimously. For the time being, consensus was lacking. Jarvis was especially reluctant to go down that path because he thought more had to be done to make the best case for a criminal proceeding. Everyone agreed that it was time to start talking to the people involved, including suspects.

The willingness to begin interviews sparked another concern among investigators. They worried that French – who was now their primary focus – might flee to the United States. The prospect was problematic because extradition was impossible without a common crime; giving or receiving secret commissions was a criminal offence in Canada but not in the United States.

The core group reconvened on May 30th. Consodine, Pickett, Guernsey, and Beckett met with Glassco and William McKee of the FECB and agreed on several next steps.[6] For one, everyone believed it was best to continue having the FECB serve as the public face of the investigation, keeping the role of Howe's department quiet until the Americans were prepared to disclose their own involvement. That time was coming quickly, however, as Consodine pledged to involve representatives of the Treasury Intelligence Branch immediately upon his return to Washington. He wanted them to visit Toronto as soon as possible to see the evidence the Canadians had uncovered. For the Americans, the case involved not only fraud but also tax evasion. Reviewing documents from some of the American companies in the Church Street cache would give Treasury officials a head start before they paid a visit to French and Pregel at their American corporate offices.

The meetings at the end of May made it clear that the investigation was just getting started. The original concern about contraventions of foreign exchange regulations had quickly blossomed into what Thomson described understatedly as "an extremely important matter," given its obvious connections to the nuclear program and the resulting international implications. He recognized the need for more staff, and asked that Williams be seconded formally from the RCMP to the Department of Munitions and Supply to help. The commissioner himself was happy to oblige.[7]

The Hunt for Radioactivity

When he was interviewed, French told investigators that he had refined radium – 6.3 grams that should have been subject to import/export controls but was not, and whose whereabouts was now unaccounted for – from radioactive waste and scraps. Investigators believed it had really come from the Belgian ore owned by African Metals Corporation (Afrimet) and refined by Eldorado. Either way, it had to be found, and everyone agreed that the investigation's technical adviser, Leslie Cook, on loan from the National Research Council, was the best person to lead the effort. In the meantime, officials at Munitions and Supply agreed to prepare a full list of radium sales from Eldorado to Radium Luminous Industries. If investigators were going to recover the stolen radium, they needed to know how much had been sold legitimately and what it was worth. Given the price, investigators began to appreciate there was the very real possibility the discrepancy was worth many hundreds of thousands of dollars.

Born in Paris, Ontario, in 1914, Cook studied chemistry and physics at the University of Toronto, graduating with a bachelor's degree in those two subjects in 1936. For the next two years, he studied in Berlin at the Kaiser Wilhelm Institute for Chemistry. With war brewing, Cook decided to leave Germany and arrived in 1938 in Cambridge, where he studied at the Cavendish Laboratory. As luck would have it, he was at home in Brantford, Ontario, on vacation when war broke out the following summer. Unsure what to do next, he took a teaching job at the local high school for a few months before joining the research subsidiary of the Aluminum Company (Alcan) in Montreal. After dividing his time between Montreal and Toronto, Cook soon transferred to the company's research lab in Kingston. By 1944, the government sought him out to join the British nuclear lab in Montreal.

By the spring of 1945, Cook was Guernsey's technical adviser on the Eldorado investigation. Investigators needed to understand not just the financial side of Eldorado but the substances the company sold, and Cook helped to prepare questions so they could figure out how the radium was being stolen and where it might be located. As Guernsey and the other investigators came to him with questions about what they were finding in the Church Street documents, Cook became increasingly worried. Soon, worry became alarm.

As the lead Canadian and American investigators met in Ottawa in late May, Cook and Guernsey set out to find the missing radium. They decided to focus on Toronto-area buildings owned by Carl French. The most obvious starting point was 103 Church Street, but there were other avenues of exploration. Radium Luminous Industries Ltd. had a laboratory nearby at 54–56 Lombard Street, near the city morgue. There was also a rural address in Scarborough, an area that was predominantly farmland. As they searched for the address on Lombard Street, Guernsey and Cook turned their work into a bit of a game, proposing to drive down the street with a Geiger counter to see if they could find the address just by looking at radioactivity readings. They did not anticipate what they found.

The contamination was so significant that their equipment picked it up as the two men sat in the car in front of a three-storey building on Lombard Street. The building had a mix of tenants; the laboratory was on the second floor, sandwiched between a heavy electrical machinery and equipment shop below and a Canadian cigar chain store above. At ground level outside and behind the building, near the shipping dock, the Geiger counter registered ten times the acceptable level of radioactivity.[8] As Guernsey and Cook entered the building and made their way to the second floor, their instruments stopped tracking radioactivity halfway up the stairs. As Cook later recalled, "Our instruments went right off the scale and we could take no more measurements, from which it was apparent that there must be an enormous amount of radioactivity higher up."[9]

Arriving at the lab, they saw three men busy at work:

> There were flasks of solutions bubbling and boiling on hotplates all around. It was perfectly clear to me that they were engaged in the final purification

> of major amounts of radium and indeed there must have been major amounts because, as I say, our instruments were completely off the scale ... My instincts told me that there was nothing we could do there in that situation and the sooner we departed the better.[10]

Based on some rough calculations, Cook figured there must have been between 20 and 30 grams of radium cooking in the laboratory. He was well aware of the health implications of so much radioactivity, not only for himself and Guernsey but, even more alarmingly, for the lab workers. As he later explained, "I knew immediately that this was a very serious situation for the people involved."

The Ivanenko Farm

The next day, Cook and Guernsey drove out to Scarborough to find a farmhouse that turned out to be owned not by French but by one of his employees, Nicholas Ivanenko – at least on paper. As they drove up to the farmhouse and barn, Cook's Geiger metres "went up very considerably." When he and Guernsey got out of the car, they noticed numerous metal oil barrels outside the barn filled with all manner of junk, from rags and plastic tubing to bundles of airplane dials. Confident they had found what they were looking for, the men decided to measure the amount of radiation in each container, but the level around the barn was so high they determined it was safer to back away.

As they did so, the level of radiation increased rapidly, spiking as they were about 18–21 metres from the barn. Puzzled, they walked around the property to see what they could find. As Cook recalled more than forty years later, it "took a little bit of circling around until we realized that there must be a great deal of radioactive material in a little shack which was on the right hand side of the lane much near[er] the road."[11] Inside the shack was a small oil drum that seemed to be the epicentre of the radiation. Having pulled it into the yard in an attempt to isolate the material, they peered inside. It was full of ash.

Carl French had accompanied Cook and Guernsey to the farm and was willing to answer their questions. Having heard his characterization of the business as a "radium luminous paint dial-painting establishment," Cook assumed the dials had been used for airplane instrument panels, along with the other waste. But what about the ash?

As French explained, it was residue from dirty rags, rags used by "the girls who did the dial painting [and] did it with camel hair brushes and from time to time had to wipe the brush with a rag to clean the tip." He went on, describing how the rags were collected and brought to the farm, where Mrs. Ivanenko burned them in the small stove inside the shack. After each round of incineration, the Ivanenkos transferred the ash from the stove into a rock shaker with a sieve to separate the ash from the larger, unburned clumps. The clumps were returned to the stove for further incineration. The ash was stored in drums around the property. French had been using the farm as a storage site for radioactive waste but also as a miniature refinery to recover radium. Guernsey and Cook tried to estimate the amount of radium in the barrels: perhaps a gram, not anywhere close to the 6 grams that Munitions and Supply thought was missing.

French's explanation of his method didn't really make sense. "Personally, I don't know how that could have been," Cook thought, "because the boxes and barrels were still there." When Cook and Guernsey pressed, French conceded that he couldn't explain the origins of the full 6 grams. Puzzlement aside, the bigger concern was the extent of radiation exposure. Even a tiny quantity of radium interacts chemically with the human body, as was well known as early as the 1910s. Cook worried that anyone using the shaker French described would be breathing in the radioactive dust. As little as a hundred-thousandth of the ash contained in the barrel would be dangerous in the lungs. Cook estimated that whoever was operating the stove at the farm would have received their daily limit of radiation in about one minute because of the radioactive concentration in the ash. In a laboratory setting, it would take an eight-hour work shift to receive ten times the allowable radiation.[12]

Cook documented everything in a formal report. He was so worried about the health hazards that he recommended notifying the provincial Department of Health, ordering a cessation of all operations at the farm, and examining the Ivanenkos for radon levels at the National Research Council in Ottawa to determine how seriously they had already been poisoned.[13] William McKee, the FECB inspector working with Glassco, agreed and passed along Cook's report to the deputy minister of health for Ontario, flagging the key health hazards in the accompanying cover letter.[14]

Guernsey also wrote a report, this one in plain language. There was a "definite reaction" at "street level" at 103 Church Street and a "milder reaction" at X-Ray Radium Industries on Davenport Road. At Carl French's home at 263 Dawlish Avenue in Toronto, "gamma ray radiation was indicative,"

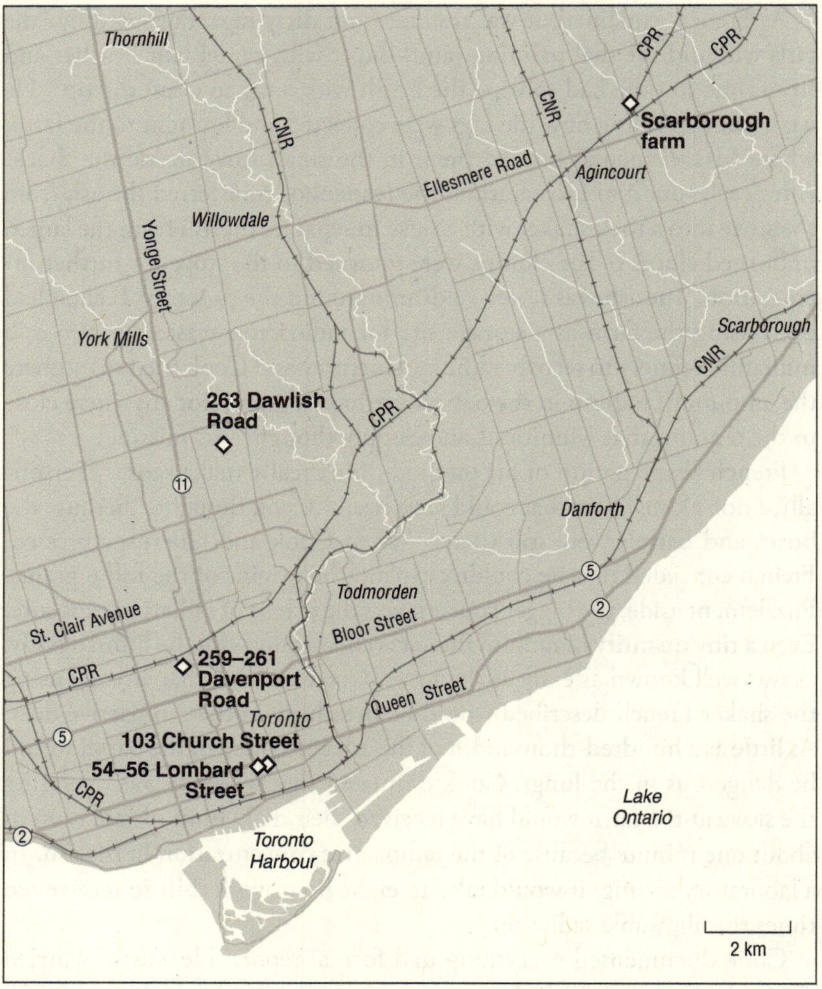

Radioactive sites in the Greater Toronto Area | Cartography by Eric Leinberger

but at the Scarborough farm, "the radiation was so intense in the vicinity of one shack that the [Geiger] Counter could not be used."[15]

The Department of Health

These discoveries left Guernsey so horrified that he speculated whether Carl French could be prosecuted criminally and held liable civilly for any harm befalling the people working in either location. He quickly discounted the possibility: "I am somewhat doubtful if the Provincial authorities would take criminal action unless representation were made through the proper channels."[16] Indeed, the department's response was well intentioned but inadequate in the long term.

At least one member of the health department actually knew about French and Pregel already, along with the associated concerns about radioactive waste, having recently discussed similar issues with New York State Department of Labor officials who were worried that radioactive scrap might fall into the wrong hands. That department had also started to investigate Boris Pregel's International Rare Metals Refinery Inc. in Mount Kisco and was preparing regulations to respond to his activities there.[17]

In the days after Guernsey and Cook uncovered radioactivity in and around Toronto, health department officials visited the same sites and held various discussions with French, with personnel working on-site, and with experts at the Montreal lab. They ordered French to wash down the Radium Luminous Industries labs and remove the ash from both the farm and 103 Church Street, and they tested everyone for exposure to radiation. They were less alarmed about the radium at the various sites because, unlike the ash, it was stored in lead cases. They were also not overly concerned about personnel. Dr. Bulmer, the senior Ontario official, thought they were safe based on his own experience; having worked with radium for ten years, he had never seen a case of radium poisoning. To be certain, he consulted a colleague in his department and an expert at the Montreal lab, who confirmed the conclusion.[18]

Guernsey was not impressed, observing, "The Provincial Department may be somewhat embarrassed on this hazardous situation due to the fact that such comes under their supervision and which has obviously been overlooked."[19] The situation may in fact have been the product of wilful ignorance; even in 1945 it was known that health department investigators had worked part-time for Carl French and Radium Luminous Industries, even publishing articles for the company.[20]

Lawrence Park

With the discovery of radioactive materials in locations associated with French, it was natural to worry about radioactivity in other parts of the city. An obvious concern was his house at 263 Dawlish Avenue in Lawrence Park. He assured investigators there was none, so when they knocked at the door on a midsummer evening, it was to look for more documents, not radium.

On June 25th, as Glassco's team prepared for interviews with French, Pregel, and Pochon, the investigators decided to look for more documents. Executed under FECB regulations, not Glassco's own authority, the search went as well as one might have predicted: poorly. The two investigators, J.M. Clish and McKee, did not receive proper authorization until mid-afternoon, and then McKee was tied up for several hours. That meant they arrived at Dawlish Avenue around sundown, 8:45 p.m. Mrs. French was not amused and refused to let them in without her husband being present.

Invoking the name of her husband's lawyer, *Senator* Bench, Mrs. French staved off the FECB officers. As they explained to her, investigators did not require anyone's consent to search the house but they preferred not to enter without permission.[21] Having failed to execute the search, they left, never – as far as we can determine – to return.

Pregel Returns to Toronto

Boris Pregel returned to Toronto on the same day that the FECB tried to search French's house. As usual, he stayed at the Royal York Hotel, his arrival preceded by two representatives of the US Army Corps of Engineers. A third had arrived in Toronto on the same train as Pregel, with "supervision equipment" (i.e., tape recorders) in tow.[22] Pregel's meetings with Ray Birks, a director at Eldorado, and with Maurice Austin, his lawyer from New York, were thus recorded. In part, the men discussed the terms of Pregel's next sales contract with the company. Then, after lunch, Pregel was served with a subpoena to appear before Glassco just two days later, on June 27th.

Pregel did what anyone else would do in his position: he called his Canadian lawyers, Arthur Slaght and Senator Joe Bench, the same people representing French in the FECB investigation. Slaght and Bench immediately understood that they needed time to prepare their client for the interview, and arranged with Glassco to reschedule for July 10th. Pregel returned to New York the next day on nothing more than the pledge to return to answer questions. Apparently, no one was concerned he might refuse to do so, in contrast to the fear that French might flee to the United States when faced with the prospect.[23] Perhaps the "supervision equipment" had turned up no mention of staying in the United States to avoid questioning.

Surveillance gave investigators a road map to make sense of the papers they had already seized from 103 Church Street. Pregel and French knew they were under a microscope, and they talked – a lot – to one another and to their lawyers. Not only did Pregel tell Arthur Slaght all about "the special project," including where experimental work with uranium was being carried out in the United States and Canada, but he detailed the legal liability he faced. Investigators learned, for example, which transactions were "problematic," because Pregel and French told their lawyers all about them during those meetings at the Royal York. Their candour gave the lawyers everything they needed to mount a defence, but it also laid bare the full extent of their crimes.

Their greatest concern involved the 700-ton contract concluded in the summer of 1943 between the Americans and Eldorado – for uranium ore that included Belgian ore from Staten Island – because that was the largest source of Pregel's radium, 29.98 grams of it. They spoke freely about taking the radium from Eldorado without payment, and French was especially worried that investigators would find the smoking gun in the documents taken from 103 Church Street: an invoice for the transaction in Eldorado's papers "for which they did not appear to have any defence."

But there were other transactions, too. Pregel and French feared investigators might figure out that they had taken another 20 grams of radium from the original contract with Afrimet. To compensate, Pregel planned to offer the company $360,000 "in an effort to overcome any embarrassing questions that may be asked."[24] French was part of another troublesome transaction for 118 grams of radium in which he guaranteed recovery of 74.75 percent. Finally, the two worried that investigators might piece together the details of the purchase and sale of radium through Industrial Radium Corporation in Chicago.[25] Pregel explained the scheme generally to his lawyer: Eldorado had "sold" that radium to him for $6 per milligram (a discount on the market price), which he then "sold" at $20 per milligram (much higher than the market price) through the stock sale of Industrial Radium created in late 1943 specifically for the purchase of discounted radium. He freely conceded there was no way to explain or justify the premium. He simply hoped his luck would hold and no one would notice.

Pregel and French also discussed how they had made extensive use of Eldorado's resources, particularly personnel. Pregel was worried investigators would learn more about the full extent of his relationship with Marcel Pochon. As Pregel explained to Slaght, he had been paying Pochon while he was working as Eldorado's chief chemist and a director. For that payment, Pochon had given the company advice about the contracts it was negotiating with Pregel's Canadian Radium and Uranium Corporation (CRUC).

With a fuller understanding of their clients' transgressions, the lawyers developed the first glimmers of a defence strategy. Part of it involved blaming Lesslie Thomson and the RCMP, but the centrepiece was Gilbert LaBine. In Pregel's telling, both men had disparaged him in different ways in order to make him look bad to C.D. Howe.[26] Pregel told Slaght that LaBine had in fact practically begged him to buy Eldorado's radium to save the company. It was outrageous that he was now being accused of a crime for having merely done Eldorado's president a favour. Missing was an explanation for the premium paid to Industrial Radium or the discount given by Eldorado. Of course, there was none. Similarly, in telling Slaght about Pochon's work for CRUC, Pregel knew it contravened the chemist's agreement with Eldorado. Why else would he have contrived to bless the arrangement with nothing more than a verbal agreement with LaBine that could not be disproved? But the strategy was not entirely negative. Almost certainly, it was counsel who suggested they try to promote Pregel's war work with the Americans as a sort of shield from prosecution.

The Fruits of Surveillance

Once Pregel left Toronto, the US Engineers packed up their equipment and returned home late on June 27th. They planned to return for the start of Glassco's interviews on July 8th.[27] Thanks to surveillance, the investigators were aware of the likely defence strategy, and knew it was not just logical but plausible.

They also knew something that exacerbated LaBine's weakness as a witness: he simply would not stop talking. Whatever he found out, whether from the questions asked by Glassco's men or his own observations, he shared with his brother, Charlie, who passed along the information to J.H. Greenberg, Eldorado's lawyer. And whatever Greenberg learned, he shared with French and Pregel.

What investigators had learned about the 700-ton contract and the radium it produced was crucial to making sense of the papers they had seized. Now that the auditors knew what to look for, they set out to find it in the company's files. And find it they did: an invoice that detailed the sale of U_3O_8 from Eldorado to CRUC, Pregel's company in New York, for the sum of $554,000. The sales invoice had been shown to the company's auditors when it was created, but then French had torn it out of the record book and substituted a different one.

This second invoice broke out a separate item: 29.98 grams of radium. That meant CRUC paid a total of $554,000 for both the U_3O_8 *and* the 29.98 grams. Pregel had told the US Engineers and everyone else that he would simply waive his commission under his sales agreement "for the interests of the war effort." That commission would have amounted to $55,400, while the almost 30 grams of radium was worth more than ten times that amount. At $20 per milligram, Pregel managed to obtain $600,000 worth of radium free of charge. In fact, he had waived nothing.

What a difference a month made. Thanks to the information gleaned from surveillance, investigators changed their minds about laying charges. In late May, Jarvis had thought it was premature to do so, but by the end of June he and others were on board. The Departments of Justice and Munitions and Supply cleared the way for Robinette and Glassco to begin preparing those charges.

It was now only a matter of time, but first investigators really needed to know how much radium had been stolen or was otherwise missing. Hazards notwithstanding, on July 4th, Guernsey and the others completed an inventory that spanned the laboratories on Lombard and Church streets. The materials had to be gathered, measured, and then catalogued. It was painstaking work. Guernsey worried about both double-counting and overlooking what was there. French had his own representative in the room to oversee the process. At the end of a long day, the inventory – prepared in triplicate – included twenty-eight items, not including some containers that were too large to be removed and measured.[28]

Glassco Meets the Defence

True to his word, Pregel returned to Toronto on July 8th, ready to meet with Glassco. This time, four members of the US Army Corps of Engineers security team listened in.

Pregel understood the gravity of his situation. Two days earlier, he had called in to the Manhattan Engineering District office in New York to show off his subpoena. Although he couched his visit in terms of fears about the type of information he might be required to provide to Glassco, it came across as a bit of a threat. His testimony, he warned, would involve "the disclosure of information pertaining to secret contracts to which he was a party with the United States Government." Regardless of his motivation,

Arthur Slaght, 1952 | Arthur Roy, Library and Archives Canada, PA-047630

Pregel's concern was easily addressed. The Engineers told Glassco that a representative from their office intended to be present during the questioning. Lieutenant Winston Pickett was the obvious choice.[29]

Whether the meeting with Glassco was a formal hearing or merely an interview hardly matters. When it began on July 10th, Pregel arrived with counsel prepared to do battle. Arthur Slaght led the charge, along with Joseph Sedgwick, Herman Rogers, and Senator Joe Bench. Maurice Austin was also by Pregel's side. His expertise was not criminal law but tax disputes involving the Internal Revenue Service. Pregel clearly knew exactly what was at stake and the full extent of his potential jeopardy.

Arthur Slaght was the most notable of Pregel's defence lawyers. The oldest and most experienced of the team, he had earned a reputation as a fiery speaker. In the spring of 1945, he had just returned to full-time legal practice after ten years as a Liberal Member of Parliament.[30]

Born in May 1877, in Simcoe, Ontario, Slaght attended local schools before graduating from Osgoode Hall Law School in Toronto in 1898. In 1906, the discovery of silver led Slaght to move north to the area of Cobalt and Haileybury, not unlike Gilbert LaBine. Eventually, he returned to

Toronto, where he specialized in mining law. Today, that specialization would typically focus on transactions and raising capital through securities. Slaght did some of that work, but he cut his teeth on the criminal cases that arose from life in the mining camps. In the process he came to learn everything about mining operations.

It was his corporate work, however, that made him fabulously wealthy.[31] He owned a big, baronial property made of stone that sat on 35 acres of lakefront in Parry Sound on Georgian Bay. There he spent his summers, working on files delivered by his legal assistant, who would make the trip from Toronto. For the rest of the year, Slaght lived in a large house in a fashionable Toronto neighbourhood, complete with a housekeeper and chauffeur.[32]

Slaght built an enviable reputation as a litigator during the 1920s and '30s, tackling a slew of high-profile financial disputes.[33] Like most prominent litigators of his time, he took on clients in both civil and criminal proceedings. Many of his cases involved the latter, with murder becoming something of a specialty. It was a job he did well, having defended nineteen murder trials without losing a single client to the hangman's noose.[34]

Big P politics was key to Slaght's success. He was a Liberal and active in party circles both federally and provincially. He was known to be a crony of the Liberal premier of Ontario, Mitch Hepburn, who was particularly identified with mining interests and noted for drinking and carousing at Toronto's King Edward Hotel, with Slaght as an enthusiastic participant.[35] That did him no good with Prime Minister Mackenzie King, who refused to have a Hepburn crony in his cabinet. After ten years on the back benches, Slaght gave up and retired from politics. As an MP, he had supported the death penalty for sabotage, treason, and espionage as a way to "minimize the number of Canada's enemies from within," a view that was mainstream at the time. During his career, he also worked extensively with the RCMP, whose work he described as "second to none."

By all accounts, Arthur Slaght earned a lot of money thanks to his legal practice and political connections. He also spent a lot of it. Perhaps his exit from politics had been prompted by the need to recharge his bank account. Once again able to practise full time, Slaght was made to order for a wealthy client accused of financial crimes – and Pregel, who would do anything to preserve his reputation, had deep pockets.

With Slaght on board, Robinette had his work cut out for him. As Slaght's grandson – also a highly regarded Toronto litigator – once recalled, Robinette acknowledged what so many others did about Arthur Slaght's legal talents: "Mr. Robinette said ... he was the best jury lawyer that he had ever seen and probably the best jury lawyer that Canada had ever produced. He had this incredible way ... of persuasive advocacy in front of a jury."[36]

What about the others who represented the objects of Glassco's investigation? In addition to Slaght, two other "Joes" – Bench and Sedgwick – were the most prominent of the defence counsel retained by Pregel and French.

Joe Bench had two clients before Glassco and Robinette. He represented Dial and Instrument Finishers Ltd. as a corporate entity and Carl French in his personal capacity as company president. Having been called to the bar in 1928, Bench was a mere baby compared to Slaght but still senior to John Robinette. A devout Roman Catholic from St. Catharines, Ontario, Bench made his mark in local politics, serving as chair of the Catholic School Board and the St. Catharines Chamber of Commerce, and on the board of St. Catharines Steel Company. He was also a faithful Liberal provincially and federally. Defeated when he ran for Parliament in 1940, he somehow managed to claw his way into Mackenzie King's favour. King rewarded him by making him a senator at the very early age of thirty-three.[37] Being a senator had cachet, and that was what Pregel and French were probably buying.

Joseph Sedgwick was another matter entirely. Second to Slaght's lead, he was separated from the senior counsel by a generation; when Sedgwick

Joseph Bench, 1928 | https://digitalcommons.osgoode.yorku.ca/class_comp/35

Joseph Sedgwick, 1943 | Library and Archives Canada, Karsh Collection, Sitting #8739

was called to the bar, Slaght was already regarded as being among the leading criminal counsel.[38] Like Slaght, Sedgwick represented Carl French, but during the Glassco inquiry he also represented Boris Pregel and Bay Securities, in which Pregel had a controlling interest. Famous for his "brilliant defences and rich oratory," Sedgwick became a prominent criminal lawyer in the 1960s and '70s, having made his reputation in the 1930s and '40s by representing accused murderers and alleged spies.

A lifelong Tory and Anglican, Sedgwick was born in Leeds, England, in 1898, and moved with his family to Toronto when he was seven years old. He volunteered for military service in the First World War after lying about his age, returning to Canada after the war with the rank of staff sergeant. Once he was home in Toronto, Sedgwick decided to become a lawyer. As a veteran, he qualified for an expedited call to the bar because the Law Society of Upper Canada had made a special provision for returning soldiers to article for three years (like university graduates) instead of the five years usually required for matriculants.

Sedgwick, called to the bar in 1923, shone in his chosen profession. Starting as a junior in a small firm, he attracted the favourable attention of one of his superiors, just when the latter was appointed deputy attorney general of Ontario. Sedgwick joined him at the department and was soon arguing cases before the Ontario Court of Appeal. The department handled all criminal appeals, and Sedgwick was kept very busy. In the process, he became what he described as "a pretty good trial lawyer." When he left government service in 1937 after a blow-up with Premier Hepburn, Sedgwick set out on his own. "By that time," he recalled, "I had had a great deal of litigious experience and junior counsel were not in great supply, so I set myself up to do counsel work."[39]

Like Robinette and Slaght, Sedgwick worked as both prosecutor and defence counsel. He helped to prosecute the kidnapper of John Labatt, the beer magnate from London, Ontario, along with Tim Buck, the leader of Canada's Communist Party. He investigated the improvident contracts entered into on behalf of the Dionne quintuplets from Callander, Ontario. He also defended people before the FECB.

Sedgwick developed strong views on criminal law and procedure. He supported capital punishment and had great faith in the jury system for criminal matters. Like all defence counsel, he understood it was his duty to make the best case he could with the facts at hand, without necessarily believing everything a client told him. He liked to quote poetry and classical literature to make his point. He was described as having "a talent for the witty, the unusual, the trenchant that made him well known beyond the area of his greatest influence and impact, his home town of Toronto."[40]

In a view he held his entire career, Sedgwick believed that a good lawyer was bound to examine all new laws and challenge them as required.[41] And thus, he and Slaght challenged the very authority of Grant Glassco and John Robinette to question their clients in July 1945.

Investigation Delayed

Robinette may have been intent on questioning Pregel, French, and Pochon, but Slaght and Sedgwick had other plans.[42] After objecting to questions on the first day of interviews, the two persuaded Glassco and Robinette on the second day to adjourn indefinitely. Counsel appealed to

Robinette's sense of fair play, arguing that the Crown investigator lacked the proper legal authority to examine the witnesses. Although he was under no obligation to do so, Robinette took the arguments seriously and adjourned to consider them. The interviews had accomplished little.

Over the summer, Robinette revisited the order in council that had launched the investigation in May.[43] After weeks of careful thought, he amended and expanded the order to give investigators significantly more power to act. Although the objections to the original order in council are no longer a matter of record, they are apparent from the changes that were included in the amended version that was adopted 5 September 1945.[44] That new instrument, PC 5782, specifically expanded the scope of the investigation in dramatic ways. The heart of the original mandate gave Glassco general powers to investigate "any or all matters relating to or arising out of the affairs and operations of Eldorado and the sale or disposition of its products," including anything related to the sales agency agreements with Boris Pregel. As noted previously, Glassco was expressly given all the powers and authority of a commissioner under the *Inquiries Act*.

The September authorization was both detailed and expansive. In addition to naming twenty-two individuals and twenty-three corporations, the new mandate conferred broad investigative powers on the RCMP to investigate anyone affecting the control, management, operation, or affairs of any of the named companies, whether they were Canadian, British, or "foreign." Not only did investigators have broad powers to compel attendance, production of documents, and disclosure of evidence, but failure to do so was now an offence under the *Department of Munitions and Supply Act*. Moreover, Glassco was entirely immunized from every type of lawsuit or legal proceeding. With the war now over, it was anyone's guess what this would mean for the next stage of the investigation.

Although the examinations had been adjourned, the audit of Radium Luminous Industries continued over the summer of 1945. The decision to lay criminal charges remained with Glassco and Robinette, subject to the consent of C.D. Howe. But, if those three men thought the amended order in council would resolve the impasse, they were wrong. Instead, it simply marked the beginning of a new, more contentious phase.

9
Going Public

The endless war had ended. On August 14th, Japan announced its surrender, and the formalities were complete by September 2nd. Just over a week later, on 10 September 1945, Igor Gouzenko, a cipher clerk at the Soviet embassy in Ottawa, defected with documents detailing the existence of an espionage ring in Canada. As the scandal unfolded – though Canadians did not hear the news until February 1946 – cabinet amended the order in council to investigate financial chicanery at Eldorado, expressly expanding J. Grant Glassco's authority.

A month earlier, the Americans had applied the fruits of their labours at the Manhattan Project, dropping atomic bombs on the Japanese cities of Hiroshima and Nagasaki. By the beginning of September, the war in the Pacific was over. Yet concerns remained about maintaining nuclear secrets and the extent of Canada's uranium stockpiles.

In Toronto, Glassco's team was busier than ever reviewing files and documents. By mid-September, five full-time auditors from Clarkson Gordon had been pulled into the investigation and five more were on the way. Glassco needed more still, so Lesslie Thomson arranged for the military to expedite the release of eight men who had previously worked with Glassco at Clarkson Gordon. With the final stages of the Royal Canadian Mounted Police's (RCMP) investigation into financial wrongdoing at Eldorado came the decision to lay criminal charges. In the proceedings that followed, the veil of secrecy was finally lifted.

By the autumn of 1945, investigators were focusing their attention on Carl French and his work with Radium Luminous Industries. Glassco was sure the company lay at the very heart of the conspiracy to defraud Eldorado of radium. It was a measure of the firm's significance that two of Glassco's auditors were dedicated to reviewing the company's documents, compared to three who were reviewing Eldorado's. Under the careful watch of J.E. Beckett, the supervising auditor, and RCMP investigator Terry Guernsey, the auditors began to find the documents that showed how French had fabricated transactions to evade taxation, even though the corporate records removed from 103 Church Street some five months earlier were in "a deplorable condition." As Guernsey observed, "It is said that common-sense bookkeeping methods have not even been used, and that the correspondence files are in even a worse condition."[1]

Despite their condition, the documents were a revelation: "amazing irregularities," especially within the radium and uranium sales accounts, sat alongside Boris Pregel's commission account records. By mid-September, these irregularities were such that Glassco and his team were confident the trio of French, Marcel Pochon, and Boris Pregel had defrauded Eldorado of more than $1 million.[2] It was an astonishing amount of money in 1945. The auditors were able to piece together several fraudulent schemes designed to hide both profits and radium, often in plain sight.

The 700-ton Contract

The first involved the US Army's uranium ore purchase, negotiated in late 1942 and delivered in August 1943. The 700-ton contract provided materials that were crucial to the Manhattan Project's early success. French and Pochon represented Eldorado in the negotiations and were thus able to assert that the company would sell uranium to the Manhattan Project only through its agent, Boris Pregel, and his company, Canadian Radium and Uranium Corporation (CRUC). But Pregel and CRUC did not actually own the ore they purported to sell; only with a deal in hand did Pregel try to purchase the requisite tonnage. Recall, too, that although the Americans had failed to see Pregel's value to the project, initially they reluctantly agreed to include him in the transaction. It was Leslie Groves who demanded to deal directly with Eldorado. The general went so far as to cancel the original agreement, eliminate Pregel's role as intermediary, and negotiate a new contract for $438,000. Despite these efforts, Pregel was impossible to ignore altogether, and he somehow convinced Groves that he would do the work gratis for the good of the American war effort.

While French and Pochon purported to represent Eldorado in talks with the Americans, they were also working for Pregel and CRUC, unbeknownst to C.D. Howe or even Eldorado president Gilbert LaBine. What's more, as we have seen, French and Pochon both had a financial stake in CRUC and were, in effect, negotiating with themselves. The trio thus benefited monetarily by including CRUC in the contract, and Pregel also took a percentage of the contract in commissions, both as Eldorado's sales agent and as CRUC's representative. All three owed Eldorado a duty of loyalty as directors and, in Pregel's case, as agent in sales negotiations. It counted for nothing.

The largest amount of missing radium could be traced to the contract for 700 tons of uranium. French had calculated the amount of radium that would be derived from refining that much uranium as 29.98 grams in carbonate form. He then lied to the Americans, telling them that Eldorado owed Pregel the radium as compensation in kind for his commission on the contract, and persuaded them to simply hand over the residual radium free of charge to Pregel after they had received the uranium from Eldorado. The Americans were not in the mood to quibble, and duly did as requested. How would they have known any different?

Pregel then sold his newly acquired radium to International Rare Metals Refinery Inc. in Mount Kisco for just $44,000, or under $1,470 per gram. At the time, the value was almost ten times that amount: $438,000. By selling the radium to his own company for one tenth its value, Pregel avoided paying the full amount of tax owing in the United States while acquiring a significant quantity of radium that he could then re-sell or lease.[3]

Buy Low, Sell High

As French and Pregel had discussed when they met at the Royal York in late June 1945, another suspicious transaction involved 118 grams of radium derived from uranium-bearing ore owned by African Metals Corporation (Afrimet), the North American subsidiary of the Union Minière du Haut-Katanga (UMHK), refined by Eldorado in Port Hope, and destined for the Manhattan Project. As part of this arrangement, Eldorado was also supposed to refine the radium derived from the 1,200 tons of ore, and it did – but not completely. As auditors reviewed the documents, a complex and audacious scheme came into focus in which Eldorado sold a substantial quantity of radium to CRUC at a significantly discounted price and discounted refining fees.

Shortly before Christmas 1942, Afrimet, CRUC, and Eldorado – represented by French – entered into a supplementary agreement to refine the radium from this enormous cache of ore. Under this subsequent agreement, Eldorado agreed to refine 60 grams of radium, and Afrimet agreed to pay the full refining fees, which were $6,000 per gram. But there was still more radium that could be extracted from that much ore; of the approximately 336 grams of radium still available, roughly a third – about 118 grams – was thought to be recoverable through the refining process.

What made the subsequent arrangement of December 1942 so unusual was CRUC's role. Eldorado had agreed to refine the 118 grams only to a "stage" (i.e., a level of purity) to be agreed upon at a later date. For this partial refining, Eldorado would earn fees of just $1,000 per gram instead of the full $6,000, because CRUC would supposedly complete the refining process, earning $5,000 per gram in fees in the process. That "later date" arrived in mid-August 1943 when the parties came to terms. Eldorado – represented by French and Pochon – agreed with CRUC that Eldorado would complete 90 percent of the refining process, and CRUC would finish the balance. But CRUC had no refining facilities; almost certainly, Pregel never intended to have his company finish the process on its own.[4] Instead, under his direction, CRUC subcontracted the work to Radium Luminous Industries.

The arrangement defied credulity. It made no sense to give a small manufacturing company with buildings in downtown Toronto and an experimental farm in Scarborough a job that Eldorado, with its world-class refining facility in Port Hope, supposedly could not – or would not – complete. That is, Radium Luminous Industries, like CRUC, had no significant refining capacity to speak of.

There was more. Under the December 1942 agreement, CRUC could buy up to 30 grams of radium from Eldorado, paying just $13,500 per gram on radium worth $20,000 per gram. The provision was said to cover any shortfalls in the final refining process, a form of insurance to protect CRUC from what was described as "excessive losses" that might occur in completing the refining process.

Agreements with Afrimet covered the refining fees paid to Eldorado, CRUC, and Radium Luminous Industries. Here, too, Eldorado got the short end of the stick. The company recovered $18,521 in excess of its estimated refining costs but had no right to sell the radium or recover its administrative costs. By contrast, CRUC and Radium Luminous Industries received a whopping $595,478 for performing work thought to have cost no more than $16,792. In practical terms, Eldorado had sacrificed profits of close to $600,000 to two companies that did next to nothing.

What about the excessive loss provision under the December 1942 agreement? Since Eldorado took the refining to approximately 90 percent, CRUC simply could not have suffered substantial losses in completing it. Nevertheless, Pregel's company exercised its right to buy 9.77 grams of "lost" radium for $13,500 per gram. Considering the discount of $6,500 per gram on the market rate that was $20,000, Eldorado lost over $63,500 in the transaction. When combined with the unwarranted fees that CRUC and Radium Luminous Industries earned from the transaction, this entire scheme cost Eldorado $642,236 in potential profits.[5]

The company also lost radium because French used the opportunity to recoup "residue" from test tubes and "recovery from scrap." That substance was radium that properly belonged to Afrimet, supposedly lost through the refining process at Port Hope and then "recovered" at the Scarborough farm. To add insult to injury, Eldorado had also agreed to make up a further 8 percent refining loss on 25 grams of radium for which CRUC was supposed to share responsibility.

As Terry Guernsey later observed wryly, "Pregel, to make a good fellow of himself, waived all commissions and profits on this deal [the original 700-ton contract], but by swinging the 118-gram contract with French was able to make much more than he would have through commissions, the profits from which should rightly have been Eldorado's."[6] At the very same time, he finalized the arrangement with French and Pochon to have Eldorado complete the refining process to 90 percent. Some coincidence.

About this series of transactions, Grant Glassco later wrote in his report: "It will be observed that the contractual position at this date [August 1943] between Eldorado and [CRUC] in respect of their joint ventures was extremely confused by the agreements entered into between them as to the manner in which the refining was to be carried out." When one factored in the company's administrative costs along with the expenses incurred by French and Pochon to negotiate the various agreements, Eldorado had actually lost money, at least with respect to radium.[7]

Other irregularities were less elaborate. For example, Pregel's sales agreement entitled him to recover his expenses from Eldorado, but his claims were excessive. Another anomaly was the low price Pregel paid for radium from Eldorado and the much higher price – over $6.00 more per milligram

– at which he sold it to "his" customers. That kind of mark-up was contrary to the terms of his sales agent agreement. CRUC also received an unexplained trade discount worth $34,000, the credit for which was found on an unnumbered invoice in French's files without any supporting paperwork. It had all the hallmarks of a fake. From what auditors could tell, CRUC had reversed a debit and converted what was owed to Eldorado into a credit to CRUC without any justification. French also profited personally, earning $5,000 from the transaction.[8]

Challenging Glassco in Court

Guernsey presented his review in mid-September 1945 derived from materials seized from 103 Church Street in early April and supplemented with material obtained under the order in council issued in early May. His analysis and conclusions were not based on anything obtained under the September order in council, which particularized more clearly Glassco's authority to obtain documents and records after Slaght and Sedgwick had adjourned the interviews in mid-July.

But the September order did not satisfy defence counsel, and they went to court to fight it. In October, acting on behalf of their corporate clients Bay Securities Ltd. and Dial and Instrument Finishers Ltd., Slaght and Sedgwick filed a writ with the superior court in Toronto to have both orders in council declared ultra vires. In other words, they asked the court to say that Glassco had no authority to conduct an investigation that was by then well underway. They wanted to quash the investigation and prevent the lead investigator from publishing his findings.

Robinette took the complaint seriously, but the initiative also put the government in a bind. Slaght and Sedgwick almost certainly gambled that, "for security reasons," the government would not wish to lay out its case in open court to justify the scope of Glassco's investigative powers.[9] They had not counted on C.D. Howe's pragmatism.

Rather than fight about the scope of the investigation, Robinette and Glassco simply decided to work with what they had. And they had a lot, not just from the Church Street documents but thanks to American surveillance records. That knowledge made it easier to push forward without compelling anyone – not Pregel, not French, and not Pochon – to answer questions. It also meant the trio did not get the chance to explain what Glassco later described diplomatically as "apparent irregularities."[10]

Press, Parliament, and Publicity

During the same period, Parliament debated whether to extend the government's wartime powers with the National Emergency Powers Bill. Then, on October 20th, the Toronto *Evening Telegram* broke news of Glassco's investigation and the challenge to it. Perhaps recognizing the limits of legal action, someone had decided to plead their case in the court of public opinion via the *Tely*, as it was known, a Conservative-leaning daily broadsheet. Sedgwick was the likely source of the article, given its tone and pitch. The short piece said that Bay Securities Ltd. and Dial and Instrument Finishers Ltd., represented by Sedgwick and Bench, "object to the drastic nature of the order and its amendment saying that among other things it deprives them of the right to appeal to the courts."[11]

Media reports probably came as no surprise to investigators. They had known that defence counsel intended to challenge Glassco's authority to act, perhaps even seeking an injunction to stop the investigation, but did not know when.[12] The day after William McElhone, J.M. Clish, and Terry Guernsey searched Marcel Pochon's home in Port Hope, investigators had their answer. Slaght and Sedgwick seem to have turned to the courts and the press at the same time.

With the writ filed, a flurry of stories began to appear in other Toronto newspapers. The *Tely* ran another piece, and the *Toronto Daily Star, The Globe and Mail,* and *The Financial Post* soon followed. Each took a side, and over the next two weeks, readers learned the basics of the alleged fraud at Eldorado along with the identities of the people and firms said to have perpetrated it.

The court filing was a chance to open up more of the investigation – some MPs knew all about it – to the public. Opposition politicians also weighed in. The Progressive Conservatives were especially keen to paint the governing Liberals as heavy handed, if not downright tyrannical. The Tories made clear their dissatisfaction and demanded the government release the text of the orders in council, which had not yet been made public. The *Tely* dutifully reported their concerns along with complaints from counsel, who lamented Glassco's investigation as an unprecedented power grab. The paper implied that investigators had turned to interrogating unrepresented individuals when the documents had come up dry, and suggested that defence counsel had stepped in to stop government abuse.[13]

H.R. Armstrong took a different approach in the Toronto *Daily Star,* which was generally sympathetic to the Liberals. His account was more detailed than the one in the *Tely* and focused on the rationale for the investigation, a seeming response to the allegations of overreach. Part of the opposition's outrage was a reaction to government efforts to use the National Emergency Powers Bill to formalize the orders, but Armstrong's report stressed that cabinet had been concerned for months that the company's radium and uranium "may have been channelled to unauthorized sources," with the clear implication of nefarious purposes. "These metals are the base for making atomic bombs," he reminded readers, declaring, "The investigation and steps taken to stop it transcend the legal aspects of the actions which will be brought into court in due course." His reference to the involvement of two unnamed Canadian senators also created some added intrigue. Claiming to tap the knowledge of the "highest government informants," Armstrong portrayed the government as cautiously trying to get to the bottom of the matter with an investigation that would not be derailed. Court applications notwithstanding, "sources" insisted that Glassco intended to carry on. With several "hearings" under his belt, others scheduled imminently would "proceed as though no court action has been initiated."[14]

The story was even bigger news the next day when *The Globe and Mail* published a Canadian Press account on its front page: "Eldorado Report Near, Howe States, as Suits Brought to Nullify Probe." The minister was said to "not know whether there had been any unauthorized deliveries," but the investigation seemed to be nearing completion. According to Canadian Press, Glassco had found the necessary information from sources other than "the parties in question."

Sedgwick was also quoted: "Speaking for my clients, we have not the slightest objection to an inquiry providing it is conducted on a fair and proper basis." The government's approach was the objectionable part. Sedgwick laid it on thick: "This was a hole-in-the-wall affair – a Star Chamber – conducted under Orders-in-Council that make the presence of counsel a privilege instead of a right."[15] He complained that his clients had been "barred access to the courts" and "took issue with the secrecy clause of the orders at this date." There had been no misuse of any uranium, he declared, rejecting the suggestion that it had found its way into the wrong hands.[16]

Wellington Jeffers, *The Globe and Mail*'s financial editor, offered his own take in the "Finance at Large" column. Canadians had a right to know what was going on at "their" company since Eldorado had been nationalized. There ought to be more government scrutiny – not less – and civil liberties be damned. He went so far as to propose a double investigation now that the war was over: one to explain what had happened at Eldorado, the other what the government was doing about it:

> Perhaps they would give each other clean sheets or sheets not too dirty. Insiders may know the answers to all these questions, but the very interested public does not. This is not meant as a comment on the writs as such. Whatever they mean or succeed in doing, there is a public right to be informed on policy and performance which should not be overlooked by those in power.[17]

Although the *Evening Telegram* echoed Jeffers's concerns, there was little reporting about the activities of Thomas Sutton, the self-appointed chair of an Eldorado shareholders' committee, who urged the government to create a formal royal commission to investigate the allegations currently subject to Glassco's remit. Sutton had ulterior motives; the committee was formed originally to complain about the price offered by the government when Eldorado was nationalized.[18] In fact, few seemed to pay Sutton much heed.

The Orders under Scrutiny

Then, as now, Saturday was a prime day for newspapers to publish investigative work. On 27 October 1945, the newspapers did not disappoint. *The Globe and Mail* stuck mostly to describing the contents of the orders that Howe had decided to table the day before.[19] The *Tely* offered some detail, and *The Financial Post* provided still more.

Among these accounts, only Warren Baldwin of the *Globe* included the names of the people – including French, Pregel, and Pochon – and individual companies listed in the amended order in council, and thus the targets of Glassco's investigation. Others focused exclusively on the two companies, Bay Securities and Dial and Instrument Finishers, that brought the court application. Baldwin expressed mild concern about the approach investigators were said to be taking, particularly an allegation that Glassco was questioning witnesses without the presence of counsel, which, as we know, was incorrect.

At the *Tely*, staff writer J.H. Fisher provided a fuller account. After going over the contents of the orders in detail, he noted that the nature of the so-called irregularities had not been described nor had charges been laid, "but involved are questions relating to the ownership of radioactive substances of great importance in connection with the development of atomic power and the atom bomb." He also outlined parliamentary discussions about the investigation, especially the concerns of Progressive Conservative leader John Bracken, who claimed simply to be trying to get to the bottom of the investigation.

Beyond the basics, Howe's statements in the House had been vague. He offered no more than the barest overview of the investigation, the subject matter, and who was leading it. "The investigation is still proceeding," he told the House. "A report has not been received. When the report is received consideration will be given to tabling it in the House."

Fisher knew exactly why Slaght and Sedgwick had turned to the courts. Although the opposition probably knew of Glassco's investigation, few would have known about its substance or the contents of the orders in council without court involvement. Fisher's news report also noticed something others missed; while investigators had been focused on French's business affairs in Toronto, the *Tely* staff reporter was the first to discuss Pregel's previous work with the Belgians, including the radium cartel involving Eldorado and the UMHK in the 1930s.[20]

But Kenneth Wilson's front-page story in *The Financial Post* that weekend was the most comprehensive. "Court Action Raises Lid on Radium Embroglio" was the headline above the article written by the Ottawa editor of the *Post*. Wilson was the most thorough and best-connected reporter in Ottawa, and his account of the intricacies of what he described as a "sweeping" investigation into the company's affairs was so rich in detail that many of the participants must have served as sources.

Copies of the judicial applications, which would have contained the details of the orders in council, have not been located. In fact, most of what can now be unearthed about the suit is derived from Wilson's far-reaching article, including that Senator Bench represented French and his company Dial and Instrument Finishers Ltd., that Slaght acted for Pregel personally, and that Sedgwick represented Pregel's firm Bay Securities.[21]

Wilson echoed the sentiments of defence counsel and Tories in the House, describing the order as "arbitrary," though it did not stop him from listing every single one of the forty-five individuals and companies caught within its web. Nor did he end there, detailing the contents of the order, including its justification under the "peace, order, and good government" powers of the constitution and its retroactive application due to "the state of the war."

He lingered over the final point, which was especially troubling given the bill before Parliament. If it passed, the National Emergency Powers Bill would extend the emergency for another year and validate all existing orders in council, including the ones empowering Glassco. Why, Wilson asked, would the government rely on emergency wartime authority after the cessation of hostilities? Even the amended order under which Glassco operated with expanded authority had been passed one week after Japan formally surrendered aboard the USS *Missouri* in early September.

If Slaght and Sedgwick had talked to the reporter hoping for some good publicity and a bit of sympathy, they must have been disappointed. Notwithstanding his concerns, Wilson's account was no mere puff piece in support of the defence. Most of it focused on what Glassco and his team were investigating – and why. Wilson captured the essence:

> What the Government was seeking by means of these orders and powers was certain factual information bearing on operations alleged to have taken place in the sale and transfer of radium and uranium. The aim of the enquiry was to find out if any criminal acts have been performed; to find out if there has been any monetary loss to the Government through unauthorized sales of these metals, and also to trace alleged disappearance of certain physical stocks of these precious metals.

Acknowledging that the investigation was not likely to have become public without the court challenge, Wilson nevertheless accepted the government's view that secrecy was necessary, not just in the weeks and months leading up to Hiroshima but even after the war out of concern about "possible international complications."

Of course, if Glassco or even Howe had hoped to keep the investigation secret, they failed. Wilson had a pretty good handle on what was going on. He provided real context for the investigation, including why radium was so important for Eldorado and the existence of a cartel agreement with UMHK to keep radium prices artificially high. He also had enough information to describe quite accurately the activities of the various players, especially Pregel, French, and their companies. He knew that Glassco was investigating "any unauthorized transactions ... in the transfer and sale of radium and uranium" as well as "any sales agreements between Eldorado and Pregel which might have resulted in monopoly of the sale of Eldorado products." Only the comment about monopolies was wide of the mark.

It's surprising just how much information Wilson had – enough to lay out a clear and accurate timeline of the government's efforts. He knew about the work of the Foreign Exchange Control Board, not just Glassco's team, and about the use of "various orders and directives," including an order of the metals controller. He even knew about Glassco's thwarted attempt to interview Pregel and French in July, postponed indefinitely after two days of consistent objection from counsel.

Wilson's sources must have come from within the investigation, or he would not have known that "it may not be necessary to hold another public enquiry and that Glassco may make his report to the Hon. C.D. Howe, Minister of Munitions and Supply on the basis of present information."

Diefenbaker Joins the Fray

With news of the investigation buzzing about, John Diefenbaker jumped into the fray. A Progressive Conservative MP from Saskatchewan first elected in 1940, Dief had a nose for publicity. When it came to Howe, irascible, imperious, and sometimes incautious in his statements, Diefenbaker scented opportunity. In early November, he rose during Question Period to demand that the minister table transcripts of the evidence Glassco had taken and pledge to publish any resulting reports. Howe's response was vague and non-committal:

> No report has been received from the investigator. In the meantime, there have been a good many representations in the newspapers, most of which are wholly unwarranted. As soon as the report is received it will be considered by the government, and if public policy indicates that it should be tabled I can assure my hon friend that it will be.

Dief understood exactly what Howe meant, so he pressed on: "The minister did not answer my question with respect to the transcript of evidence, except that part of it the production of which may be contrary to public policy."

Howe committed to nothing: "Much of the investigation has no reference to evidence." Conceding that "a few witnesses were heard in the early stages," he half-heartedly agreed to consider doing something – maybe: "If it is of any interest I suppose I can get the transcript of evidence and table it. I have not seen it myself, but I shall be glad to ask if the transcript is available. If so I shall read it, and consider tabling it."[22]

The Financial Post Weighs In

Two days later, *The Financial Post* picked up where Diefenbaker left off.[23] Some of the concerns expressed in its op-ed were legitimate, others were fearmongering. Recognizing that the courts would determine whether the orders were constitutionally permissible, the paper nonetheless worried that "order-in-council government" would replace Parliament. The piece echoed the rhetoric of Slaght and Sedgwick, asking whether secret boards of inquiry would subvert "the normal processes of the courts." The op-ed also complained that witnesses were permitted legal representation "only after vigorous protest." This was untrue; lawyers had always been permitted under the order and attended every interview. How else could Slaght and Sedgwick have objected so strongly to the questioning? Why else would Robinette have reconsidered the original order in council and put forward the more detailed amended one in September?

Yet the *Post* got it right when it questioned the government's continued reliance on national security to justify its secrecy. The secrecy may have been warranted to protect the atomic bomb project, but not now. There was also a valid concern that the order expressly empowered investigators to compel testimony without the presence of counsel.[24] Although judges have, and had, the power to compel attendance to give evidence, the power to prohibit access to counsel – even if Glassco did not invoke it – was genuinely problematic. In the days before the *Charter of Rights and Freedoms,* access to counsel was a common law right that could be overridden by statute. And, as Canadians would soon learn with the espionage trials arising from Gouzenko's revelations, judges were often all too willing to dispense with counsel in certain circumstances.

The *Post* urged the government to let the courts determine the fate of Eldorado's executives in the ordinary course, to dispense with the "Star Chamber" system: "If this sort of thing can happen in Canada, all our rights as citizens are in jeopardy."

The *Post* also ran a lengthy front-page story on Boris Pregel, detailing his involvement with the radium trade generally and Eldorado more specifically.[25] But it was a flattering feature that left readers with the impression that the rationale for investigating Eldorado's sales agent was a mystery.[26] Of course, it was not.

The RCMP Investigation Continues

Diefenbaker made a fuss about the process, but no one rose in Parliament to defend anyone under investigation. Auditors continued to review their cache of documents, and investigators continued to prepare their criminal case. By American Thanksgiving, thanks to a so-called confidential informant in New York, investigators had abundant evidence that French and Pregel had worked together to steal radium from Eldorado.

The identity of the "Confidential Informant" in archival records is unclear, but given the level of detail provided about the views and thoughts of Pregel, French, and Pochon, the who was most likely a what: surveillance, namely wiretaps. Little else would explain the specifics that were summarized in RCMP reports. For example, in late November, based on information from the informant, Guernsey recounted several conversations involving French and the Pregel brothers. They discussed the whereabouts of various quantities of stolen radium and their efforts to dispose of it, despite needing more radium than they had. With the heightened scrutiny of an investigation, they were evidently scrambling, worried someone was going to figure it out – and soon.

It's not clear whether French had lied to Pregel about the state of their mutual radium stockpile or if they were simply commiserating about their looming problem, but the difficulty was this: French had claimed to have control over 18 grams, only 7 of which were still in Canada. That was insufficient to meet his business needs. French had said he extracted 6 grams of radium from scrap materials imported to Canada for processing, but that was untrue. Despite their efforts, operations at the Scarborough farm had yet to extract any usable radium from the collected scrap material, so French had borrowed from the stockpile that belonged to Afrimet. Returning the radium was not an option because it had been delivered to purchasers. There was nothing to return. At some point, those supplies needed to be replaced.

The paper trail – or lack of one – was now top of mind. Unless they could conjure up radium from thin air, they would have to explain where it was. French had a plan: they could "sell" the radium to Insurance Appraisal and Rating Agency Inc., a company in which French had an interest, as a way of explaining the missing supplies. The scheme was an obvious sham and smacked of despair. The agency's Canadian office shared space with French's desk at Eldorado – at least until he resigned – and there was no reason to believe that an insurance firm needed its own supply of radium.[27]

As mentioned previously, just as these financial contortions were known to the RCMP, French and Pregel knew a lot of what was going on with the investigation thanks to the LaBine brothers and Eldorado lawyer Jack Greenberg. Everything Gilbert LaBine learned about the investigation he told his brother, Charlie. Anything Charlie learned, he told Greenberg, who passed along the information to French or Pregel.[28]

Thanks to this trail of information, French saw the writing on the wall by late November 1945. Now, his biggest fear was being charged, and once more he pondered leaving Canada to evade prosecution. When Guernsey got wind of the news he told Glassco and Robinette, and talks resumed about whether to prepare charges immediately.

While prosecutors considered how to proceed, Parliament enacted the *National Emergency Transitional Powers Act*.[29] The legislation came into force on December 18th, and with it, the controversial orders in council that Slaght and Sedgwick had challenged became law as a matter of statute. It wasn't impossible to challenge a statute, but it was certainly more difficult to do so.

The Charges

Carl French's fears became a reality three days later, when two RCMP officers arrived at his office on Church Street and arrested him. They took him to Police Station 1 at 10 Court Street, where he was charged with five criminal counts related to fraud: one for omitting to make proper entries in Eldorado's corporate records with the intent to defraud the company and four involving the acceptance of secret commissions. Bail had been prearranged at $5,000 – a sizable sum in 1945. French was released almost immediately and remanded to mid-January by the magistrate J.L. Prentice.[30]

The press was waiting, but French declined to comment. Senator Bench, who drove in from his home in St. Catharines to represent him, was not talking either. Nor was C.D. Howe, who had left to spend part of the Christmas holidays in Bermuda. Most other ministers had left Ottawa, too. Lesslie Thomson, however, was available. Speaking to the *Star,* he stressed that French had been charged under the *Criminal Code,* and not pursuant to the orders in council.[31] It was disingenuous to say, as he did, that the charges were altogether "independent" of the Glassco investigation, but the point that these were offences under legislation that pre-dated the investigation was important.[32]

Given the media's interest in the investigation, it was not surprising the charges were front page news in *The Globe and Mail* on that final Saturday before Christmas.[33] The *Star* offered the most detailed account of the arrest and charges, which were reprinted in full as sworn by Terry Guernsey.[34] The first count concerned records related to the agreement between Eldorado, CRUC, and the US Army Corps of Engineers over the uranium sale of August 1943. French was alleged to have violated section 413 of the *Criminal Code,* a provision designed to address corporate fraud and specifically aimed at company officers who falsified corporate accounts. The violation involved the fabrication of an invoice dated 21 August 1943, which provided for the delivery of radium from Eldorado to CRUC as part of the uranium sale to the US Engineers.[35] The other four charges involved contravention of section 504,[36] which criminalized receipt of secret commissions. In French's case, those charges related to payments he had received between 1942 and 1944 from Pregel, Radium Luminous Industries, CRUC, and International Rare Metals. At the time, French was supposed to have been acting for the benefit of Eldorado, not his own. It made no difference whether the payments were an inducement or reward for doing business with the entities in question.[37]

French's trial was expected to begin in a few months – February or March 1946 – by which time Howe was supposed to have received Glassco's report, even if the findings were not made public.[38] Such a speedy trial is unimaginable today.

Instead, fifty-four days later, Pochon and Pregel were charged alongside French. Each was charged with conspiracy to commit fraud with one another and their various companies – Radium Luminous Industries, International Uranium Mining Company Ltd., and CRUC – against Eldorado for radium and cash worth at least $500,000.[39] Guernsey and McElhone had hoped to turn Pochon into a Crown witness against his co-conspirators, but after a long day of questioning at his home in Port Hope on February 13th, he remained obdurate.[40] The Mounties then arrested him and drove him to Toronto to be charged. According to Guernsey, Pochon burst into tears, and appeared in police court the following day. Boris Pregel had to be charged in absentia since he was still in New York. Finally, French was charged with additional counts relating to the company's records more generally, not just a single invoice.

The First Court Appearance

The trio were scheduled to appear in Magistrates' Court before S. Tupper Bigelow on February 18th. Bigelow, nicknamed the "Hanging Magistrate" for being something of an authoritarian on the bench, was still new to the job that would later make him so well known within the Toronto legal community.[41]

Only two defendants appeared before Magistrate Bigelow that day in February. Sedgwick appeared for French, and H.C. Walker appeared for Pochon. Sedgwick had the good sense to ask for the particulars about the charges against French and then sit down. Robinette agreed to consider the request.

Pregel was in New York and had not the slightest intention of travelling to Toronto to be arrested. Instead, Arthur Slaght read a statement into court on his behalf based on the strategy the two had devised at the Royal York in June. Feigning confusion and denying all wrongdoing, especially the allegations of fraud, Pregel refused to appear, saying the charges were "political and malicious and not judicial and fair."

The statement portrayed Pregel as cooperative, even helpful to investigators. He had already appeared before Glassco's inquiry and provided "as complete information as was requested." His compliance had been ongoing: "Since July, 1945, I have, through my counsel, volunteered a considerable amount of information to Mr. Robinette, and on at least two occasions, my counsel, on my instructions, has written to Mr. Robinette, offering him the fullest cooperation in conducting a complete inquiry into my connection with Eldorado from the outset, which offers to date [have] been ignored."

Not only had he done nothing wrong, but it was *he* who had been treated badly. "As to my connection with Eldorado," he declared, "far from having defrauded that company, or having conspired to do so, the facts will show that I, more than any other person, am responsible for what success the company has had, and for what assistance it was able to give during the recent war to the allied nations." Indeed, all his actions had been "done with the full knowledge of Mr. Gilbert LaBine," who had not been charged as a conspirator. The implication was clear: If LaBine was not before the court, why was he?

Just as Pregel and Slaght had strategized, the statement framed his wartime work as patriotic. Beyond helping Eldorado, he had assisted in the development of atomic energy more broadly. "Those competent to judge have said that my efforts had much to do with the early development of atomic energy," he wrote. "I am at a loss to understand how it can be charged that I was other than a great benefactor to Eldorado. Whatever I or companies associated with me did receive was an inadequate reward for the labors performed."[42]

Robinette understandably disagreed entirely with Pregel's characterization of his activities – and said so in court.[43] Even Slaght seemed to have difficulty stomaching his client's statement; at one point, he lowered his glasses over his nose, looked at the magistrate, and said, "Your Honour, I want you to know that this is my client's letter and not mine."[44]

The Move to Close the Courtroom

The parties reconvened before Magistrate Bigelow in May to determine whether to close the preliminary hearing to the public. Robinette, acting under Howe's instructions, argued that national security required an *in camera* hearing to allow the Crown to make its fullest case for prosecution.[45] In an affidavit, Howe made the case that a public hearing was not in the public interest because the prosecution involved Eldorado and nuclear secrets. Defence counsel opposed the move, with Slaght continuing to act for Pregel, and Sedgwick for French. They argued that the Eldorado conspiracy trial had been mistakenly linked to the Gouzenko spy case in popular imagination, so the accused had not been able to properly defend themselves. "This story should be told fully and in detail," they asserted.[46]

Open courts were the rule, and any deviation from that principle required a careful assessment of circumstances. Bigelow sided with Robinette. Released in mid-May, his decision relied on section 679(d) of the *Criminal Code,* which gave the judge discretion to close the courtroom. He invoked an English precedent from 1913, closing public access in cases involving delicate or confidential evidence.[47] As the House of Lords had held, the ability "to secure that justice is done" sometimes required excluding the public. That decision had to be based on necessity, not expedience or convenience.

Slaght and Sedgwick had tried to convince Magistrate Bigelow that their clients would not be able to defend themselves without disclosing certain information about the contracts in issue. Bigelow was dubious. The so-called prohibition against disclosure claimed by the defendants – their confidentiality agreements – applied whether the proceedings were open to the public or closed. The prohibition was supposed to prevent disclosure of *any information anywhere*. For Bigelow, the issue was whether the government would waive the obligations of secrecy for the purposes of mounting a legal defence.

Bigelow did not simply reject the defence position; he found quite the opposite, suggesting that the government would be *more* likely to release the accused from their obligations to maintain secrecy about certain details of their wartime work if the preliminary hearing were held behind closed doors. This point probably tipped the case in favour of the government, and Bigelow allowed the preliminary hearing to proceed *in camera*.

Slaght and Sedgwick had also complained that their clients could not get a fair trial because the press was biased against them. Again, Bigelow was unsympathetic:

> A good deal has been said in argument about the unfavourable and indeed inaccurate statements which have been made about the accused in the press. This is a matter which does not concern the Court and has nothing to do, as I see it, with answering the ends of justice. Justice is administered by the Courts and the duty of the press in this connection, with which the Court has no right to interfere, is simply to report accurately and fairly the Court's proceedings.[48]

Pregel Talks to Groves

The US Army Corps of Engineers were attentive to the proceedings in Toronto's Magistrates' Court, and not just because key members knew they would be called to testify at the criminal trial. Even before Bigelow announced his decision, Pregel wrote to Leslie Groves to complain that he could not defend himself.

In support of the motion to close the court, Howe had testified that it would be undesirable for the US Engineers to give evidence in open court. Pregel now dismissed that argument, writing to Groves that "from the point of view of secrecy, except for the fact that the press and the public are not physically present, there is absolutely no difference between 'in camera' hearings and open court procedure." Plainly, this was wrong, so why say it?

Despite the breezy tone, Pregel's letter was not simply recounting the opinion of his lawyers. It was also a threat, as his elaboration made evident:

> The defendants and their counsel retain all rights of the ordinary procedure, including complete cross examination of witnesses, and ... all witnesses, attorneys, and defendants, are not and cannot, by any stretch of imagination

> or point of law, be prohibited from releasing any part or full information, including ... testimony and cross examination, either to the press or to whom else they see fit, thus reducing the 'in camera' proceeding, for security purposes, to nothing but sham and pretext.

That is, no one had any intention of staying quiet about what was going on in the courtroom, regardless of the magistrate's decision. He closed his letter with a certain fawning insincerity, implying, once again, that he was somehow helping Groves: "I believe that having cooperated for many years with services under your command, as well as a number of other government organizations, in the strict maintenance of secrecy regulations, it is my duty to inform you of the factual situation."[49]

Groves and the others in his office were unperturbed. When Bigelow granted the Crown's application, the general wrote to each of the accused formally releasing him from his obligation to keep secret Eldorado's role in the Manhattan Project. Groves expressly stated that the waivers were limited to discussions with counsel and testimony in court; no one was authorized to talk to the press.[50]

With the decision to close the preliminary proceeding to the public, counsel now had to schedule the hearing. More disagreement followed as Slaght and Sedgwick continued to plead their case, now with Robinette, urging the special prosecutor to "do more to raise the secrecy ban, particularly with Canadian authorities." Robinette agreed to adjourn for two weeks to consider the point, assuring the court that "something has been done on the Canadian angle, and we may expect some development in the next week."[51]

Returning to the Courtroom

The parties returned to Bigelow's courtroom at the end of May. Again, defence counsel argued in favour of holding the preliminary inquiry in open court. Again, they focused on their clients' potential liability for revealing state secrets. Again, Bigelow was unmoved. Although Groves had waived the contractual limits between the US Engineers and the accused, he could do nothing to immunize them from prosecution under Canada's *Official Secrets Act*.[52]

Defence counsel now argued that their clients remained potentially liable as a result: "Without freedom to disclose such secret information as may be necessary in order adequately to instruct counsel and to offer a complete defence to the charges against them, the accused are at such a disadvantage that it is not possible for a fair trial for them to ensue."

Bigelow was characteristically unsympathetic. For one thing, the Crown had ensured that the accused did not have to maintain an obligation to keep secret information related to the Manhattan Project at the expense of mounting a defence in the Canadian proceedings:

> Counsel for the Crown has, as they have pointed out, motivated by courtesy, and certainly not by any legal or even ethical obligation devolving upon them, provided to each of the accused a release from the appropriate American authorities with respect to Canadian proceedings against them which, although perhaps not a perfect example of legal draughtsmanship, nor yet a document which provides for all imaginable contingencies, in the course of what will doubtless be a preliminary inquiry and trial of considerable complexity, is, in my view, in all the circumstances, the manifestation of more than a reasonable endeavour on the part of the Crown to assure to the accused a fair trial so far as their American duties and obligations are concerned.

For another, Bigelow was unwilling to order the Crown to grant immunity. It's also possible that he already decided that the three were guilty as charged, remarking, "The position in which the accused find themselves due to this alleged disadvantage is one brought about by their own volition." But his argument had more to do with his understanding of the boundaries between the court's authority and the Crown than his own views about the potential guilt of the accused. As he amplified, "I do not think the Court is competent, indeed, I think it would be presumptuous, to direct counsel for the Crown to provide immunity to the accused or to dictate the provisions of that immunity."

If the real concern was prosecution under section 4 of Canada's *Official Secrets Act,* why was Bigelow untroubled by the prospect? Because he understood the Crown's role and attendant ethical obligations in prosecutions. As he noted, the section might make it an offence to communicate material protected under the *Official Secrets Act,* but the court expected the Crown to act consistently:

> This section provides ... that any person who communicates secret documents or information to any person other than a person to whom he is authorized to communicate with or a person to whom it is in the interest of the state his duty to communicate them, commits an offence under the

> *Official Secrets Act*. I can imagine no more pressing duty of the accused and their counsel in the interest of the State, than to communicate to a British Court a complete defence to charges which may be laid against such accused. For the Crown in the case at bar to urge that the accused are protected by the *Official Secrets Act* and in another case at a later time against the same accused to urge that they should be convicted for a violation of the same Act they had earlier condoned and indeed approved, is so unthinkable and so contrary to all principles of British justice that I cannot regard it as a reasonable hypothesis.[53]

Bigelow's remark might have been a warning to Robinette and his junior counsel, Peter Wright, to keep on the straight and narrow, but it was more likely a statement of the obvious. Nevertheless, Slaght and Sedgwick appealed Bigelow's order to the High Court of Justice to stop the preliminary hearing on the grounds that the trio could not defend themselves. At the end of June, Justice Barlow, the judge who heard the appeal, easily rejected the request.[54]

In truth, the criminal proceedings had run into a brick wall. The issue of whether the trial would be held in open court had now been resolved, at least for purposes of the preliminary hearing, but getting witnesses to testify was another matter. There was also the risk of an acquittal. As clear as the case was on paper, conveying all its complexity to a jury was far less straightforward.

10
And Just Like That, Trial and Settlement

The announcement of charges against Carl French, Marcel Pochon, and Boris Pregel was sensational. Based on the relatively speedy trials of the day, court watchers might have expected the Eldorado case to be wound up by the summer of 1946 or, in the event of appeal, at least concluded by the fall. It was not.

As each side consolidated its position, sending occasional salvos toward the enemy, 1946 unfolded like siege warfare. Gradually the sensationalism drained away. Between summer 1946 and spring 1947, no public news about the proceeding emerged, with good reason. After mid-1946, the criminal case being fought out in a Toronto courtroom took a backseat to a civil suit in the Southern District of New York between Eldorado on the one side and Pregel and French on the other, as the Crown corporation sought to recover its damages. February 1947 saw a dénouement as a civil settlement was reached via a package of agreements between Pregel and Eldorado. Charges were withdrawn.

Like the criminal case against Pregel and his co-conspirators, the civil suit shows how a lawsuit was handled in the 1940s when managed by a first-rate lawyer. Like the criminal case, the civil suit never came to trial. (This was not atypical at the time, and indeed, most sensible lawyers today would advise their clients to settle if possible.) Legal cases are rarely self-contained: other forces, other influences, can be at play. That, too, is true of the civil suit described in what follows.

It might seem odd that Eldorado chose to pursue Pregel and French civilly. Pochon was not included in the civil suit because he did not seem to have any assets in the United States, or at least none worth trying to seize. The prosecution under John J. Robinette had prepared a thorough brief, choreographing in minute detail the Crown's criminal case. The documentary record was full, with Mounties, accountants, and lawyers having worked tirelessly to make their case by gathering comprehensive evidence that would be understandable to a Canadian judge and jury. Then, having secured an *in camera* preliminary hearing, the prosecution stopped. Why? The documentary record is silent on this point, but there are more than a few suggestions.

Financial cases were notoriously hard for a jury to grasp, and the Eldorado case was among the most complex to reach a Canadian court. Even Robinette estimated the chances of success to be no better than 50 percent, but complexity was not the only reason.[1]

Any discussion of the progress of the Eldorado case must begin with the man who authorized it: C.D. Howe. As minister of munitions and supply he had organized the Canadian economy for war, by and large effectively. When the conflict was over, his executives returned to their peacetime jobs singing the praises of the minister who had trusted them and supported them against criticism in a devolved management style that had proven successful. Most of these temporary wartime executives, men in their forties and fifties, proudly called themselves "Howe's boys." Although most did not share his Liberal Party identification, they remained personally attached to him for what turned out to be a long political career.

Howe's wartime efforts had impressed another constituency: the Americans. That Howe was American-born helped make him persuasive when it came to dealing with the United States, and the Americans liked his confident attitude and no-nonsense approach. Leslie Groves and Kenneth Nichols, who oversaw the Manhattan Project, trusted him. They knew they had a common interest and could talk bluntly. It was natural to carry on helping one another as they had during the war.

With that war over, Howe became the minister of reconstruction and supply, rolling over his wartime responsibilities to convert the economy to civilian production. He retained some of his wartime powers, but they were understood to be temporary. Even so, it was a point on which he was vulnerable, since his political opponents liked to claim that he was imperious, arbitrary, and power hungry. Howe did like to get things done quickly.

As his dollar-a-year men departed, he had more time to focus on one of the few executives left: Gilbert LaBine.

In 1943, Howe and those around him had regarded Eldorado's president in positive terms: a bit rough and crude perhaps, but also charming and presentable, a man of real achievement. As we have seen, LaBine was the author of his own legend, and there was enough to draw upon to create a convincing picture. But the image began to show cracks over time. By 1945, they were affecting his position in Ottawa. This giant of the mining frontier had shown that he could found a mining company, but there were increasing doubts he knew how to run it. Four men close to Howe were instrumental in what came next.

Lesslie Thomson was the first in Howe's circle to sound the alarm, but until 1945 his concerns were focused on conflicts of interest and inefficiencies that had LaBine at their heart. As Thomson remained an indispensable aide to Howe into 1946, he focused increasingly on atomic matters, and especially on Eldorado.

C.J. Mackenzie was the second of Howe's key advisers on Eldorado. After the war, he remained president of the National Research Council. Interested in the scientific end of Canada's atomic energy program for the most part, Mackenzie was nonetheless both curious and gossipy, especially with a scandal in the offing. He also kept a diary, which makes it possible to track what Howe and his office knew.

Howe's principal legal adviser was Guy M. Jarvis. We know little of Jarvis's personality except that the minister trusted him and that he was consulted on all serious legalities, especially those relating to Eldorado. He was also cautious when it came to the investigation and the possibility of charging French, Pregel, and Pochon.

Finally, there was W.J. (Bill) Bennett, Howe's executive assistant. Thirty-four in 1945, Bennett had been managing Howe's office for the previous decade. Howe was drawn to his efficiency, loyalty – and indefatigability. Bennett saw more of Howe than any other aide, and Howe saw more of Bennett. Most of their exchanges were spoken, and thus now lost to history, but it's clear that Howe had begun to pay attention to Bennett's opinions by the end of the war. Like Thomson, Mackenzie, and Jarvis, Bennett was profoundly unimpressed by Gilbert LaBine.

John Robinette shared that view. His careful trial preparation involved the anticipated testimony of many witnesses, many more than the twenty-nine who were selected to go to court. Royal Canadian Mounted Police (RCMP) officers Terry Guernsey and Bill McElhone interviewed most of them, but Robinette interviewed LaBine because his testimony was essential for the success of the criminal prosecution; the Crown needed to prove beyond a reasonable doubt that Eldorado's president had been deceived and knew nothing about the activities of Pregel, French, and Pochon. A judge and jury had to be convinced that French had acted without LaBine's knowledge or consent. LaBine, however, thought he would look like a fool if he acknowledged in open court what had been going on in his company right underneath his nose. It was Robinette who broke the news to Howe that this most important witness was unreliable and even ready to contradict the most important elements in the Crown's case to save his reputation. At least that was the explanation according to Bill Bennett, who told the story many years later.[2]

In March 1946, Bennett became executive vice-president of Eldorado, and thus had reason to be in the room. Although LaBine remained president, he was now little more than a figurehead. It was Bennett and a rejuvenated board of directors who ran the company, moving its head office from Toronto to Ottawa, away from the mining speculators. Clearly, LaBine was on his way out. He resigned a year later – with other irons in the fire through mining speculations and properties – and Bennett became president.

An easy exit was Howe's tried and true way of dealing with executives whose time had passed or whose usefulness had expired.[3] LaBine had been treated considerately. His inadequacies as president had not been exposed, thanks in large part to the decisions of Howe, Robinette, and J. Grant Glassco.

Although LaBine accepted his fate, he was neither grateful nor gracious. He was bitter.[4] Later, he told people he had been cast aside by an unappreciative government, Howe having taken away "his" company. Canada's Mining Hall of Fame honoured the man and his story – just as LaBine told it – and people believed it because his reputation was intact.

Legal Doldrums

The winter of 1946 was a busy time for the Glassco investigation as preparations for the trial of French, Pregel, and Pochon accelerated. The accountants worked tirelessly, identifying no fewer than two hundred exhibits to be introduced at trial, an extraordinary number at the time. Newly promoted Sergeants Guernsey and McElhone interviewed Manhattan Engineering District (MED) officers and transcribed the results.[5] The result of these collective efforts was formidable. Anyone who touched the case – American, Canadian, or British – was sure that French, Pregel, and Pochon were guilty. But every prosecutor believes that, or they would not proceed to trial. Would a court see it the same way? Would a jury understand the reams of evidence, much of it highly technical?

To secure a conviction for fraud, Robinette would have to prove beyond a reasonable doubt that the three men had deceived the US Army Corps of Engineers into signing the contracts at issue. To prove conspiracy, he would have to prove, beyond a reasonable doubt, that they had worked together to plan the deception.

The prosecution team decided that Nichols, Major Phillip Merritt, and his superior, Colonel John R. Ruhoff, should testify. They could detail the circumstances surrounding the Manhattan Project's decision to buy uranium from Eldorado and have the Canadian company refine the Belgian ore from African Metals Corporation (Afrimet) in its Port Hope facility. The Crown also needed witnesses to explain who knew what about the various contracts governing the sale of uranium and radium. Nichols had participated in the September 1942 negotiations, and all three were involved with the later, larger orders.[6] Between them, the Americans could explain what French had told them about the necessary role of Pregel and his Canadian Radium and Uranium Corporation (CRUC), while also making clear their intent to exclude Pregel from the contract. Other witnesses would describe the market value of radium, the true cost of refining, and how Eldorado and the Americans had been deceived. In late February 1946, Groves agreed to allow the three to participate. So far so good.

In the spring, a hitch developed when Edgar Sengier decided to return to Belgium. Whether he was really needed in Europe or simply wanted to avoid testifying is unclear. Investigators strongly suspected the latter. In interviews, Sengier had claimed not to recall key details, which seemed difficult to believe. Instead, he proposed that one of his subordinates, Charles Notebaert, testify. Notebaert was a Canadian and had served on the Afrimet board. Through Afrimet, he had first-hand knowledge of the contracts between Eldorado, CRUC, and the Union Minière du Haut-Katanga (UMHK), having signed several of them.

Nevertheless, Notebaert's testimony would lack some of the personal familiarity that Sengier could have brought. Sengier, after all, had known Pregel for more than twenty years. He could have commented on whether there were patterns in Pregel's behaviour, though that was unlikely to have been a permissible line of questioning under the rules of evidence. It's also possible that Sengier wondered how Pregel would respond to testimony perceived to be hostile. The Belgian had got to where he was in business and in life by knowing when to remain silent.[7]

The Arrival of James Tully

For all the time and effort that went into preparing the case for prosecution against French, Pregel, and Pochon, there was a bigger question. What did *Eldorado* stand to gain? Monetarily, nothing; that is not the point of a criminal prosecution. To make the company whole financially required a civil suit. And if, as prosecutors believed, most of the radium and proceeds were stored in the United States under the control of Boris Pregel or one of his many companies, maybe it made more sense to look to US courts for relief and remedy. In February 1946, acting at Howe's behest, and possibly with advice from Groves's staff, Glassco contacted James H. Tully, a lawyer in New York.[8]

Called to the New York State bar in 1922, Tully had served briefly in the army during the First World War before earning a law degree at night from Fordham University. Eventually, he served as counsel in New York to what was then called the Patrolmen's Benevolent Association, the largest police union in the United States. A staunch Roman Catholic, Tully was also active in a host of church charities. As a young lawyer, he had represented notable Broadway entertainers such as Florenz Ziegfeld Jr., founder of the Ziegfeld Follies, and Vincent Youmans, a composer and producer. When Tully died in 1964, he was general counsel for a charitable foundation established by Herbert Hoover.[9]

But in 1946, Tully was a partner in the firm of Wood, Molloy & France, whose New York office was located at 25 Broad Street in the Broad Exchange Building, just across the street from Afrimet at number 41. The address was one of the city's most prestigious office spaces, a Beaux-Arts building about a block south of the New York Stock Exchange.

Tully arrived in Ottawa in February to meet with Jarvis, Glassco, and his team. In addition to a briefing, Tully also received Glassco's account of his entire investigation, including the business history and relationship between French, Pregel, and Pochon, plus reports about Radium Luminous Industries and Insurance Appraisal and Rating Agency Inc.[10] Soon, Tully knew as much as anyone about what the auditors and investigators had found.

Tully, meticulous in his approach, offered some initial advice. He saw three preliminary issues. The first involved the future of Pregel's 1940 sales agreement with Eldorado. The second was the question of how much radium was missing. And the third was the issue of how to recover it.

Terminating the Sales Agreement

The Canadians worried that terminating Eldorado's contract with Pregel might not be recognized in New York, with implications for their rights and benefits in that state. Tully agreed and warned that neither state nor federal courts were likely to accept an order for termination from a Canadian court. The problem lay with the doctrine of *international comity.*[11] Under the doctrine, a nation is free to regulate its affairs within its own borders, and its actions ought to be recognized by other states. But it cannot extend its jurisdiction outside its borders. As Tully advised, the United States had consistently refused "to give any extra-territorial effect to any such governmental action where to do so would be to produce a result repugnant to the public policy of the forum in which the controversy arises."

What could possibly be repugnant about the Canadian government terminating a sales agreement with Boris Pregel? Recent experience was part of the problem. The most recent lawsuits involving the termination of contracts with state actors involved insurance policies held by American citizens in the Soviet Union. The Soviet government had unceremoniously terminated these contracts without compensation. As Tully explained, the courts would give effect to governmental acts as a matter of international comity, but the destruction of contract rights under the insurance policies had been viewed as "little more than confiscation." Without proper compensation, such confiscation was "repugnant to the public policy of the United States," as informed by the legal protection of property and contract rights outlined in the US Constitution.

Tully feared that simply cancelling Pregel's contract might be viewed in the same light unless there were some sort of "appropriate compensation" for the rights involved. Absent a treaty between Canada and the United States that permitted termination of contract rights for the purposes of prosecuting the war more efficiently (for example), Tully thought the Canadian government was out of luck.[12] At the very least, it was a risk that might give Pregel sufficient hope to warrant turning to litigation.

Despite his gloomy initial prognosis, Tully nevertheless thought there was a solution. If Eldorado could establish that Pregel, acting as its agent, had perpetrated "fraudulent transactions, dealing with the subject matter of the contract," then the company would have grounds to terminate or rescind the agreement. He set out the relevant details. Pregel had committed "various frauds" by diverting Eldorado's property for his own use, while "conspiring with others," and "seriously" injuring the company's interests. "It is assumed," Tully concluded, "that these breaches, the facts of which are not completely known, amount to what the Courts of this country, both Federal and State, would describe as disloyal, dishonest and contrary to the best interest of Eldorado."[13]

Disloyal. Dishonest. Contrary to the best interest of Eldorado. That closely described the activities of both Pregel and French over the previous several years. Pregel was no mere *sales* agent, neither an employee nor a director of Eldorado. He was the company's sales *agent*. As an agent, Pregel owed his principal, Eldorado, "an absolute duty of loyalty and has the further duty to act honestly and to account for all monies or things of value received by it for the benefit of the principal." Tully continued:

> If there is any suggestion of any untrustworthiness on the part of the agent, his agency may be forthwith terminated. If the agent has made any secret profits as the result of his agency, he must account for those profits to the principal. If the agent's conduct has been such as to warrant a termination of the agency agreement, then the agent may be deprived of the right to remuneration as provided to be paid to him under the contract and may in addition be deprived of any right to be reimbursed for any monies laid out on behalf of the principal.

There was a clear benefit to this approach. Someone acting in breach of their fiduciary duty should be deprived of any benefit.

The essence was this: case law strongly suggested that an agent who acted against the interests of his or her principal would be required to relinquish any benefit received in the process. Such a finding could end Pregel's agency agreement, negate any claim for lost commissions, and require repayment of commissions already received. Tully was sure of it, whether brought under federal or state law.

The one caveat was timing. Under this approach, Pregel's sales agreement would end, but it would not be void *ab initio* – as if the agreement had never existed. That would require Eldorado to prove that Pregel had used deception to bring about the agreement or had entered the contract for fraudulent purposes.

The Possibility of Arbitration

Tully noticed a potential wrinkle. Pregel's sales agreement required the parties to submit any dispute to arbitration subject to the rules of the International Chamber of Commerce (ICC), effectively precluding either party from taking the issue to court.[14] As a matter of law, courts were supposed to decline to hear any dispute properly covered by an arbitration clause, as determined by a panel of arbitrators. This is precisely the way arbitration clauses typically function today.

Arbitration offered several benefits. Usually used when parties want more control over the process by which their disputes are resolved, arbitration allows the two sides to predetermine the applicable rules and procedures. Arbitration is also a way to preserve a relationship that is important to maintain, dispute notwithstanding, and enables the parties to keep the outcome confidential.

Unfortunately, in 1946, nobody quite knew where the ICC was. It was rumoured to have moved from its original home in France to Sweden during the war, but Tully could find no representatives of the organization in New York or anywhere else in the United States. He was at a loss about how to proceed if Pregel were to invoke the clause when it might not even be operable. After pledging to see what more he could discover, Tully eventually learned that the ICC had returned to Paris and seemed to be up and running.

Nevertheless, he strongly advised against submitting to its jurisdiction. The ICC had its own rules, and as is typical with arbitrations, there would be no right to appeal its decision. Was Eldorado willing to make that kind of gamble? With Tully's advice against it, there is no evidence to suggest that the company seriously contemplated doing otherwise.[15]

Who Owned the Radium?

The second key concern on which Tully issued advice was the missing radium. If Eldorado were to sue to recoup its losses, it was essential to determine just how much was missing. In the winter of 1946, Glassco and, by extension, Tully, still did not know.

Early on, Tully contemplated bringing an action for *replevin,* a type of lawsuit that allows a plaintiff to retake personal property that was wrongfully taken or withheld.[16] But Eldorado would have to prove ownership to succeed, and that basic requirement turned out to be surprisingly difficult to meet. "I am somewhat disturbed by the looseness with which Eldorado has dealt with this all-important factor," Tully noted in a letter to Glassco in mid-March. Referring to an August 1943 agreement between Eldorado and Pregel's International Rare Metals Refinery Inc. (which may well have been CRUC and not International Rare Metals given that both entities were owned by Pregel and incorporated in New York State), Tully appeared to indicate that Eldorado owned the material that was further refined for a fee. Recall that an agreement from December 1942 between Eldorado and CRUC required the former to refine radium to a certain "stage," to be agreed upon later, which occured in August 1943. At that time, the two parties agreed on the applicable "stage" of completion, but CRUC lacked refining capacity, and thus sub-contracted the work to Radium Luminous Industries. Whether International Rare Metals was somehow involved with this earlier arrangement is unclear, but the fact that French was named the company's production manager and distribution supervisor the same month seems like too much of a coincidence.[17] Aside from the ridiculous arrangement to pay fees, the agreement was explicit that the material remained the property of Eldorado. Everyone understood this. Or did they? As Glassco – and now Tully – discovered, the paperwork was actually opaque on the point.

As Tully reviewed the records, he found troubling documentation. First, despite Glassco's investigation, Eldorado had continued to deal with both of Pregel's companies, carrying on with International Rare Metals and CRUC as if nothing were amiss. No investigation. No searches. No seized documents. No RCMP. Nothing. Business as usual.

Then, as Tully discovered, in November 1945, Eldorado's new secretary-treasurer, J.W. Gemmell, had written to International Rare Metals about 28.6 grams of radium that had supposedly been sent to Mount Kisco for refining. Gemmell might have been acting on his own, but who could be sure? After all, LaBine's oblivious management style was still the order of the day at Eldorado. Gemmell requested either the radium or payment of $13.50 per milligram, and asked Pregel to advise which alternative he preferred. He even offered to accept payment in monthly instalments.[18] These terms – the possibility of buying the radium and doing so at a reduced rate – were new, as was the cache of radium.

Pregel leapt at the offer. Under the original terms, the refinery was expected to produce 3 grams per month. Now, International Rare Metals would advise Eldorado each month whether it intended to keep the radium it refined and pay $13.50 per milligram for it, or return it to the Canadian company. In fact, Pregel said, International Rare Metals intended to purchase 3 grams of radium that it had just sent to the National Bureau of Standards for assessment.[19]

Tully was horrified. "Obviously," he remarked,

> Mr. Pregel's letter demanded a quick and definite refutation of the many self-serving declarations which it contains and in particular an absolute denial of his unwarranted assumption of the right to purchase the radium element at $13.50 per [milligram] in such quantities as he would from time to time require and to the purchase of approximately 3 grams of radium which were shipped for measurement to the National Bureau of Standards on November 1, 1945.

Writing in March 1946, he observed, "It would appear that Eldorado has thus far failed to dispute Mr. Pregel's declared intent to purchase such radium, and I therefore urge that this be done immediately."[20]

It is perhaps a sign of how confusing the documentation was that Tully's initial recommendation to seek replevin was premised on a fundamental misunderstanding. Originally, he believed that Eldorado owned all the radium Pregel took to Mount Kisco, but Afrimet – that is, UMHK – actually owned much of it. But there was still uncertainty about how much radium belonged to Eldorado and what documentation existed to prove it. For greater certainty, Tully asked to review the complete correspondence between Eldorado, International Rare Metals, and CRUC from the fall of 1945. As he did so, he came to see clearly that there was a difference between what Glassco believed and what could be proved.

It was the timing of the flurry of correspondence between Gemmell at Eldorado and the Pregel interests that raised the biggest red flag. The letters were sent *after* Pregel and French had been subpoenaed by Glassco and Robinette, *after* interviews were adjourned, and *after* news of the investigation had been shared in the newspapers. How could Eldorado and International Rare Metals set out a production and payment schedule as if nothing had happened?[21]

That Eldorado would even consider discussing radium sales with International Rare Metals after April 1945 seemed inconceivable, and as such to have been engaged in for nefarious purposes. Yet Tully decided to treat the correspondence as tantamount to clerical error. Gemmell had been in the job for about six months when the exchange began. By September, he was still inexperienced, or at least uneasy in the job. With great understatement, Glassco observed to Tully, "I have for some time been dissatisfied with the calibre of the existing management of the company."

It is unlikely that Gemmell would have acted without LaBine's approval, and the incident served as yet another reminder of his negligence.

Referring to Bennett's impending appointment as president, Glassco also mentioned that there were "steps to correct the same, but they are not yet effective. In the meantime, I suppose you will have to do the best you can with the facts."[22]

A Legal Theory for Recovery

As springtime arrived in New York, Tully continued to search for a legal route to recover Eldorado's missing radium and funds – the third issue under consideration. The contracts and correspondence were muddled and confusing, perhaps by design, as were the details about the amount of radium carbonate sold, shipped, refined, or owed. But where Robinette and Glassco focused on the August 1943 sales agreement at the heart of the criminal prosecution, Tully went all the way back to an agreement dated 22 December 1942.

As he worked his way through the successive letters and contracts between December 1942 and August 1943, alongside Glassco's interpretation of them, Tully developed two competing legal approaches to recovering the missing radium and monies owed. One embraced the refining agreements of December 1942 and August 1943 to create a legal co-adventurer relationship between Eldorado and CRUC that limited recovery. The other rescinded the December agreement and all the subsequent contracts based on fraud. What did each entail?

In New York, and within the common law more generally, the law recognized a separate legal entity called a *co-adventure*. As Tully explained to Glassco, a co-adventure created a legal partnership in which profits and losses were shared equally. It was a terrible arrangement for Eldorado.

Under the 22 December 1942 agreement with the US Engineers, Eldorado was supposed to refine ore owned by Afrimet. As part of that arrangement, Eldorado also agreed to refine two different quantities of radium: 60 grams to be refined outright, and an additional 118 grams treated under an agreement with CRUC, whereby Eldorado would refine the amount only "to a stage agreed upon" at a refining fee of $1,000 per gram. CRUC would then "finish" the refining process for a further $5,000 per gram. The August 1943 contract filled in the details and committed Eldorado to refine the radium to between 90 and 95 percent. Under Tully's theory, Eldorado could rescind that agreement and require an accounting under which each party would recoup its expenses and then share any profits equally: "Naturally, under such an accounting, if either party had more than its share of the profits, it would have to account to the other for the excess."

Tully's other proposal treated the December 1942 agreement as modifying an existing contract. Under this scenario, Eldorado would have to credit CRUC and Radium Luminous Industries for the costs those companies had incurred to carry out the venture. Since Eldorado's own costs were limited in proportion to the 118 grams at $1,000 per gram, regardless of what the company spent to refine the ore, such an approach would be risky, if not potentially ruinous. There was already an imbalance between the two sides and sticking to the December agreement would make it worse.

The August 1943 agreement exacerbated those differences. Under the arrangement, CRUC surrendered its right to profits in exchange for an indemnity from Eldorado for any losses incurred to perform the contract. Framed differently, CRUC would be entitled to reimbursement for its expenses in carrying out the joint venture, but nothing more. Tully feared, however, that the company's inflated refining fees would be categorized as expenses, and thus subject to reimbursement. Once more, CRUC could come out ahead.

Rescission based on fraud – the second legal approach – looked far more promising to make Eldorado financially whole. Withdrawing the December 1942 agreement would also rescind the August 1943 agreement, which would entitle Eldorado "to all of the proceeds of the venture" while exposing the company "at most" to reimbursing CRUC for its expenses, and those "would probably be negligible." In fact, a conclusion of fraud might eliminate even that requirement. As Tully explained,

> It is quite possible that even these items would be disallowed ... on the broad theory applying to fiduciaries under which they are held to be disentitled to claim for reimbursement for expenses incurred where they have acted in gross dereliction of the fiduciary duties imposed upon them, and where the expenses for which they seek reimbursement are directly involved in the acts of misbehavior of which they are guilty.

This was key. If the December 1942 agreement were rescinded due to fraud, every subsequent arrangement would be tainted and thus invalid.[23] Tully favoured this approach because it would give Eldorado "the greatest latitude" to establish its claim against CRUC for the maximum amount.[24]

Tully explained the underlying fraudulent statements in a letter to Glassco:

> The material statements contained in Eldorado's letter of December 22, 1942 are in all respects false as shown by your report but the trickery of that letter is demonstrated by the chicanery of those who purported to represent Eldorado in good faith in their deals with companies in which they had an undisclosed interest by the agreement they reached, as set forth in Eldorado's letter to CR&U under date of August 20, 1943. The other facts and circumstances fill in to complete a pattern of unconscionable conduct on the part of those who had a fiduciary relationship to Eldorado.[25]

Under this approach, Tully believed the company could recover more than the obvious lost profits. Eldorado might well receive the $6,500 per gram difference between the cost of radium on the open market and the price at which CRUC had bought it from Eldorado under the December agreement. Based on its contractual agreement to make up losses incurred through refining, Eldorado had sold radium to CRUC for just $13,500 per gram when the market price was $20,000.

The challenge, according to Tully, would be establishing that CRUC's claimed loss was fictitious, created by the company and Radium Luminous Industries as co-conspirators. It was a lot to prove, but the fraud and deceit were so outrageous, so boldfaced, that Tully thought the prospects of recovery were excellent. The extent of the fraud was breathtaking.

The focus on refining was also important because Pregel's sales agreement did not permit commissions for refining. As Tully wrote to Glassco,

> Your reports indicate quite clearly the extent and nature of such fraud. Under such a theory, the claim of Eldorado would be as if the original refining contracts were taken solely in the name of Eldorado such that the work would have been done and the profits realized exclusively by it. Your report contains an estimated cost of the entire refining process of $1,540 per gram and on that basis the profits should be $4,460 per gram. As I read the agency agreement of November 7, 1940, I see no provision therein for the payment of a commission to Pregel for refining work. The fraud which is indicated with respect to the refining contracts with African Metals is the misrepresentations made by Pregel, French and Pochon to the United States engineers to the effect that Eldorado would not accept such contracts unless CR&U were made coadventurer under them.

Without a contractual basis on which to claim a commission, Pregel should be required to repay those funds, too. What's more, the foundation for his claim that he and CRUC were entitled to be party to every refining contract as a co-adventurer would crumble.

Lowell Wadmond, the Attorney

Boris Pregel had not been idle. He understood his peril. His complicated business affairs often required legal work, and it is not surprising that he engaged New York attorneys to help him with his contracts. The 1940 contract with Eldorado, for example, bears the imprint of legal advice, though we do not know whose.

According to his brother, Alexander, in 1942 Boris retained Lowell Wadmond, one of the most prominent litigators at the white-shoe law firm of White & Case. Founded in 1901, White & Case was and is one of New York's leading corporate law firms, built on a client base of financial institutions. It seems likely that Pregel retained the firm not only for its corporate law expertise but also for its standing and reputation in New York society. For White & Case, Pregel's old-world charm would not have seemed amiss, assisted by his million-dollar bank account at Chase National Bank and his office in the Rockefeller Center.

By the time Pregel retained Wadmond, he was one of the firm's rainmakers, a rarity for a litigator.[26] Wadmond had represented Winston Churchill in 1936; it was the kind of reference that helped the lawyer's public image. He had also brought in the business of Arabian American Oil Company (Aramco), then a rapidly growing business though not the corporate giant it would later become. It helped to have prominent clients, even if they were not rich – yet.[27]

Wadmond and Pregel were well matched. In his youth, the lawyer had contemplated becoming a musician, and he retained this interest all his life, culminating in the 1950s with a stint as president of the New York Philharmonic. In his spare time, Pregel composed – for example, a piano concerto, the Concerto Pathétique. In the 1940s, Wadmond and his wife regularly appeared in the society columns of *The New York Times*. There was an element of the old-boys club about Wadmond, deals done over lunch, an index of friends and their phone numbers, arrangements made in private. It was a level of recognition that Pregel craved, and he did not want lawsuits and press coverage to stand in the way.

Pregel told Wadmond that he was in trouble – totally unjustified trouble. We know that Pregel rated his own performance highly, and after 6 August 1945, there was no need to conceal his accomplishments. Wadmond already knew who General Groves was. In Pregel's view, the general had an unreasonable dislike of him that endangered his good name, the most valuable thing a salesman could have.

Armed with Pregel's version of the truth, Wadmond decided the best way to resolve the situation was to talk lawyer to lawyer. The most prominent lawyer at the Manhattan Project was Groves's confidential aide, Colonel William A. Consodine. Recently demobilized, Consodine was practising law in Newark, New Jersey, in the summer of 1946 when he received an unexpected phone call from Wadmond.

Wadmond explained that he was representing Boris Pregel in his dispute with Eldorado, and that the accusations against him were baseless, the product of both spite and misunderstanding. The personal animosity of not just Groves but also Lesslie Thomson motivated the suit. Together they had concocted unfounded stories about Pregel: a patriot, a philanthropist, and a devoted public servant. Given these distortions and misrepresentations, surely Consodine could help "straighten out" a few things for his client.

Surely, he could not. Consodine was appalled. He made it clear that his previous position "in a legal capacity with General Groves" meant that any such assistance, formal or otherwise, would be unethical. Wadmond seemed unbothered. He tried again. Ethics were subjective, he said. Consodine disagreed. There were certain professional obligations and standards of behaviour that were objective and universally recognized. He could not act, directly or indirectly, against his former employer. Wadmond was persistent. Consodine pushed back, emphasizing that animosity was not the root of Pregel's difficulties. The most he could offer was to arrange a meeting between Pregel and Groves, not that Eldorado's sales agent needed help to see the general. Wadmond thanked him so profusely for this small gesture that Consodine thought it necessary to reiterate that the offer was "purely gratuitous and would in no way be attached to any fee or compensation."

Pregel's lawyer understood but kept going. He sought common ground in one final attempt to ingratiate himself, as one member of the bar to another. He knew that "you people" at the Manhattan Project had "investigated everybody and have files on everybody." The appeal: "If there is anything in your file concerning Pregel that you feel as a brother lawyer I should know and can tell me I would appreciate it if you would."

Consodine was noncommittal and desperate to get off the phone. As he later explained to Groves in a letter detailing the encounter, "Mr. Wadmond did not seem to be abashed at all that he was in my mind offering a highly unethical proposition to me." Groves, in turn, passed along the information to Thomson. Taken with Pregel's comment that he would not be bound by any *in camera* proceedings to maintain the secrecy of his testimony in the Toronto criminal proceeding, he noted that it sounded like more than a veiled threat.[28] If it was, it did not achieve its purpose.

The Southern District of New York

On Monday, 9 September 1946, Tully filed the main complaint in the Southern District of New York. The lawsuit on behalf of Eldorado represented much more than the views of the Crown corporation. Groves and his staff had been kept apprised of Eldorado's thinking, and had reviewed drafts that passed back and forth between Washington and Ottawa.

Tully had settled on a legal theory in the spring, but the formal filing did not occur for months. In an age before computers and technologically assisted review, it had taken that much time to determine the quantity of radium involved, even with many details known through surveillance. He and Glassco corresponded regularly and warmly over the spring and summer. By mid-August, Glassco had prepared a list of commissions and trade discounts paid to Pregel and CRUC, along with the differences between the undervalued radium sold and the inflated refining fees paid to CRUC and International Rare Metals. With the assistance of Consodine, Tully helped by tracing sales of radium concentrate through Pregel, CRUC, and International Rare Metals to third parties. Altogether, Tully and the Canadians had documentation to support a claim for damages totalling $2,663,362, equivalent to more than $50,000,000 today.

By summer's end, after the Canadians – Glassco, Robinette, his junior counsel Peter Wright, and Howe's executive assistant Bill Bennett on the general allegations, Jarvis and accountant E.B. Richards on the details – had reviewed several drafts, the civil complaint was almost ready to go, subject to considerations about national security. The concerns surrounding the criminal proceeding in Toronto also raised potential problems in New York, so Tully sent Groves a draft copy of the complaint for his review. He was confident that Pregel, French, and Pochon had not defrauded the Manhattan Project directly, but he still wanted to ensure the complaint contained nothing sensitive.[29]

Groves formally cleared the document two weeks later, though he didn't want to publicize the finances and contractual obligations of the Manhattan Project if he could avoid it, and asked Tully to secure the same sort of *in camera* proceeding as the Canadians had won. At the very least, it would not hurt to try. "The proof of the allegations in the complaint and the defense thereto might well be dangerous to security," he cautioned, though he mustered no evidence to demonstrate this was so.[30]

The lawsuit was not front-page news, though it did make page 11 of *The New York Times* sports section under the headline "Suit Charges Fraud in Deal for Uranium." The first sentence said it all: "Damages of $2,500,000 are asked by the Eldorado Mining and Refining, Ltd. of Canada, in a suit on file in Federal Court yesterday, which alleges fraud on the part of Carl B. French, secretary and treasurer of the company from 1939 to 1945, and Boris Pregel, a French citizen, who was the company's sales representative." The article outlined the allegations that Pregel and French had misrepresented obligations to Pregel and CRUC in their dealings with both the US Engineers and Afrimet. The account made clear that the two were accused of diverting business from Eldorado and defrauding the company of millions.

The suit, which also named CRUC and International Rare Metals, was the first detailed public account of the various fraudulent schemes that had given rise to criminal charges in Canada. Anyone following those proceedings would have known about the allegations of fraud, but the New York civil suit set out precisely how the three had duped Eldorado out of millions. Although Groves wanted the hearing to be held *in camera,* he didn't ask Tully to seal the court file, so the pleadings were publicly available.[31]

The claim outlined the misleading inclusion of Pregel and CRUC in transactions, the various schemes to undervalue the radium purchased from Eldorado, the reduced fees paid to Eldorado, and the excessive fees paid to International Rare Metals by Eldorado for refining that radium. It described how Pregel, CRUC, French, International Rare Metals, and Radium Luminous Industries took advantage of improper trade discounts and commissions to which they were not entitled, and took corporate property and assets that were not theirs, including radium concentrate from Eldorado that they stored in the United States. Pregel was alleged to have sought reimbursement for expenses ten times greater than the actual figure.

The legal basis for recovery did not depend on common law or statutory provisions but on equity. In equity, a plaintiff may demand an account of profits in cases of fraud, which was precisely what Tully proposed. It was a way for Eldorado to recoup all the profits flowing from the contracts with the US Engineers that improperly included CRUC. Pregel was not merely a salesman, but Eldorado's sales *agent,* which carried a lot of weight. It meant that he had fiduciary duties to the company, just like French had as a corporate director.

After much thought and consultation, Tully – and, by extension, Thomson – had agreed to forego the action for replevin. Given the existing documentation, it was going to be too messy to meet the requirement to prove ownership. They remained open to the possibility of amending the claim later if it made sense to do so. It never did.

Reaching a Settlement

Pregel responded to the suit by filing a counterclaim against Eldorado. He turned the tables, alleging the company had defrauded him of commission payments by misrepresenting the state of the business in 1942. In his version, he had been duped into sacrificing his commissions by management's claims of financial hardship. There was more. Eldorado owed him the residues of the radium ore that had been refined – and kept – pending resolution of Glassco's investigation. Altogether, Pregel claimed more than $1 million in damages. Glassco's team dutifully reviewed the cache of documents for anything that could substantiate the claim, but none could be found.[32]

Tully and Wadmond exchanged missives through the winter, eventually reaching a deal in late February 1947.[33] The settlement agreement was as complicated in its details as the dispute was complex in its origins. In mid-March, Robinette appeared before Magistrate Bigelow for the court's permission to withdraw the criminal charges. The lawyer explained in open court that the dispute was more properly civil than criminal. The magistrate obliged.

With settlement in hand, the claim and counterclaim were discontinued in the Southern District of New York. When he wrote to his client, Wadmond hyped the result: the criminal charges had been "without merit" and he had always thought they "would be discontinued or dismissed, before even a preliminary hearing." Eldorado's civil complaint was also weak, with no evidentiary basis and doomed to failure, whereas Pregel's counterclaim was strong enough to stand on its own. "Because of the evidence which we adduced in preparation for examinations before trial, of the civil action," Wadmond wrote, the counterclaim had had "every likelihood of success."

Yet, as wise counsel know, a settlement is better than a loss: "There being an old adage that a settlement once made is a good settlement, I suppose that on balance the relinquishment of your civil counterclaim in return for a stipulation of discontinuance of the entire civil action is probably a good thing, since it frees you from the annoyance and inconvenience and expense of protracted litigation."[34] In Wadmond's positive interpretation, Pregel had given up nothing he was not already planning to return, paid for nothing he was not willing to pay for, and lost nothing of any value.

Wadmond told his client he had seen no evidence to support Eldorado's claim, which makes one wonder whether Tully had shown him any of the evidence against Pregel and the others. In 1947, the rules of evidence and discovery were more limited than they are today. Now, the discovery process lays bare the evidence of both parties: the good, the bad, and the ugly. Although disclosure rules were becoming more comprehensive in the 1940s, many counsel still withheld their most valuable evidence to be disclosed at trial by surprise.[35] It was a strategy that Wadmond appreciated. "Trial lawyers are trial lawyers and should depend on surprise," he once said.[36] Today, a court would prohibit such a tactic.

The full record of depositions isn't available – in fact, it's unknown if the lawsuit reached that point – and Tully may have chosen not to tell Wadmond about the fraudulent sales invoice involving his client. Tully certainly knew about the two different invoices from August 1943 pertaining to the 700-ton contract, since the issue featured prominently in the draft of Glassco's report he had received in February 1946. The invoicing imbroglio explained the source of the 30 grams of radium that had magically appeared for purchase. If Wadmond had seen the revised invoice alongside the original, he may have been less convinced of his client's innocence and the strength of his civil suit. Of course, it's equally possible he had seen the evidence and for that reason worked hard to get Pregel to accept the settlement.

The settlement and related events give rise to a series of reasonable questions. Did Robinette use criminal charges as a bargaining chip to get French and Pregel to return the stolen radium? Or even to break the agency agreement that was so very favourable to Pregel? Were factors outside the courts and the lawsuits involved?

On the most important point – whether the criminal proceeding was genuine – no documentary evidence suggests otherwise, and quite a bit supports the opposite conclusion. More plainly, it would have been unethical for prosecutors to use criminal charges as leverage to secure the settlement of a civil suit, just as it is today. There was also great bitterness on the part of some investigators when the criminal proceedings were withdrawn in 1947.[37] The rationale for a civil suit was simple pragmatism; it was the only way to secure the return of the radium and money held by Pregel in the United States, and the only way to terminate his sales agreement.

The settlement detailed quantities of radium and sums of money that were to be returned or paid by Pregel and his companies to Eldorado. The list was lengthy and complicated, and it saved the best till last: Pregel's prized sales contract. With the New York litigation settled, Pregel's agency agreement (and all related agreements) with Eldorado, dating back to November 1940, would finally come to an end.

Considering that the weaknesses in Eldorado's case might not have survived the test of a trial, Tully's rationale for pursuing the matter civilly makes sense. He wrote to Howe:

> An exhaustive study of the evidence in preparation for trial led me to the conviction that Eldorado's interest would be best served by a fair and equitable adjustment of the various matters in dispute. My appraisal of the available evidence upon which we were to rely in the establishment of our allegations of fraud left much to be desired, and I so reported to you. The terms of settlement produced a result, which I should hesitate to risk by subjecting our claims to the vagaries of litigation.[38]

The End of the Affair

Allegations of fraud, even on the civil standard, are often difficult to prove in court. The Eldorado case was no different, and it presented unique challenges. Not only did the existing documentary record make it difficult to bring a claim for replevin, but the continued communication between Eldorado and Pregel's companies even after the investigation had begun would almost certainly have made it more challenging to persuade a court Eldorado had been defrauded.

Tully's account of the settlement differed in almost every way from Wadmond's. At the very top of the list of points covered by the settlement, Tully put the termination of Pregel's agency agreement and all sub-agency relationships, including the one involving CRUC and mysteriously guaranteed by Eldorado. In Wadmond's account, this was the last point. Next was the immediate return of 120.3 milligrams of radium, which CRUC held "on consignment under the agency agreement," and the "prompt return" of 35,681.65 milligrams of radium from International Rare Metals, the product of "a certain refining agreement between Eldorado and International, dated August 20, 1943."

Tully also included a payment schedule, which would have come as a surprise to someone who read only Wadmond's version. As part of the settlement, CRUC agreed to pay Eldorado for radium held by the company or leased to third parties. The payments were significant, totalling almost $325,000 over eight instalments of approximately $40,500 each over the next twenty months. There was also a catch. If CRUC declared bankruptcy or missed a payment, the entire balance was due, subject to thirty days' grace. CRUC and International Rare Metals also agreed to pay Eldorado $152,572.42 "representing the total net indebtedness owed by such companies to Eldorado as shown upon the books of Eldorado." Finally, Eldorado would receive a lump sum payment of $100,000 cash from either CRUC or International Rare Metals, both of which agreed to drop their counterclaims against Eldorado.

For its part, Eldorado agreed to ship certain residues left from refining ores belonging to Afrimet, along with 23 tons of radioactive lead oxide. The returned residues related to refining contracts with Afrimet dating from October 1942 to August 1943.[39]

Why did Eldorado agree to settle? The company got the better part of the deal, walking away with more than $2 million in "money or money's worth," as well as the invaluable benefit of terminating Pregel's agency and sub-agency agreements. The cost was "but two minor obligations": the residues and the lead oxide.

With that, Eldorado's dealings with Boris Pregel, Carl French, and Marcel Pochon ended, avoiding the kind of publicity that surely would have followed a trial, even if parts of it were conducted behind closed doors. As it turned out, the closed doors were not those of a courtroom but of the US Internal Revenue Service. We cannot confirm that Robinette knew of the pressure being exerted on Pregel by the taxman, though it's likely; investigators on both sides of the border certainly did.[40] Later, Major Phillip Merritt, the US Engineers geologist who had been so closely involved with the case, thought the IRS had been crucial in pressuring Pregel not merely to settle but to do so on terms highly favourable to Eldorado.[41]

Another incentive for Pregel was the possibility of deportation that would have followed a conviction for tax evasion. Having acquired French citizenship in 1939, he had at least eliminated the prospect of an involuntary trip to Romania, his country of previous citizenship and a place he may never have been. More important, however, Pregel wanted to stay in the United States, having already applied for American citizenship.[42]

Because of the secrecy that veils the detailed administration of tax accounts, we'll never know what Pregel had to pay into the US Treasury and what, if anything, his co-conspirators, French and Pochon, had to pay the Canadian Department of National Revenue. Nevertheless, we can reasonably conclude that a series of monetary and radioactive exchanges in 1946–47 ended their liability, whether for fraud, tax evasion, or simple breach of their fiduciary duties. The slate was wiped clean.

Among the most active participants in the Eldorado case were the two Mounties, Bill McElhone and Terry Guernsey. It had been their responsibility to collect the evidence, interpret it, organize it, and have it ready for trial, or trials, because the same evidence set would have been used in either the criminal or civil case. McElhone's police career was built on his ability to investigate financial crime, and his keen work was eventually rewarded with promotion to inspector. Guernsey moved farther, and faster, and had more exposure to a broader world.

McElhone was present in the Toronto Magistrates' Court in March 1947 to watch the Crown withdraw the charges against Pregel, French, and Pochon. He had recently resigned from the Mounties, though whether that had anything to do with the withdrawal of charges is impossible to say. Certainly he was still indignant about it when interviewed almost forty years later. Sitting in that busy courtroom, waiting for the case to be called, he had watched various criminals receive sentences of greater or lesser severity, and in some cases be sent to the penitentiary for thefts in the double digits. Pregel, French, and Pochon had tried to steal millions, their guilt was beyond question, and they got off scot free. Justice, said McElhone, was not done.

Guernsey's view was different. Interviewed shortly after McElhone, he shook his head. No. "Money was their god. We took their money. We gave them ulcers." Justice, of a kind, was done.

Conclusion

When residents of the Malvern subdivision in Scarborough woke on 20 November 1980 to learn that their homes sat on land contaminated with radioactive waste, the revelation came not from government officials, scientists, or regulators. It was the work of two journalism students, Frank Giorno and Jane Glassco. Giorno had begun the project of assembling a rudimentary list of radium and uranium companies while working the summer before at Pollution Probe, a Canadian environmental organization. One name – Radium Luminous Industries Ltd. at 103 Church Street – stood out. Giorno presented his findings to an investigative reporting class that fall, and Glassco approached him to collaborate. The project was large and the archival trail obscure, so Giorno, after some initial hesitation, agreed.

Neither could have anticipated the cascade of coincidences that followed or how the story touched Glassco's own past. Roughly a month into their work, she found a reference to a confidential 1947 report written by an accountant, J. Grant Glassco, who was her former father-in-law. Jane was the daughter of Walter Gordon, a former Liberal cabinet minister and an acquaintance of C.D. Howe. She had married into the Glassco family in the early 1960s, and Grant Glassco died in 1968. Although she was long divorced from his son by 1980, the connection was striking.

The report delivered to C.D. Howe in May 1947 detailed the findings against Carl French, Boris Pregel, and Marcel Pochon.[1] With charges stayed and the civil suit settlement announced, Howe never made it public. To obtain a copy, Giorno and Glassco had to apply through what was then a largely informal archival access system. It arrived, as expected, several weeks later.

Concerned about the implications of possible radioactive contamination, Glassco sought advice from a friend from her university days, an oncologist named Nicholas Perkofsky. He happened to be the nephew of an elderly chemist named Nicholas Tschernosoff. Unbeknownst to Glassco, Tschernosoff, now in his eighties, had worked for Carl French both at 103 Church Street and on the Scarborough farm and was willing to speak with them. His memory was excellent, and he recalled with great detail how he and farm owner Nicholas Ivanenko had burned radium waste in a makeshift incinerator, storing the ash in barrels and then spreading it as fertilizer to test its effect on crops. Even in the 1940s, Tschernosoff had been worried about radiation, monitoring his blood counts at a local hospital. In 1980, he still believed he had some radioactive material in his body though, as he proudly told them, he was "still going strong." Ivanenko, now living in a seniors' home, confirmed Tschernosoff's story. More important, he recounted how he had spoken with provincial health officials in the 1940s, and again in 1975, when radiation was detected at 103 Church Street. Glassco and Giorno began to see that a sort of collective forgetfulness was at the heart of the story.[2]

Exploiting hints in the Glassco report and the recollections of Ivanenko and Tschernosoff, the journalists turned to land records, aerial maps, and even the spacing of telephone poles in the Malvern area to figure out the location of French's wartime operations. Eventually, they identified two parcels of land on McClure Crescent. Quietly, they tested soil nearby. The readings were troubling. To verify their findings, they consulted Arthur Holloway, a University of Toronto specialist in radiation exposure. His readings confirmed that radiation levels were three times the federal limits. It raised an unsettling question: If two students could find this, why had the government missed it?

As *The Globe and Mail* prepared to run the story, reporters contacted the Atomic Energy Control Board (AECB) for answers. The AECB had none. Conscious of public anxiety, senior officials asked the newspaper to delay publication so they could review the circumstances and be prepared to respond. The regulator ordered a new round of testing the day the article appeared.

The new tests uncovered not just a hotspot but institutional amnesia. After *The New York Times* ran a story in February 1975, the AECB had investigated French's Toronto properties.[3] Those tests had been limited – just twenty-four bore holes over 10 acres – and missed the Scarborough site by just 50 metres. In 1980, the AECB drilled seventy-two bore holes, and found contamination well above acceptable limits.

Even so, officials continued to minimize the risk. The AECB president reassured homeowners the exposure posed little danger, likening it to smoking "an extra pack of cigarettes a day." Perhaps not a big deal in 1980 – when roughly 40 percent of Canadians older than fifteen smoked – but shocking today. Even at the time, the comparison did little to reassure residents whose home values were collapsing. Removal of soil proved impossible because Ontario had no approved disposal site, and no community was willing to receive the contaminated earth. The homeowners were stuck with properties they could not sell.

Returning to Court

In this vacuum, the law intervened. Without the benefit of class action legislation, George Heighington led more than forty homeowners in filing a lawsuit against the province, the Ontario Housing Corporation, and Carl French. The central questions were simple: What did Ontario know, and when did it know it?

Leslie Cook and Terry Guernsey had documented French's activities at the Scarborough farm in the summer of 1945. Cook's report to Ontario's Department of Health was explicit, and it was ignored. By the time Giorno and Glassco rediscovered the site, the province had no institutional memory of the contamination. The lawsuit brought the facts back into view.

A trial before Justice Holland in May 1987 distilled the complexities of an investigation that had occurred decades earlier. Fortunately, key witnesses were still alive and willing to testify on behalf of the plaintiffs. John Robinette, in meticulous detail and supported by forty-year-old records, reviewed the legal case he had helped to prepare against French, Pregel, and Pochon, whose activities had contaminated the Scarborough site. Guernsey, now retired from the Royal Canadian Mounted Police, was available to detail the discovery of contamination in Scarborough. Cook, also retired, explained what was understood in 1945 about the hazards of radiation. It was clear that his report, delivered to the Department of Health at that time, had laid bare the contamination at the Scarborough farm. Together, Guernsey and Cook offered convincing evidence that provincial officials knew about the problem in 1945.

In its defence, the province tried to argue that the passage of time, personnel changes, and the development of the subdivision meant officials could not reasonably have been expected to foresee harm. Justice Holland disagreed. In his judgment in July 1987, he held that Ontario knew about the contamination in 1945 and had an obligation under the province's *Planning Act* to protect future residents.[4] Failure to keep track of the contaminated land breached that duty. Reasonableness – not perfection – is the standard in negligence law. By any measure, the actions of the province fell short of the standard.

Two years later, the Court of Appeal agreed, upholding Holland's decision. The appeal panel acknowledged that there had been some confusion at trial about the layout of French's farm sheds, but it did not change the central point: the province had been warned and did not keep track of the information. The homeowners were entitled to recover their financial losses. Eventually, they secured a settlement of $4.1 million, having spent more than $500,000 to do so; ultimately, each of the families involved in the suit received $5,600, having lost about $7,000.[5]

The homeowners' victory in court did not expedite the clean-up. More than 4,000 tonnes of contaminated soil remained in place until late 1995, fifteen years after *The Globe and Mail* published the story and the AECB confirmed the existence of radioactive soil.[6]

The contamination long outlived the principals in the Eldorado scandal who had brought radium to Scarborough.

What Became of Them?

After leaving his position as Eldorado's Port Hope refinery manager in the spring of 1945, Marcel Pochon remained a respected citizen of the town of Port Hope, where he worked as a consultant using his own small private laboratory. He died in 1958 at the age of sixty-nine. Whether the lung cancer that killed him stemmed from radiation or from the cigarettes he smoked profusely is impossible to know.[7] By the time of his death, some of his legacy was being questioned. It became evident that many properties around the town had suffered radioactive contamination, and there were demands that it be cleaned up.[8] His household goods were marked with yellow and black radiation tags, awaiting transport to what was then Canada's only radiation dump, at Chalk River, Ontario, where they were destroyed. In 1976, a federally funded clean-up began. Among its subjects was Pochon's stately home on Port Hope's most prestigious street. Pochon had named it "Muidar" – "radium" spelled backwards – and project officials later revealed that he had painted the banisters on the staircase with luminous paint so he could see his way upstairs after dark without turning on the lights. It seemed he was also personally radioactive, for they claimed that they could tell his favourite leather chair (leather absorbs radiation easily), and trace his presence in the library.

Gilbert LaBine left Eldorado in 1947 and stopped prospecting in 1949. In his later years, he dedicated himself to two other interests, Gunnar Mining Ltd. and Nesbitt LaBine Mines, and to protecting his mythic status as a prospector extraordinaire. When he spoke to a biographer in 1959, he described himself as a details man, as did his acolytes. He called the nationalization of Eldorado, to which he had consented and from which he had profited handsomely, "high-handed burglary." As he had during the war, LaBine missed the point. The company was burgled all right, but not in the way he described.[9] He died in June 1977 at the age of eighty-seven.[10]

Until his death in 1976 at the age of eighty-three, Boris Pregel lived in the same apartment overlooking Central Park in Manhattan that he had acquired in the summer of 1939. Various investigations – including before the House Un-American Activities Committee – into his wartime and early Cold War business activities came to nothing.[11] After navigating naturalization hearings that were complicated by allegations of wartime uranium sales to the Soviets, he secured US citizenship in 1950, and worked hard to become a respected figure in scientific and cultural organizations. His obituaries called him a philanthropist and scientific leader. It was true enough: he had been president of the New York Academy of Sciences and chair of its board of trustees, president of the American division of the World Academy of Art and Science, vice-president of the American Geographic Society, president of the French University in New York, and a trustee of the New School for Social Research.[12] He had composed and performed a cello concerto at Carnegie Hall. His obituaries said nothing about Eldorado, the fraud, or his refinery at Mount Kisco, New York – contaminated like Scarborough, and like Scarborough cleaned up at public expense.[13]

Carl French became a high-profile and respected citizen. He was asked to join various boards of directors, especially of mining firms. He continued with his own companies, such as Radium Luminous Industries, and expanded into medical supply firms. He became a member of Toronto's most socially prominent clubs. On the model of Boris Pregel, he reinvented himself as a pioneer in cancer treatment and research, especially in fundraising to support that work. Internationally, he participated in the International Union against Cancer, one of Pregel's causes from the 1930s.

French claimed to have received a medal from a prestigious French arts and science organization in 1967, and if so, it is likely that Pregel had a hand in it. As the first national chair of the Canadian Cancer Society, he cultivated an image of civic responsibility. He was not shy about his wartime accomplishments either, boasting in his *Canadian Who's Who* entry that he had been associated with Leo Szilard and Enrico Fermi, and that he had been in on the secret of the atomic bomb. When Giorno and Glassco interviewed him in 1980, he readily discussed his philanthropic work. But when they turned to his introduction to the world of radium and his involvement with Radium Luminous Industries, he ended the interview abruptly, accusing them of deception.[14]

Named as a defendant when the Malvern lawsuit began in 1983, French died the next year. The suit did not carry on against his estate, which may have been a missed opportunity.[15] French was quite wealthy, having sold his company X-Ray and Radium Industries Ltd. to Westinghouse in 1969. The company was a leading supplier of medical radium and associated minerals in the Western hemisphere, and its sale made French a fortune. His obituaries praised his charitable work; like those for Pregel, they omitted any reference to the criminal charges and civil suits. His image had been rehabilitated entirely.[16]

The lawyers who were integral to the wartime legal proceedings also had legacies worth noting. Arthur Slaght had been nearing the end of his career when he defended Pregel and French in the Eldorado investigation. At that time, he had already been regarded as leading counsel for decades. He died in January 1964 at the age of eighty-six, having retired from the practice of law seven years earlier.

By contrast, Joseph Sedgwick's involvement in the investigation came closer to the mid-point of an exceptional career in criminal law. A formidable presence in any courtroom for more than fifty years, he maintained a busy defence practice while also serving as a bencher with the law society and member of assorted commissions related to criminal law before retiring in 1975. He died in 1981 at the age of eighty-three.

Of the leading counsel, only Joe Bench, the young Liberal senator who often served as the public face for the defendants, did not enjoy a long career in the law. He died suddenly in 1947, at the age of just forty-two.

As for John Robinette, he was just finding his stride professionally in 1945. His reputation was made not by his work on Eldorado or any other wartime retainer, but by his involvement with a notorious murder case in 1947. His skillful advocacy on appeal saved his client, Evelyn Dick, from execution after she was convicted of murdering her husband and infant son. Robinette won a new trial for his client, who was acquitted of murdering her husband but found guilty of manslaughter in the death of her son.

Although he is now best known as a civil litigator, Robinette actually did a lot of criminal work, saving sixteen clients from the gallows before losing one.[17] The loss transformed him into a lifelong advocate for the abolition of the death penalty and helped to push him into focusing more exclusively on civil litigation and regulatory work. He became one of Canada's leading constitutional litigators and appeared regularly before the Supreme Court of Canada on all manner of disputes, including major constitutional cases such as the patriation reference and early *Charter* challenges. Sadly, within months of testifying in the *Heighington* trial, Robinette was diagnosed with dementia. He formally retired from his law firm, McCarthy Tétrault, in 1991, and died just shy of his ninetieth birthday five years later.

C.D. Howe served another twelve years as a minister in the Canadian cabinet. In 1947, he received the American Medal of Merit for his efforts during the war, a year after Sengier, who received his from General Groves himself. Afterward, he piloted the postwar reconstruction of the Canadian economy and organized defence production during the Cold War; he built two transcontinental pipelines, turned Canada into a major producer of iron ore, and inspired a generation of businessmen – "Howe's boys" as they called themselves. Gilbert LaBine, as we have seen, was not among them. Howe died in 1960.

And what of those who had worked so closely with Howe on this matter? Lesslie Thomson was remembered, and honoured, for his work facilitating Canada's nuclear programs during the war, receiving the Order of the British Empire and the US Medal of Freedom with Golden Palm. He died two years before Howe, at the age of seventy-two. Howe's assistant Bill Bennett became president of Eldorado after LaBine's departure, as we have seen.[18] He stayed in that role until 1958. Later, he became president of an iron ore company and remained engaged in what had become a substantial Canadian nuclear industry. Bennett died in 1991.

As noted above, Grant Glassco died at the age of sixty-three in 1968. After the war, Glassco remained a trusted adviser to Canadian governments, Liberal and Progressive Conservative, and was a major figure in the accounting profession. Although he played a crucial role in the investigation of Eldorado's wartime finances, he is actually best known for leading a royal commission on government organization under Prime Minister John Diefenbaker.

On the American side, Leslie Groves is remembered as an organizational phenomenon, successfully managing one of the largest and most important projects of the war. He is also remembered for his ambition and self-promotion, though he never achieved his larger goal: to become a full general in charge of the US Army Corps of Engineers. He retired in 1948 at the rank of lieutenant general and died in 1970. Groves's deputy, Kenneth Nichols, became a major general, and in retirement became general manager of the US Atomic Energy Commission. He died in 2000.

Edgar Sengier continued his notable career after 1945. He and the Union Minière du Haut-Katanga (UMHK) prospered extracting the mineral wealth of the Belgian Congo. The Americans recognized his role in supplying uranium with the Medal of Merit, the same award as Howe, though Sengier's role in the atomic story was largely a matter of luck and last-minute timing. Otherwise, he might have had to share the credit with his former colleague Boris Pregel, who came within days of buying Sengier's stock of uranium. Sengier retired as UMHK director in 1949, full of honours (Belgian, American, and British, among others) and loaded with prestige. He remained on the company's governing board until 1960, just as the Congo secured its independence, and died three years later in Cannes.

As for Gustave Lechien, it's uncertain what happened after he fled to Guatemala in late 1941. His name abruptly disappears from the UMHK board minutes and other records, and does not turn up elsewhere. There is no evidence that he was ever arrested or brought to trial for his presumed embezzlement of UMHK radium.

Private Proceedings and Public Awareness

We are left with questions about how an apparently clear case of fraud frustrated Canada's legal system. The law engaged extensively with the allegations of fraud at Eldorado but left their substance unresolved. This was true in both the criminal case in Toronto and the civil suit in the Southern District of New York.

That the allegations weren't resolved formally by a judge or jury was not – is not – entirely unusual. Then, as now, most disputes don't get to trial; in criminal law, the accused often takes a plea, just as parties in civil suits often settle disputes before they reach a trial on their merits. Lay readers may be taken aback, but those involved in the legal profession know that the justice system simply couldn't function if every proceeding ended with a trial. In this regard, the disputes involving Eldorado's finances are not out of the ordinary, dollar value notwithstanding.

The preceding account of fraud at Eldorado has shown not just why and how three men defrauded a Canadian company of millions of dollars' worth of radium, leaving a trail of environmental contamination in their wake, but why it was worth doing. Despite well-publicized criminal charges and a civil suit in New York, people soon forgot about what had happened. All three died as upstanding citizens, reputations intact or, at the very least, not obviously tarnished. And why not? The criminal charges were withdrawn without a trial. None of their court appearances dealt with the allegations on their merits.

Justice must not merely be done but be seen to be done. Would a public trial have made a difference in this instance? The Canadian investigation received extensive newspaper coverage in the autumn of 1945 and into 1946, and a criminal trial on the merits would have been sensational. The personalities involved would have offered the kind of courtroom drama that newspapers relish. A public airing of the evidence would have created a collective memory of the fraud and, crucially, of the contaminated land in Scarborough. Forgetting would have been much harder.

A public trial might also have influenced American authorities. Activities at Pregel's refinery at Mount Kisco were not seriously scrutinized until the 1950s, long after wartime operations had ceased. A Canadian criminal trial could have heightened awareness in New York. The 1946 civil suit, which received a small burst of attention in *The New York Times*, might also have made a difference had there been a trial rather than a settlement. We will simply never know what difference public proceedings on the merits could have made in terms of the public's awareness.

The Fragility of Institutional Memory

Why, then, were the facts allowed to drift out of institutional memory? This too is a difficult question to answer. In *Heighington*, the court did not determine why the province had lost track of the 1945 warnings. In fairness, doing so was unnecessary for a finding of liability; the mere fact that the province had been notified in 1945 was sufficient. But there is something unsatisfying about a trial record that offers no documentary evidence to suggest what happened. Were papers misfiled? Discarded? Simply forgotten as immediate wartime concerns receded, staff retired, and offices were reorganized? All we know is that the urgency that had animated the Eldorado investigation dissipated once the company settled the New York civil suit in 1947, and the information was lost.

It's tempting to attribute these lapses to the secrecy that comes along with national security. In the immediate aftermath of war, secrecy was invoked to justify holding the preliminary inquiry behind closed doors. Superficially, it was a fair enough position. Canada was a participant in the Manhattan Project, uranium was essential to the construction of the first atomic weapons, and officials were anxious about revealing anything that might compromise the Allied atomic program. Yet, as we know, key facts about Canada's uranium supply were already public. Geological survey reports were widely available. Eldorado's production levels were reported in *The Northern Miner*. Even the wartime expansion of refining facilities was known to those following the industry. The secrecy surrounding the inquiry was therefore not strictly necessary to protect classified material. Rather, it served to shield an awkward wartime scandal from public scrutiny at a potentially delicate political moment. The same could be said for the American approach; recall that Groves, too, sought to have the New York civil suit heard *in camera*. He failed, and the day the suit was filed, *The New York Times* published its contents. No harm resulted.

The broader shadow of national security is real enough. It influenced how governments discussed radiation, uranium production, and industrial hazards. But even here, secrecy was uneven. What French and others did at the Scarborough farm was not clandestine; it was dangerous, irresponsible, and poorly supervised, but not secret. Perhaps the claim of secrecy became a convenient shorthand, a rhetorical shield, and later an excuse for not knowing or not remembering. What was hidden was not so much the information itself but the political will to maintain it.

The deeper problem is not secrecy but the failure of diligence. Records were not well organized or preserved. Investigations were not coordinated. Key details were not passed from one generation of officials to the next despite reasonable wartime coordination to investigate what happened, if not to prevent it. Bureaucratic structures may have presumed that the next office or division would remember what the previous one had learned, but records to support the presumption cannot be found. The costs of this mistake were borne not by the officials who made it but by unsuspecting families who bought houses on land that should have been known to be hazardous.

The story of fraud at Eldorado and the contamination it left behind is therefore not solely about three men who manipulated wartime contracts for personal gain. It's also about the fragility of institutional memory. Governments, corporations, and regulators have long struggled with the issue of how to preserve and transmit the lessons of the past. Too often, once a crisis has been resolved – or seems to have been resolved – the incentive to maintain detailed records recedes, especially when the underlying issues are technical, complex, or embarrassing. In that sense, the story of Scarborough is a case study in how we forget the past to our peril.

It was not inevitable that the contaminated land would be forgotten. Cook's 1945 report was clear and precise. Guernsey remembered enough about the investigation to urge ministry officials to talk to Cook. Robinette, decades later, with the help of contemporaneous documents, recounted events in a persuasive narrative. But without institutional structures, none of this was sufficient to prevent building on contaminated land. It took more than forty years for the wartime efforts of Cook, Guernsey, and Robinette to make a difference. In the end, two journalism students accomplished what government systems had not.

Legal and Personal Accountability

We are struck by how differently the principal actors fared after 1947. French, Pregel, and Pochon left legacies that bore little visible trace of the fraud. Their professional lives continued with their reputations intact. French reinvented himself as a philanthropist; Pregel became a patron of scientific societies; Pochon returned to private research. None lived long enough to see the full consequences of their actions.

The *Heighington* case offered a legal reckoning of sorts. Justice Holland's decision, affirmed by the Ontario Court of Appeal, was firm in the view that the province had a duty to protect future homeowners from harm. It was a reminder that legal accountability may still be possible even after decades. But the environmental proceeding did not replicate what a criminal trial might have delivered, nor offer the kind of resolution that might have been possible had the civil proceeding gone to trial in the Southern District of New York. Nor can it explain the deeper reasons why the contamination had been allowed to become part of a housing subdivision even while it resolved liability for that oversight.

It's said that sunlight is the best disinfectant. What, then, does the story tell us about the relationship between law, memory, and public accountability? It is proof that the absence of public proceedings can have profound consequences. When allegations of wrongdoing are addressed behind closed doors, our collective memory suffers. Government cannot rely on informal or improvised systems for preserving knowledge of wrongdoing, especially with respect to hazardous activities. The Eldorado investigation was treated as exceptional, a wartime anomaly, and once it ended officials allowed its details to be overlooked. That gap in institutional diligence allowed a contaminated site to be forgotten long enough to be expropriated, subdivided, and turned into affordable housing. Though invoked repeatedly, secrecy was not the central cause of that failure but a rhetorical veil. An absence of political will to maintain and share potentially embarrassing information is the fault at the heart of the matter.

The affair also reveals something about the human desire to move on from crisis. After the war, Canada turned toward reconstruction, prosperity, and peace. It became a trusted ally within the Western bloc of nations that united in the early days of the Cold War against the Soviet Union. Eldorado became a Crown corporation focused on uranium production for a growing nuclear industry. Regulators moved on to new responsibilities. It's natural in such moments to put aside complex challenges with no easy answers.

And yet, as the Scarborough story shows, the past does not always stay buried. Sometimes it literally resurfaces. The contaminated soil in Malvern was not just a residue of wartime fraud but a physical reminder that decisions made in haste, concealed for convenience, or forgotten through neglect can carry consequences far into the future.

In the end, the rediscovery of contaminated land in 1980 forced the past into public view. The investigative efforts of two young journalists exposed a forgotten history and compelled multiple levels of government to confront what they had previously overlooked through negligence – or simply ignored. Their work exemplifies how accountability sometimes emerges not from formal legal mechanisms but from individuals willing to ask difficult questions.

It seems fitting to end on a note that is at once cautious and hopeful. Cautious because it shows the consequences of forgetting about our past, of secrecy used loosely, and of diligence not maintained. Hopeful because it demonstrates that truth can re-emerge, even decades later, through the work of lawyers, citizens, journalists, archivists, and historians. The story of Eldorado is not only a tale of fraud and contamination, hidden within the shadows of secrecy that accompanied claims of national security. It is a reminder that there is a collective responsibility in the pursuit of justice, and that the past, when uncovered, can still demand – and achieve – accountability in the present.

Notes

Introduction

1 Pat McNenly, "J.J. Robinette Gets His Day out of Court," *Toronto Daily Star*, 26 April 1971. See also "The Grand Old Man of the Ontario Bar Recalls over Half a Century of Change in the Legal Profession," *Ontario Lawyers Weekly*, 8 July 1983, 6–7.

2 "J.J. Robinette Renowned as Top Courtroom Lawyer," Obituaries, *Toronto Star*, 19 November 1996, A4.

3 Richard Holland, interview, 1997, Osgoode Society for Canadian Legal History, Oral History Program (Osgoode Society Oral History Program), file C 81-4-0-10, 35.

4 *International Corona Resources Ltd. v Lac Minerals Ltd.*, (1986) 53 OR (2d) 737, 25 DLR (4th) 504. The Supreme Court of Canada upheld Holland's decision, in what is now a leading case on the existence of fiduciary duties in business relationships. See *Lac Minerals Ltd. v International Corona Resources Ltd.*, [1989] 2 SCR 574. See also Robert Reid and Richard Holland, *Advocacy: Views from the Bench* (Aurora, ON: Canada Law Book, 1984).

5 *Heighington v Ontario*, 1987 CanLII 5417 (ONSC), also reported at 60 OR (2d) 641, and affirmed by the Court of Appeal in 1989 at 69 OR (2d) 484. It was an important environmental law decision dealing with government liability for historical contamination.

6 Mary Gooderham, "Four Years of Living with A-soil Makes Activists of Housewives," *Globe and Mail*, 26 December 1984.

7 Walter Sullivan, "Radium-Soaked Concrete Found in Toronto Building," *New York Times*, 27 February 1975, https://timesmachine.nytimes.com/timesmachine/1975/02/27/76524869.html?pageNumber=14, picked up what the Canadian newspapers had said five days earlier, with added colour about the hazards of radiation.

8 James Jefferson and Ross Laver, "Radioactive Traces Found in 2 Scarboro Backyards," *Globe and Mail*, 20 November 1980.

9 Ibid; James Jefferson and Ross Laver, "AECB Feared Radiation Tests a Worry to Malvern Families," *Globe and Mail*, 21 November 1980.

10 Jefferson and Laver, "AECB Feared Radiation Tests." In 1984, Cosgrove was appointed to the Superior Court in Eastern Ontario. He resigned from office in 2009 after the Canadian

Judicial Council held an inquiry into his conduct during a criminal trial in 1999 and recommended to Parliament his removal from office.

11 Dealing with historical currency is at times more an art than a science. When dollar figures are provided in relation to radium and uranium, they are in American nominal amounts. Otherwise, the dollar amounts are Canadian. A dollar in 1940 had approximately twenty times the purchasing power of today. During the Second World War, one Canadian dollar was worth roughly US$0.90.

Chapter 1: The Most Valuable Metal on Earth

1 Lucy Jane Santos, *Half Lives: The Unlikely History of Radium* (London: Pegasus Books, 2021), 23.

2 James Mahaffey, *Atomic Awakening: A New Look at the History and Future of Nuclear Power* (London: Pegasus Books, 2010), 37–38, Kindle.

3 Quoted in Santos, *Half Lives*, 27.

4 Pierre Curie, "Radioactive Substances, Especially Radium," Nobel lecture, 6 June 1905, https://www.nobelprize.org/uploads/2018/06/pierre-curie-lecture.pdf.

5 Barbara Goldsmith, *Obsessive Genius: The Inner World of Marie Curie* (New York: W.W. Norton, 2005), 131–32.

6 When the Curies' bodies were reinterred in 1995, they were found to be free of radiation. Given that the half-life of radium is 1,600 years, it would have been noticed if it were present.

7 This would be repeated many years later in a house in Port Hope, Ontario, belonging to one of her students, Marcel Pochon.

8 Marcel Guillot, a chemist who worked at the Curie laboratory from 1927 to 1930, is quoted in Susan Quinn, *Marie Curie: A Life* (Lexington, MA: Plunkett Lake Press, 2011), loc. 8634, Kindle.

9 Bertrand Goldschmidt, in discussion with Robert Bothwell, c. 1982. Goldschmidt studied at the Institut Curie in the mid-1930s. As we will see in chapter 2, there is a second part to Curie's comment.

10 Santos, *Half Lives*, 26. The Central Chemical Products Company, as Santos renders it, was headed by André Debierne, another former student of Pierre Curie.

11 Timothy Jorgensen, *Strange Glow: The Story of Radiation* (Princeton, NJ: Princeton University Press, 2016), 128–29.

12 Jerome Halpern and John M. Heslep, "Radium in Military Surplus Commodities," *Public Health Reports* 81, 12 (1966): 1057–63.

13 Santos, *Half Lives*, 159.

14 Jorgensen, *Strange Glow*, 127.

15 Roger F. Robison, *Mining and Selling Radium and Uranium* (Cham, Switzerland: Springer International Publishing, 2015), 474.

16 Herbert Hoover, *An American Epic: Introduction, the Relief of Belgium and Northern France, 1914–1930* (Chicago: H. Regnery, 1959), 43.

17 Translated from "SENGIER (Edgar)," *Biographie Belge d'Outre-Mer*, 7-A (Brussels: Académie Royale des Sciences d'Outre-Mer [ARSOM], 1973).

18 Jacques Vanderlinden, "À propos de l'uranium congolais," *Classe des Sciences Morales et Politiques Mémoires in-8*, new series 51, 1 (Brussels: ARSOM, 1991), 22. Interestingly, as late as 1940, a British geologist commented on the "considerable secrecy" being maintained over

the ore body at Shinkolobwe and the method of extracting it: C.F. Davidson, "A Brief Report on the Uranium Deposits of the World," c. 1940, National Archives, United Kingdom (NA), Records of the United Kingdom Atomic Energy Authority and its predecessors, AB1/281.

19 Anne Adams, "The Origins and Early Development of the Belgian Radium Industry," *Environment International* 19 (1993): 491–501.

20 Boris Pregel, interview by Spencer Weart, 6 January 1975, Niels Bohr Library and Archives, American Institute of Physics (NBL), College Park, MD, www.aip.org/history-programs/niels-bohr-library/oral-histories/4833.

21 Adams, "Belgian Radium Industry," 493; Vanderlinden, "À propos de l'uranium," 27.

22 Vanderlinden, "À propos de l'uranium," 27.

23 Pregel, interview by Weart, 6 January 1975.

24 See Gustave Lechien, 2 November 1941, National Archives and Records Administration, United States (NARA), RG 85, Records of the Immigration and Naturalization Service, 1787–2004, Passenger and Crew Lists of Vessels Arriving at New York, New York, 1897–1957, T715. The ambassador is listed as a contact, perhaps because his name came to mind as useful and impressive: the two men would certainly have met either in Brussels or in the United States, and it may be true that the count was a friend. On Lechien's son-in-law the marquis, see "Colombian Envoy to France Arrives," *New York Times*, 12 December 1940. On the same ship as the envoy came Lechien's two daughters and their husbands, the marquis Guy de la Roche du Ranzet and Gerard Jacob, a former Belgian who had worked as a press attaché for the Franco fascist regime in Spain and become a Spanish citizen. De la Roche du Ranzet stayed in the United States for the time being, but Jacob was probably en route to a diplomatic posting in Guatemala.

25 Vanderlinden, "À propos de l'uranium," 28.

26 Sofia Pregel, *Moe detstvo* (Paris: Novoselé, 1973), 215, 280.

27 MI5, the British foreign intelligence service, erroneously claimed that Boris was born in Romania in 1884: Brigadier Sir David Petrie (MI5), letter to S.T. Wood (Commissioner RCMP), 9 July 1945, Library and Archives Canada (LAC), RG 18, vol Waste Not Wanted Inc. (WNW).

28 Boris's grandfather read a French newspaper, and there are references to a maid speaking German. Later in life, Boris and his wife spoke Russian to each other, and preferred to speak French to those who could manage it. See Minda Zetlin, interviews by Vilma Hunt, September and October 1995, Arthur and Elizabeth Schlesinger Library on the History of Women in America, Radcliffe Institute for Advanced Study, Harvard University, Papers of Vilma R. Hunt (Hunt Papers), files 68.5, 70.7, and 70.8; Pregel, *Moe detstvo*, 24.

29 In a semi-fictional account of her childhood, Sophia Pregel describes her mother's love for theatre and singing and notes that Boris's favourite composer was Tchaikovsky. *Moe detstvo*, 30.

30 Ibid, 23, 212.

31 MI5 placed Pregel's university education at Liège and Brussels, and also in Petrograd (the wartime name of St. Petersburg). He earned a diploma as an electrical engineer. According to a much later curriculum vitae, in 1917 in Petrograd, Pregel published a pamphlet or book on electrical engineering written in French, and another in 1919 in Odessa. See Boris Pregel, curriculum vitae enclosed in a letter to Lyman Briggs, 11 December 1941, NARA, RG 227, Records of the Office of Scientific Research and Development, Bush-Conant files. See also undated draft manuscript, Hunt Papers, file 71.11; Petrie, letter to Wood, 9 July 1945.

32 Alas, Boris is almost certainly the sole source on his life and career at this stage, whether the information comes from him directly or through his younger brother, Alexander. See Boris Pregel, curriculum vitae enclosed in a letter to Lyman Briggs, 11 December 1941, NARA, RG 227, Bush-Conant files.

33 Alexander's interviews with Vilma Hunt in 1996–97 echo his brother's narrative, as they were bound to do since Boris was his source for the stories. The interviews appear in the Hunt Papers but the location and precise dates are unrecorded. See Hunt Papers, file 71.6 Writings – The Uranium Merchants, letters to A&E Pregel, 1995–99 and file 72.1 Writings – The Uranium Merchants, research and notes 1990–98.

34 MI5 reported that Pregel was "fighting in Denikin's army," which operated between 1918 and 1920, and occupied Odessa for some months in 1919. Petrie, letter to Wood, 9 July 1945. This may corroborate Pregel's story, or it may simply be a repetition of Pregel's own words. See also Pregel, *Moe detstvo*, 20, 149.

35 Commercial notice for ship *Mikhail Arkhangelsk*, *Istamboul* (newspaper), 31 January 1922, https://gallica.bnf.fr/ark:/12148/bd6t552602t/f3.image.r=Boris%20Pregel#, giving Boris's office address as the fifth floor of a building in the Galata suburb.

36 A year of riots, insurrections and runaway inflation, 1923 was not a time when one would have wanted to be in Berlin or in Germany. Though the Pregels' ancestors came from East Prussia and they themselves spoke German, postwar Germany was wracked by economic and social strife. Massive inflation and sporadic political violence, some of it anti-Semitic, created economic, cultural, and political reasons for leaving. It may not be an accident or coincidence but simple common sense that Boris Pregel chose to keep on moving from Berlin to Paris.

37 "Alexander Pregel, Uranium Dealer, Dies at 91," *New York Times*, 28 June 1998. According to Alexander's interview with Vilma Hunt, he was at the American Robert College of Istanbul for six years, probably 1920–26, and then spent two years in Paris before attending the University of Minnesota.

38 Interwar Romania had a stellar reputation for corruption. See Robert St. John, *From the Land of Silent People* (Garden City, NY: Doubleday, Doran, 1942).

39 See O.O. Gruzenberg, *Yesterday: Memoirs of a Russian-Jewish Lawyer* (Berkeley: University of California Press, 1981), xxv, 13, 54, 236. The editor of the book thanks Alexandra Pregel, Boris's second wife, presumably for information about Sofia. Sofia's father passed through Kiev and Odessa in 1918–19, possibly with his family, and she might have met Pregel there. Gruzenberg next moved to Berlin, then Riga, and finally Nice, where he died in 1940. The Pregel patriarch, Julius, lived in Berlin for a time, and Boris, who had investments there, may have as well.

40 Boris Pregel confirmed that Lechien was an engineer and, in his opinion, a good one, thus conforming to the pattern of UMHK senior management. Pregel, interview by Weart, 6 January 1975.

41 Pregel had a booth displaying his wares at a dental supply trade fair in Paris in February 1927. "La semaine odontologique et le 3ème Salon de l'art dentaire," *Excelsior: Journal Illustré quotidien*, 9 February 1927, https://gallica.bnf.fr/ark:/12148/bpt6k4607445c/f6.item.r=Pregel.

42 UMHK claimed it had not been paid; Mme Curie called that claim inaccurate. M. Exbrayant, letter to Mme Curie, 4 March 1927, recounting a conversation with M. Jadot, Governor of the Société Générale de Belgique, AIR LC.MC, part 3623, and Marie Curie, letter to Exbrayant, 5 March 1927, AIR LC.MC, part 3624, Archives, collections du Musée Curie, http://www.calames.abes.fr/pub/#details?id=Calames-20147101673416353 5.

43 In the late 1930s, UMHK asserted that the price reduction permitted the uses of radium to be expanded. "Notice sur le Radium de l'Union Minière du Haut-Katanga," n.d., UMHK Papers, Belgian State Archives, Brussels. From internal evidence the document can be placed no earlier than 1934–35 and no later than 1938.
44 Santos, *Half Lives*, 164.
45 Hector A. Colwell and Sidney Russ, *X Ray and Radium Injuries: Prevention and Treatment* (London: Oxford University Press, 1934), quoted in Santos, *Half Lives*, 209, detail just one of the many uses of radium.
46 Jorgensen, *Strange Glow*, 89–92. Radium and its daughter, radon, emit alpha particles that in the case of the factory workers settled in the bones, causing bone cancer. Radon also affects the lungs when it is breathed in, as has happened to miners, for example.
47 Robert Bothwell, *Eldorado: Canada's National Uranium Compa*ny (Toronto: University of Toronto Press, 1984), 8, quoting the British atomic historian Margaret Gowing.
48 Union Minière du Haut-Katanga, *Rapport du Conseil d'Administration et du College des Commissaires, 1932*, ss 2 and 3, https://dfg-viewer.de/show?id=9&tx_dlf%5Bid%5D=https%3A%2F%2Fpm20.zbw.eu%2Ffolder%2Fco%2F0692xx%2F069242%2Fpublic.mets&tx_dlf%5Bpage%5D=74. The African milling operations were closed, and the company proposed to survive on its inventory.
49 Devra Lee Davis, *The Secret History of the War on Cancer* (New York: Basic Books, 2007), 18, quotes "the great experimentalist Isaac Berenblum" to that effect.
50 Pregel, interview by Weart, 6 January 1975.
51 Pregel, curriculum vitae enclosed in a letter to Lyman Briggs, 11 December 1941.
52 See notice for Organisation de Secours aux Enfants in *La Tribune Juive*, 16 December 1938; Jewish Telegraph Agency (New York), "Boris Pregel, French Philanthropist, Appointed to Legion of Honor," *News*, 24 August 1939.
53 Jewish Telegraph Agency, "Boris Pregel."
54 *L'Oeuvre*, 21 July 1939. Pregel headed the financial committee of Les Amis de la République française, whose membership included many high-ranking politicians.

Chapter 2: Discovering Canada's Eldorado

1 Much of what we know about Gilbert LaBine comes from publications by Eldorado itself. For example, the company published a picture booklet called *The Romance of Canadian Radium* that includes references to testimony before the Joint Committee of Commerce of the US Congress on 8 July 1937 and production details from the company for the same period. There is no reference to any date beyond mid-1937. Eldorado Gold Mines Ltd., *The Romance of Canadian Radium* (Toronto, 1937).
2 Canadian Mining Hall of Fame, "Willet Green Miller, 1995 Inductee," https://www.mininghalloffame.ca/willet-green-miller.
3 Peter C. Newman, *Flame of Power: Intimate Profiles of Canada's Great Businessmen* (Toronto: Longmans, Green, 1959), 153–54.
4 Newman, *Flame of Power*, 153–54.
5 Robert Bothwell, *Eldorado: Canada's National Uranium Compa*ny (Toronto: University of Toronto Press, 1984), 23.
6 Ibid, 24–25.
7 Eldorado, *The Romance of Canadian Radium*, 33, citing Charles Camsell's article. It's worth noting here that although radium was consistently measured in grams, the weight of the

ore from which it was extracted was measured in two different ways. Europeans used tonnes, also known as metric tons (1,000 kilograms, or 2,200 pounds), while North Americans used short tons (2,000 pounds).

8 The following discussion of testing is based on the Mines Branch data, as discussed in Bothwell, *Eldorado*, 25–32.

9 Canada, *House of Commons Debates*, 17th Parl, 2nd Sess, vol 2 (7 May 1931), 1332.

10 Leslie Roberts, "Treasure under the Arctic's Rim," *Maclean's*, 15 July 1936, 19.

11 Bothwell, *Eldorado*, 18–19.

12 J. Peter Williamson, *Securities Regulation in Canada* (Toronto: University of Toronto Press, 1960), 3. That requirement – *full* public disclosure – is the foundation of prospectus requirements in companies legislation and modern securities regulation in England and Canada. See L.B.C. Gower, *Principles of Modern Company Law*, 5th ed. (London: Sweet and Maxwell, 1992), 39.

13 Charlotte Gray, *Murdered Midas: A Millionaire, His Gold Mine, and a Strange Death on an Island Paradise* (Toronto: Harper Collins, 2019), 46.

14 Ibid, 46; Christopher Armstrong, *Blue Skies and Boiler Rooms: Buying and Selling Securities in Canada, 1870–1940* (Toronto: University of Toronto Press, 1997), 303.

15 Gray, *Murdered Midas*, 47.

16 Paul M. Tyler, *Radium*, Department of Commerce, United States Bureau of Mines, Information Circular, August 1930, I.C. 6132, 35.

17 Société Industrielle du Radium Ltd., Records, https://www.scripoworld.com/records/united-kingdom/england/societe-industrielle-du-radium-ltd.

18 Tyler, *Radium*, 36; MI5, assessment, 28 June 1945, Library and Archives Canada (LAC), RG 18, vol. Waste Not Wanted Inc. (WNW).

19 Terrence Guernsey, "Marcel Leon Pochon – Eldorado Mining & Refining Ltd., Port Hope, Ontario," 24 November 1944, LAC, RG 18, WNW; MI5, 28 June 1945, WNW; Roger F. Robison, *Mining and Selling Radium and Uranium*, (Cham, Switzerland: Springer International Publishing, 2015), 156.

20 Both witnesses quoted in MI5, 28 June 1945, WNW. Based on subsequent documentation and personal discussions with Robert Bothwell c. 1982, the latter assessment and characterization appears to come from Bertrand Goldschmidt.

21 Bertrand Goldschmidt, *Atomic Rivals* (New Brunswick, NJ, and London: Rutgers University Press, 1990), 142; Goldschmidt, in discussion with Robert Bothwell, c. 1982.

22 See also South Terras Mine, Cornwall, timeline, www.cornwall-calling.co.uk/mines/st-austell/south-terras.htm; Courtenay V. Smale, "South Terras: Cornwall's Premier Uranium and Radium Mine," presidential address, November 1992, *Journal of the Royal Institution of Cornwall* 1 (1993), www.dangerouslaboratories.org/rcw3.html; Robison, *Mining and Selling Radium and Uranium*, 156.

23 MI5, 28 June 1945, WNW.

24 Tyler, *Radium*, 36.

25 MI5, 28 June 1945, WNW. The intelligence report cited an employee, Maurice Gregory, as someone who could provide information about the refinery, laboratory, and a confusing tangle of corporate connections. Gregory had been subject to security inquiries in the past because he had worked for Urgeirica Radium Consolidated Ltd., a British-owned radium and uranium company in Portugal. Urgeirica was located in Thames House (now Five Kings House and home to the UK's domestic intelligence and security agency, MI5), which was also the headquarters of Imperial Chemical Industries, one of Britain's largest manufacturers.

There was some concern that Urgeirica's interests might interlock with Chemical Services Industries, the Brandhurst Company, and its likely holding company, Demetra.

26 Guernsey, "Pochon – Eldorado Mining," 24 November 1944.

27 MI5, 28 June 1945, WNW.

28 Marcel Pochon, interview by RCMP officers William McElhone and Terrence Guernsey, 9 December 1945, LAC, RG 18, WNW. A further report, dated 7 January 1946, compiles all the information from the Pochon interviews, along with an excerpt of a letter from his counsel dated 4 January 1946, and indicates that he will no longer speak with investigators voluntarily.

29 Bothwell, *Eldorado*, 56–57. In Glassco's working papers, Pochon's salary in 1932 was given as $7,500, with a commission of 1 percent on sales of radium and uranium, whereas Bothwell found it to be $10,000 (*Eldorado*, 65). Glassco says Pochon's salary did not increase to that level until 1937. J. Grant Glassco to C.D. Howe, Report on Eldorado Investigation, 1 April 1947, LAC, RG 134, Glassco Commission Investigation, Eldorado Canada fonds, vol 140, file Glassco – 1947, 7.

30 Goldschmidt, *Atomic Rivals*, 142; Goldschmidt, in discussion with Bothwell, c. 1982.

31 Pochon, interview by RCMP, 9 December 1945.

32 Ibid. Pochon later claimed that he had an arrangement with South Terras Mine that allowed him to keep whatever radium he recovered during the various clean-up processes in the 1920s.

33 Frank L. Hess, "Radium, Uranium, and Vanadium," in *Minerals Yearbook, 1932–1933*, ed., O.E. Kiessling (Washington, DC: Bureau of Mines: United States Government Printing Office, 1933); Pochon, interview by RCMP, 9 December 1945.

34 Bothwell, *Eldorado*, 58–59.

35 Pochon, interview by RCMP, 9 December 1945.

36 Guernsey, "Pochon – Eldorado Mining," 24 November 1944.

37 Ibid.

38 William Lyon Mackenzie King, diary entry, 16 November 1936, LAC, MG 26-J13, item 17409, Diaries of William Lyon Mackenzie King.

39 Roberts, "Treasure under the Arctic's Rim," 30.

40 Bothwell, *Eldorado*, 61.

Chapter 3: The Mirage of the Markets

1 C.J. Mackenzie, diary entry, 12 April 1943, Library and Archives Canada (LAC), MG 30, B122.

2 Robert Bothwell, *Eldorado: Canada's National Uranium Company* (Toronto: University of Toronto Press, 1984), 46–47.

3 Edgar Laytha, *North Again for Gold: Birth of Canada's Arctic Empire* (New York: Frederick A. Stokes, 1939), 94–95; Bothwell, *Eldorado*, 65–66.

4 Tom Primrose, "Western Roundup," *Calgary Albertan*, 16 September 1964, 20.

5 Tom Primrose, "Personality of the Week," *Calgary Herald*, 1 October 1955, 5.

6 "Funeral Services Set for Harry M. Snyder," *Arizona Daily Star* (Tucson), 24 March 1972, 3.

7 Timothy Sale, email to authors, 9 July 2024.

8 Among Snyder's various businesses were R. Hotte Oil Company (1882), Loyal Oil & Gas (1917), the Automobile Owners Association (1921), United Auto Service (1922), LaSalle Petroleum Refinery (1925), Sylvestre Oil Company (1929), Adanac Oil & Gas (1929), and Excel Petroleum (1931), limited companies all.

9 In 1937, Snyder led an expedition to Glacier Lake, taking with him surveyors, geologists, and photographers. The effort resulted in his election to the Royal Geographical Society in London in December 1937. "Meetings: Session 1937–38," *Geographical Journal* 91 (1938): 96; Julie Carrington, Library, Royal Geographical Society, email to authors, 28 April 2022.
10 Snyder, unpublished memoir, n.d., on file with authors.
11 The financing arrangement is detailed in Bothwell, *Eldorado*, 66.
12 Memorandum for the Record, Subject: Boris Pregel, Re: Interview with Dr. John Leitch, 25 May 1943, Hoover Institution Library and Archives, Stanford University, Robert S. Norris Collection, MI-4-A, box 48, file Boris Pregel.
13 "Carl French Dies, Leader in Fight against Cancer," *Battle Creek Enquirer*, 4 May 1984; "Lawyer Carl French Was among the First to Know of A-bomb," Obituaries, *Sunday Star* (Toronto), 22 April 1984, A10.
14 Terrence Guernsey, Report to Inspector W.H. Williams, 31 January 1945, Library and Archives Canada (LAC), RG 18, vol Waste Not Wanted Inc. (WNW).
15 What is now known as the Northwestern Pritzker School of Law is the oldest in Illinois and world renowned. Founded in 1851, Northwestern University was the country's third largest by 1900. The law school was founded eight years after the university, originally as part of the University of Chicago. Then, in 1873, the school became affiliated with Northwestern and severed ties to the University of Chicago eighteen years later. Although Chicago-Kent is the second-oldest law school in Illinois, it is now one of the few American law schools to be affiliated with a technical university. It was founded in 1888, merged with Chicago College of Law to become Chicago-Kent College of Law in 1900, and then merged once more in 1969, this time with the Illinois Institute of Technology.
16 Having reviewed old Northwestern yearbooks, Dana Lamparello, an archivist at the university, emailed Patricia McMahon on 23 June 2022: "Boy was Carl French an engaged student! ... This may be the most I've ever found in a yearbook for an individual student!"
17 *The 1928 Syllabus*, vol 43 (Evanston, IL: Junior Class of Northwestern University, 1927), 194.
18 Ibid, 390. The circus was held annually from 1908 to 1932 with the exception of 1918. It was organized primarily by the fraternities and sororities and a board of almost fifty students who spent a year planning for the spectacle. The university cancelled future circuses because the preparations were so extravagant that they were thought to take too much time away from the purpose of the university. "Northwestern Circus Was One of the University's Greatest Shows," *Northwestern Stories* 16, 14 (25 January 2001).
19 "Lawyer Carl French Was among the First to Know of A-bomb," A10.
20 J. Grant Glassco to C.D. Howe, Report on Eldorado Investigation, 1 April 1947, LAC, RG 134, Glassco Commission Investigation, Eldorado Canada fonds, vol 140, file Glassco – 1947, 7.
21 Ibid, 9.
22 Ibid, 8.
23 Bothwell records the radium output for 1937 at "almost 24 grams" (*Eldorado*, 71), relying on "Radium Sales, Original Dox" and Carl French, "Analysis of Sales Representation in England and the Continent, June 1937," Board minutes, 25 September 1937, LAC, RG 134.
24 During the First World War, radium was priced at $125–35 (USD) per milligram. See H.H. Hughes, *Minerals Yearbook 1937*, United States Department of the Interior, Bureau of Mines (Washington, DC: US Government Printing Office, 1937), 770; "Radium," *Maclean's*, 1 May 1937; Bothwell, *Eldorado*, 72.

25 Bothwell, *Eldorado*, 72.

26 Leitch, interview by J.E. Southerland, 25 May 1943; Glassco, Report, 1 April 1947, 9. The Leitch account gets many details wrong. For example, the cartel talks took place between 1937 and 1938. Leitch says they took place in the spring of 1939. He also describes a £25 million loan from Great Britain to Romania in May 1939. There was a loan, but the amount was £5 million. See *New York Times*, 2 May 1939. Leitch was also obviously hostile to Boris Pregel, who took his job as Eldorado's sales agent in North America. However, the Leitch account still provides useful detail about the people involved with the negotiations.

27 Harry Snyder, letter to Gilbert LaBine, 22 April 1938, LAC, RG 134.

28 Leitch, interview by J.E. Southerland, 25 May 1943.

29 René Brion and Jean-Louis Moreau, *De la mine à Mars: La genèse de Umicore* (Tielt, Belgium: Uitgeverij Lannoo, 2006), 185.

30 Snyder, letter to Gilbert LaBine, 22 April 1938; Harry Snyder, Report to the Eldorado Board, agreement dated 30 April 1938, RG 134.

31 Bothwell, *Eldorado*, 72, n47. According to the *Toronto Star*, 14 May 1938, 15, Eldorado's annual general meeting was held on 13 May 1938. The board meeting would have been held earlier.

32 *Act of July 2, 1890*, 15 U.S.C. ss 1–7, otherwise known as the *Sherman Antitrust Act* after Senator John Sherman of Ohio, who introduced the legislation. The act made it illegal to have any combination "in the form of trust or otherwise that was in restraint of trade or commerce among the several states, or with foreign nations," and created an administrative structure that investigated and prosecuted violations. See *United States v E.C. Knight Co.*, 156 US 1 (1895). In 1895, the US Supreme Court held that the American Sugar Refining Company, which controlled 98 percent of the sugar refining in the United States, had not contravened the act. The Court held that although the entity controlled manufacturing, that was not the same as controlling trade.

33 *Dominion Trade and Industry Commission Act, 1935*, 25–26 Geo V, c 59. The legislation followed a series of efforts: *Combines Investigation Act, 1910*, 9–10 Edward VII, c 9; *Board of Commerce Act, 1919*, 9–10 Geo V, c 37; *Combines and Fair Prices Act, 1919*, 9–10 Geo V, c 45; *Canada (AG) v Alberta (AG)*, 1921 CanLII 399 (UK JCPC), 60 DLR 513; *Combines Investigation Act, 1923*, 13–14 Geo V, c 9; *Combines Investigation Act*, RSC 1927, c 26; *Reference re Validity of the Combines Investigation Act and of s 498 of the Criminal Code*, [1929] SCR 409; *Proprietary Articles Trade Association v Canada (AG)*, [1931] 2 DLR 2 (PC) per Lord Atkin. See also the *Constitution Act, 1867* (UK), 30 & 31 Vict, c 3, s, 91(27), reprinted in RSC 1985, appendix II, No. 5; John A. Ball, *Canadian Anti-Trust Legislation* (Baltimore: Williams and Wilkins, 1934), 69.

34 See, for example, "London Judgment Obliges Confederal Revision – Overhaul of B.N.A. Act or Tax Shift Indicated; 4 Bennett Acts Voided," *Globe and Mail*, 29 January 1937, 1.

35 The St. Joachimsthal ("Jachymov") mine in Bohemia, from which the Curies had drawn their original pitchblende, was also involved. Its role as a source of radium and uranium was compromised when the Germans occupied the area in 1938 with the rest of the Sudetenland, but in any case the two larger cartel members gave the Czech company barely a nod when drawing up the agreement.

36 Report, 30 April 1938, LAC, RG 134, File Radium Sales – Britain and Europe.

37 Robison, *Mining and Selling Radium and Uranium*, 303–4; Bothwell, *Eldorado*, 71.

38 Bothwell, *Eldorado*, 73.

39 Ibid.

Chapter 4: The Race to Build a Bomb

1 René Brion and Jean-Louis Moreau, *De la mine à Mars: La genèse de Umicore* (Tielt, Belgium: Uitgeverij Lannoo, 2006), 226.

2 Stonehaven had been a prominent Conservative politician and governor general of Australia. He brought prominence and connections but no business experience to this role.

3 Jacques Vanderlinden, "À propos de l'uranium congolais," *Classe des Sciences Morales et Politiques Mémoires in-8*, new series 51, 1 (Brussels: ARSOM, 1991), 75–76, is mistaken on this point, as confirmed by the British document "Uranium: A History of Action up to 10th May, 1939," National Archives, United Kingdom (NA), Records of the United Kingdom Atomic Energy Authority and its predecessors, AB1/37 14510. In her history of British atomic energy, Margaret Gowing relies on this document, which appears to be an accurate representation of what was said. *Britain and Atomic Energy 1939–1945* (London: Macmillan, 1964).

4 Graham Farmelo, *Churchill's Bomb: How the United States Overtook Britain in the First Nuclear Arms Race* (New York: Basic Books, 2013), part 1.

5 In February 1939, the scientific journal *Nature* published a letter from two Jewish Austrian atomic scientists who were refugees from Germany. They argued that "a new type of nuclear reaction" could be produced by bombarding uranium with neutrons, unleashing potentially unlimited energy. The letter caused a stir among scientists around the world, who shared the news with their respective governments. Lise Meitner and Otto Frisch, "Disintegration of Uranium by Neutrons: A New Type of Nuclear Reaction," *Nature* 143 (1939): 239–40, https://doi.org/10.1038/143239a0.

6 Brion and Moreau, *De la mine à Mars*, 227.

7 Edgar Sengier, "Notes relatives au concours apporté par la Belgique aux Alliés pour la réalisation de la bombe atomique," 8 November 1957, UMHK Papers, Belgian State Archives, Brussels. See also Arthur Breuer, memorandum to file, 28 June 1956, National Archives and Records Administration, United States (NARA), RG 59, General Records Relating to Atomic Energy Matters, 1948–1962, folder Pregel, Boris – Claim No. 35761, Confidential Security Material.

8 Alexander Pregel, interview by Vilma Hunt, n.d., Arthur and Elizabeth Schlesinger Library on the History of Women in America, Radcliffe Institute for Advanced Study, Harvard University, Papers of Vilma R. Hunt (Hunt Papers), file 71.6 Writings – The Uranium Merchants, letters to A&E Pregel, 1995–99 and file 72.1 Writings – The Uranium Merchants, research and notes 1990–98.

9 After the war, the US State Department communicated to the Canadian embassy the opinion of French intelligence that Pregel was a shady character. Communism was thrown in for good measure. Pregel was subjected to congressional investigation by the House Un-American Activities Committee between 1948 and 1950.

10 Pregel, curriculum vitae, enclosed in a letter to Lyman Briggs, 11 December 1941, NARA, RG 227, Records of the Office of Scientific Research and Development, Bush-Conant files.

11 Vladimir Halpérin, *Raoul Dautry: Du rail à l'atome* (Paris: Fayard, 1997).

12 Sengier, "Notes relatives," 8 November 1957.

13 "Belgian Metals Group in Consolidation Here," *New York Times*, 17 February 1926. Sengier and Lechien were Afrimet directors from the beginning. Both men visited New York

regularly and made the rounds in high society. "Luncheon Given for Alicia Ludlow," *New York Times*, 28 October 1936.

14 Ernest R. May, *Strange Victory: Hitler's Conquest of France* (New York: Hill and Wang, 2000), 537–38.

15 Alexander Pregel, interview by Vilma Hunt, n.d.

16 See Cultural Plunder by the Einsatzstab Reichsleiter Rosenberg: Database of Art Objects at the Jeu de Paume, https://www.errproject.org/jeudepaume; and Mark Masurovsky, "The Fate of the Collection of Alexandra Pregel aka Avxente," https://plunderedart.org/2020/01/08/the-fate-of-the-collection-of-alexandra-pregel-aka-avxente.

17 Scribbled note on the *New York Times* obituary of Joana Mendes, daughter of the Portuguese consul in Bordeaux, telephone conversation with Associated Press, 12 June 1997, Hunt Papers, file 71.6.

18 NARA, RG 85, Records of the Immigration and Naturalization Service, 1787–2004, Passenger and Crew Lists of Vessels Arriving at New York, New York, 1897–1957, T715.

19 "Retrait du radium de France," memorandum to Félicien Cartier (Chair, UMHK Board), 6 September 1944, UMHK Papers, Belgian State Archives, Brussels.

20 Robert Bothwell, *Eldorado: Canada's National Uranium Compa*ny (Toronto: University of Toronto Press, 1984), 81.

21 Brion and Moreau, *De la mine à Mars*, 230.

22 Brion and Moreau, *De la mine à Mars*, 228.

23 Bertrand Goldschmidt, *Pionniers de l'atome* (Paris: Stock, 1987), 174–75. Goldschmidt and Pregel were on cordial terms in 1941–43, and Pregel even gave Goldschmidt, a chemist, a job, as outlined below.

24 When Sengier and Lechien went to New York in October 1939, they left a fellow named van Stappen in charge of UMHK's radium department. Van Stappen was close to Pregel and gave him 50 milligrams of company radium at some point during that winter. During the same period, the two also sold radium to the Germans as part of a complicated balancing of debts and assets between Pregel and the company. When the Germans invaded Belgium, van Stappen packed up his department's radium and headed south to Bordeaux. The radium was divided, and Pregel received 550 milligrams to take to the United States. As for van Stappen, he remained in charge of radium in Brussels during the German occupation. At the end of the war, fellow employees accused him of collaborating with the Germans and he was dismissed. The transaction may have been compensation for shares Pregel had owned in Auer Gesellschaft in Berlin. It led the British Ministry of Economic Warfare to consider placing Pregel on its blacklist of individuals and firms dealing with Germany, though no action was taken. The deal was covered by the cartel agreement, which meant that Eldorado got 40 percent of the profit. "Retrait du radium de France," 6 September 1944. Although the memorandum refers to authorship by "les soussignés" (the undersigned), their names do not appear.

25 Edgar Sengier, letter to N.F. Hall, 24 April 1941, transcribed in handwritten memorandum by Michael Perrin, date illegible but possibly as late as April 1943, NA, AB1/541. See "B. Pregel and C. Chilowsky," 23 October 1942, NA, AB1/541. The report included details from the Federal Bureau of Investigation, which had been shadowing Pregel for some time. Much of the information about Pregel seems to have been unfiltered, but it is a good indication of the view of US intelligence, probably the FBI. Lechien left for Central America in December 1941.

26 See J. Grant Glassco to C.D. Howe, Report on Eldorado Investigation, 1 April 1947, Library and Archives Canada (LAC), RG 134, Glassco Commission Investigation, Eldorado Canada fonds, vol 140, file Glassco – 1947, 6.

27 Snyder stepped down for unknown reasons, but there are indications he was less than willing to go as he filed a lawsuit over unpaid expenses. In 1940, Snyder still held more than 19,000 shares personally and a great deal more stock institutionally. When French took his place he also got a seat on the board. Glassco, Report, 1 April 1947, 7.

28 A copy of the contract is in NA, AB1/541.

29 Bothwell, *Eldorado*, 92–95; C.J. Mackenzie, diary entry, 12 April 1943, LAC, MG 30, B122.

30 Wallace Akers, letter to Michael Perrin, 7 August 1942, NA, AB1/541. Akers conveyed the view of the British Ministry of Health that UMHK controlled Eldorado. He doubted the story but mistakenly conceded that the cartel gave UMHK control of Eldorado's radium sales. The misunderstanding suggests the level of inaccurate information then in circulation about the radium and uranium industry.

31 See David Zimmerman, "The Tizard Mission and the Development of the Atomic Bomb," *War in History* 2, 3 (1995): 259–73. By spring 1940, the Americans had reached "the same level of indifference" as the British but then began to realize the feasibility of an atomic weapon.

32 Brion and Moreau, *De la mine à Mars*, 230. They got this information from the UMHK Papers, so Sengier and Lechien most likely knew of it at the time.

33 "The Frisch-Peierls Memorandum," March 1940, https://web.stanford.edu/class/history5n/FPmemo.pdf.

34 Glassco, Report, 1 April 1947, 7.

35 Letter to Sir Edward Appleton, 1 December 1941; Dominions Office, letter to G.P. Thomson, 9 December 1941; Thomson, letter to Office of Scientific Research and Development, 16 December 1941; Carl French, letter to D.W. Boyce, National Research Council, 18 December 1941; J.T. Jackson, letter to Michael Perrin, 23 December 1941, all in NA, AB1/80. The purchase was finally authorized on 6 January 1942. British purchases in Canada were financed from outright gifts of money or war loans from Canada to Britain.

36 Murphree's Wiki biography is sketchy and does not say that he had acquired a doctorate despite various references to him as such by Lyman Briggs and Boris Pregel. See LAC, RG 134, vol 140, file Glassco Doc – 434; a Briggs telegram to Gilbert LaBine, 26 December 1941; Boris Pregel to E.V. Murphree, 29 January 1942. Murphree had joined Standard Oil in 1930 and returned there at the end of the war. When we refer to the uranium that was being traded during the war by Eldorado or UMHK, it is in all cases triuranium octoxide (U_3O_8). It was produced in varying degrees of purity and had to be reprocessed in most cases in the United States.

37 Briggs to LaBine, 26 December 1941. See also Lyman Briggs to Boris Pregel, 24 December 1941, NARA, RG 227, vol 85, file CRUC.

38 Gilbert LaBine to Boris Pregel, 6 March 1942, LAC, RG 134, vol 140, file Glassco Doc – 434.

39 Eger V. Murphree to Gilbert LaBine, 4 February 1942, LAC, RG 134, vol 140, file Glassco Doc – 434.

40 G.P. Thomson, letter to Wallace Akers, 5 March 1942, NA, AB1/541. At this stage, the British were just beginning to take a specific interest in Eldorado.

41 Gilbert LaBine to Eger V. Murphree, 7 February 1942, LAC, RG 134, vol 140, file Glassco Doc – 434.

42 The Szilard papers at the University of California, San Diego, contain a file of correspondence with Pregel, mostly concerning the procurement of radium and U_3O_8 for experiments. In that connection, Szilard seems to have paid a visit to Port Hope. The uranium oxide (U_3O_8) was available for rental. Letters exchanged between the two in the 1950s were warm in tone.

43 Compton had won the Nobel Prize in physics in 1927, and for most of his career he was a professor of physics at the University of Chicago. In November 1941, he produced a report that argued positively for the feasibility of an atomic weapon. In April 1942, he began to work with the Office of Scientific Research and Development project.

44 NA, AB1/128.

45 Boris Pregel to Gilbert LaBine, 4 March 1942, LAC, RG 134, vol 140, file Glassco Doc – 434.

46 Boris Pregel to Gilbert LaBine, 6 March 1942, LAC, RG 134, vol 140, file Glassco Doc – 434.

47 Bothwell, *Eldorado*, 98.

Chapter 5: Allies and Rivals in the North Atlantic Triangle

1 Sir Alexander Cadogan, permanent undersecretary at the Foreign Office, quoted in Clyde Sanger, *Malcolm MacDonald: Bringing an End to Empire* (Montreal and Kingston: McGill-Queen's University Press, 1995), 201.

2 Sanger, *Malcolm MacDonald*, discusses MacDonald's female attachments, which were constant.

3 Thomson was regarded as a superb committee chair, someone who listened to his interlocutors and worked ceaselessly to achieve consensus among his colleagues. His warm and open personality helped considerably, both in England and in Canada. He had come to Canada for family reasons. Graham Farmelo, *Churchill's Bomb: How the United States Overtook Britain in the First Nuclear Arms Race* (New York: Basic Books, 2013), 157–58.

4 William Lyon Mackenzie King, diary entry, 15 June 1942, Library and Archives Canada (LAC), MG 26-J13, item 17409, Diaries of William Lyon Mackenzie King; Michael Perrin, interview by Robert Bothwell, c. 1982, quoted by Bothwell in *Eldorado: Canada's National Uranium Company* (Toronto: University of Toronto Press, 1984), 120.

5 Sydney Halter, formerly of the C.D. Howe Company, interview by Nancy Perozzo, 21 July 2010, https://friendsofgrainelevators.org/wp-content/uploads/2024/03/HALTER-Transcript.pdf.

6 "Minister" is a diplomatic rank as well as a position. In the 1940s, ministers headed legations – similar in every respect to embassies. Embassies, however, were reserved for important countries, a level Canada achieved only as a result of its outstanding war effort. Today all countries are assumed to be important, and legations have vanished from diplomacy.

7 J.P. Moffat, letters to Secretary of State, 9 September 1940 and 26 February 1941, National Archives and Records Administration, United States, RG 59, Records of the State Department, 842.002/105 and 842.002/107.

8 Robert Bothwell and William Kilbourn, *C.D. Howe, a Biography* (Toronto: McClelland and Stewart, 1980), 115.

9 Ibid, 143–49.

10 In July 1941 and again in 1943, Howe was so exhausted that he was sent off on vacation. On both occasions his colleagues and associates feared that his condition affected his

judgment. C.J. Mackenzie, diary entry, 13 July 1943, LAC, MG 30, B122; Bothwell and Kilbourn, *Howe*, 162–64.

11 Mackenzie already knew two members of the British delegation when he met them in Howe's office on 15 June 1942. G.P. Thomson had been assigned as liaison officer to Canada, based at Mackenzie's National Research Council, and in the small world of official Ottawa, he knew and liked Malcolm MacDonald.

12 William McElhone, interview by Bothwell, 5 August 1981, University of Toronto Archives, Robert Selkirk Bothwell fonds.

13 C.J. Mackenzie, diary entry, 19 February 1942, LAC, MG 30, B122.

14 Wilfrid Eggleston, *Canada's Nuclear Story* (Toronto: Clarke, Irwin, 1965), 45. Eggleston's source was almost certainly Mackenzie.

15 See Bothwell and Kilbourn, *Howe*, 161, for an attempted departmental coup. Howe's position within the government was not guaranteed. He stopped a prominent industrialist turned wartime administrator from supplanting him in 1940–41, thereby enhancing his prestige and his standing with the prime minister, who admired Howe's skill in disposing of his would-be rival.

16 Lesslie Thomson, memorandum summarizing his wartime service, 1947, McGill University Archives, Montreal, Lesslie Rielle Thomson fonds.

17 The reader may have trouble believing this. The story, however, came from John Proctor in an interview by Robert Bothwell in Toronto, n.d. Proctor later became president of a major Canadian bank, and had a reputation for competence and probity.

18 Carl French, letter to Boris Pregel, 11 February 1943, transcribed by the RCMP, file G-355-0-5, Eldorado Mining and Refining Ltd., LAC, RG 18, vol. Waste Not Wanted Inc.

19 *Northern Miner*, special supplement, 25 June 1942, 62 and 168.

20 This analysis draws on Lesslie Thomson's report to the minister in 1946, as found in the Lesslie Rielle Thomson fonds in the McGill University Archives. Thomson started to draw conclusions about Eldorado and LaBine and French in mid-1943, when he was called in to examine the management of the company's contracts with the Americans.

21 See, for example, "Don't Quote Me," *Toronto Star*, 1 September 1942, 15, a regular mining column that reported the closing of LaBine's Gunnar mine in central Manitoba. It was impossible to continue, LaBine told shareholders, due to government restrictions on supplies and labour. In this and other enterprises LaBine was associated with the speculator Joe Hirshhorn.

22 See correspondence from February 1944, National Archives, United Kingdom, Records of the United Kingdom Atomic Energy Authority and its predecessors, AB1/541.

23 The hotel was built in 1917 and featured various services for its tenants, such as a kitchen on the second floor that sent meals up to their apartments via dumb waiter. On the ground floor was a chic restaurant, the Café des Artistes. Notable tenants included Isadora Duncan, Noel Coward, Rudolph Valentino, and Alla Nazimova.

24 Peter M. Rutkoff and William B. Scott, "The French in New York: Resistance and Structure," *Social Research* 50, 1 (1983): 185–214, covers the functioning of the École. See also François Chaubet and Emmanuelle Loyer, "L'École libre des hautes études de New York: Exil et résistance intellectuelle (1942–1946)," *Revue historique* 302, 4 (2000): 939-72. The Rockefeller Foundation and the New School together provided for the École.

25 Bertrand Goldschmidt, *Pionniers de l'atome* (Paris: Stock, 1987), 125, 171–72. The European scientists were employed directly by Pregel in such humble tasks as filling radium tubes, to be sold on to hospitals or to industry.

26 House Un-American Activities Committee, HUAC Notes, 1950, University of Iowa, Special Collections, Henry A. Wallace Papers, box 6. By spring 1944, Pregel had so ingratiated himself with Wallace that the vice-president asked for his help in organizing an official trip to Russia and China. Pregel gave him radium-treated portraits of Josef Stalin, Chiang Kai-Shek, and Chiang's wife, Soong Mei-ling, to present to his hosts on behalf of the United States. He also gave Wallace radioactive gifts for personal use, including a pad for an injured knee and a pair of luminous watches for his wife and him. The gifts drew on Pregel's signature enterprise involving radium, the Canadian Radium and Uranium Corporation. See, for example, Wallace, letter to Boris Pregel, 20 April 1944 and Pregel to Wallace, 8 May 1944, Franklin Delano Roosevelt Library, Hyde Park, New York, Henry Wallace Papers, container 58.

27 Francis Henri Jean Siegfried Perrin, interview by Spencer Weart, 11 and 15 November 1977, New York, Niels Bohr Library and Archives, American Institute of Physics, Maryland, https://www.aip.org/history-programs/niels-bohr-library/oral-histories.

Chapter 6: Opening Eldorado for Business Again

1 The British seem not to have pieced together that the mine was re-opening because of the substantial order placed by the US Army.

2 René Brion and Jean-Louis Moreau, *De la mine à Mars: La genèse de Umicore* (Tielt, Belgium: Uitgeverij Lannoo, 2006), 232.

3 Ibid, 233.

4 Ibid, 232.

5 Jack Greenberg, Eldorado's counsel, was among them. Reading later legal engagements, it seems likely that Pregel and French also consulted two Canadian senators who were lawyers familiar with the mining industry: Joe Bench of St. Catharines and W.H. McGuire of Toronto. Both were Liberals, though that does not seem to have meant a connection to the Liberal ministers in Ottawa.

6 Kenneth D. Nichols, *The Road to Trinity: A Personal Account of How America's Nuclear Policies Were Made* (New York: Morrow, 1987), 43–44. The Bohemian Grove meeting involved the S-1 Executive Committee, chaired by Conant. The Manhattan Engineering District came under the remit of the committee.

7 See the perceptive biography of Groves by Robert S. Norris, *Racing for the Bomb: General Leslie R. Groves, the Manhattan Project's Indispensable Man* (South Royalton, VT: Steerforth Press, 2002).

8 That included the British historian Margaret Gowing, whose official history of the British atomic project Groves preferred to the American counterpart. See *Britain and Atomic Energy 1939–1945* (London: Macmillan, 1964). Groves has been suspected of anti-Semitism, a not uncommon trait within society more generally at the time, but the charge is doubtful. If so, he made exceptions for people he got to know, like, and trust. For example, his chief scientist, Robert Oppenheimer, and Bertrand Goldschmidt were Jewish. Groves also urged the French Goldschmidt to stay in North America and become an American.

9 W.E. McClelland to N.T.G. Hackett, "Order Respecting Uranium and Radium," 20 January 1943, Library and Archives Canada (LAC), RG 28A, Records of the Department of Munitions and Supply, vol 237, file 196-8-2-42. We are indebted to Tristan Cullum for this reference.

10 Brief, Secret, Eldorado Mining & Refining Ltd., 1 August 1946, O.G. 146/117 45D 1284-E-1, LAC, RG 18, vol Waste Not Wanted Inc. (WNW).
11 Nichols, *Road to Trinity*, 43.
12 "Note pour Monsieur Coupez," 13 July 1946, UMHK Papers, Belgian State Archives, Brussels.
13 A memorandum summarizing a conversation with two State Department officials on 1 September 1942 states that Sengier did not want to give a monopoly to "Canadian Uranium" if possible. But by "Canadian Uranium," he meant CRUC and Pregel, not Eldorado more generally. See Brion and Moreau, *De la mine à Mars*, 232 and 451n38.
14 Memorandum, n.d., WDW. The memorandum, whose typeface matches other, similar documents, is almost certainly from the security branch of the Manhattan Engineering District (MED). The sources cited are from Pregel's International Rare Metals company. The army was either intercepting Pregel's correspondence or had surreptitiously copied his office files. The circumstances behind the memorandum's creation are discussed below.
15 Record of a meeting held in the Lord President's room, 12 October 1942; [Michael Perrin], "B. Pregel and G. Chilowsky," 23 October 1942, LAC, MG 27, C.D. Howe fonds (Howe Papers), vol 12, file S-8-2(32).
16 Michael Perrin, letter to Wallace Akers, 7 August 1942, National Archives, United Kingdom, Records of the United Kingdom Atomic Energy Authority and its predecessors, AB1/47.
17 We cannot be certain that it was a joint composition, but the content could only have come from Pregel, even if the fluent English is not characteristic of his arrogant but obsequious style. C.D. Howe, letter to Malcolm MacDonald, 11 January 1943, and MacDonald to Howe, 19 January 1943, which enclosed the French–Pregel response that Howe had sent on to him, "Memorandum Re: Boris Pregel," Howe Papers, vol 12, file S-8-2(32). LaBine most likely simply signed what was put before him, which was his standard practice.
18 C.D. Howe, letter to Gilbert LaBine, 26 May 1943, LAC, RG 134, Glassco Commission Investigation, Eldorado Canada fonds, file 1-75-U-12; Gilbert LaBine, letter to C.D. Howe, 28 May 1943, Howe Papers, vol 12, file S-8-2(31).
19 Nichols, *Road to Trinity*, 97.
20 Ibid.
21 Nichols, *Road to Trinity*, 98.
22 C.J. Mackenzie, diary entry, 26 July 1943, LAC, MG 30, B122.
23 Howe may have been pressed by Lesslie Thomson, who reported on the Ventures (US Army) claims in August 1943. As noted, however, Howe already knew of these claims in July.
24 The order in council was issued in the *Canada Gazette*, 25 September 1943, 3991–92, 7168, pursuant to s 130 of the *Regulations for the Disposal of Quartz Mining Claims on Dominion Lands in the Northwest Territories*, approved by Order in Council P.C. 507 [possibly 307], 4 March 1932, effective from 2 April 1932, *Yukon Quartz Mining Act*, RSC 1927, c 217.
25 Lesslie Thomson, memorandum to Howe, 1946, McGill University Archives, Montreal, Lesslie Rielle Thomson, 1886–1958 fonds. Thomson recorded the fact but not the date or the subject of their conversation.
26 Ibid.
27 "Recording of a conversation between Brigadier General Leslie Groves and Mr. Boris Pregel at a conference Monday 25 October 1943," National Archives and Records Administration, RG 77, file Boris Pregel.

Chapter 7: From State Secrets to Corporate Fraud

1 Canada, *House of Commons Debates*, 19th Parl, 5th Sess, vol 1 (28 January 1944), 6 (Hon. C.D. Howe). All the shares in the company were formally expropriated by an order in council dated 27 January 1944, issued under the *War Measures Act*, RSC 1927, c 206. Henceforth, the company was known formally as Eldorado Mining and Refining (1944) Limited and incorporated by Letters Patent 30 June 1945 under part 1 of *The Companies Act*, 1934, 24–25 Geo V, c 33. On 1 August 1946, the Governor in Council issued a proclamation directing that the *Government Companies Operation Act*, 1946, 10 Geo VI, c 24, apply to the company.

2 The few attempts the Germans made to embed spies in Canada failed, and the other enemy powers fared no better. That did not stop governments in Canada and the United States from interning members of those communities, especially the Japanese. See, for example, "World War II Enemy Alien Control Program Overview" in the United States (https://www.archives.gov/research/immigration/enemy-aliens/ww2), and Eric M. Adams and Jordan Stanger-Ross, *Challenging Exile: Japanese Canadians and the Wartime Constitution* (Vancouver: UBC Press, 2025).

3 3 Geo VI c 49.

4 Terrence Guernsey, interview by Robert Bothwell, c. 1981, University of Toronto Archives, Robert Selkirk Bothwell fonds. RDX, also known as hexogen and by various other names, stood for Research Department Explosive or Royal Demolitions Explosive.

5 *The Canada Year Book, 1943–1944*, D.B.S. 4-1100P (Ottawa: Census and Statistics Office, 1944), 1005–6.

6 Fraser Reid interview by Terrence Guernsey, 31 May 1946, Library and Archives Canada (LAC), RG 18, vol Waste Not Wanted Inc. (WNW).

7 Terrence Guernsey, evidence at trial proceedings, *George Heighington et al v Her Majesty the Queen in Right of Ontario*, Action No: 6476/83, Appeal No: 354/88, *Heighington* Transcript of Testimony, 146–47 (Court of Appeal Record); Guernsey, interview, n.d.

8 Guernsey, evidence, *Heighington* Transcript of Testimony, 147.

9 Ibid, 148.

10 After the war he was sent for formal intelligence training in England and then moved permanently into the security field. When he returned to Ottawa, he moved swiftly through the ranks, culminating in the senior rank of superintendent.

11 John Sawatsky, *Men in the Shadows: The Shocking Truth about the RCMP Security Service* (Doubleday Canada, 1980; repr. Totem Books, 1983), 100. The quotation is from Charles Sweeny.

12 Pochon had become a naturalized citizen in late 1936, unlike French, who kept his American nationality.

13 Terrence Guernsey, "Marcel Leon Pochon – Eldorado Mining & Refining Ltd., Port Hope, Ontario," 24 November 1944, WNW.

14 J. Grant Glassco to C.D. Howe, Report on Eldorado Investigation, 1 April 1947, LAC, RG 134, Glassco Commission Investigation, Eldorado Canada fonds, vol 140, file Glassco – 1947, 2.

15 Ibid, 9.

16 Ibid, 4–5; "Lawyer Carl French Was among the First to Know of A-bomb," Obituaries, *Sunday Star* (Toronto), 22 April 1984, A10.

17 Christopher Armstrong, *Blue Skies and Boiler Rooms: Buying and Selling Securities in Canada, 1870–1940* (Toronto: University of Toronto Press, 1997), ch 12.

18 Terrence Guernsey, Report to Inspector W.H. Williams, 31 January 1945, WNW.
19 George Bateman, letter to C.D. Howe, 30 March 1945, WNW.
20 Ibid.
21 Glassco, Report, 1 April 1947, 2–3.
22 Ibid, 6–9. Lesslie Thomson, letter to Gilbert LaBine, 18 January 1945, LAC, RG 28A, Records of the Department of Munitions and Supply, vol 175.
23 Robert S. Norris, *Racing for the Bomb: General Leslie R. Groves, the Manhattan Project's Indispensable Man* (South Royalton, VT: Steerforth Press, 2002), 368ff; Vincent C. Jones, *Manhattan, the Army and the Atomic Bomb* (Washington, DC: Center of Military History, US Army, 1985), ch 11.
24 Whitaker's career with the Secret Service spanned forty-six years. He joined in 1930, then enlisted during the war, leaving the army as a captain in 1946. He ended his career as the head of the New York office. "Albert Whitaker, 82, Secret Service Official," *New York Times*, 22 August 1990, D21.
25 A French scientist not to be confused with the British Michael Perrin.
26 This analysis derives from the accounts of Groves's intelligence operation in Norris, *Racing for the Bomb*, and Jones, *Manhattan*.
27 Alexander Pregel, interview by Vilma Hunt, n.d., Arthur and Elizabeth Schlesinger Library on the History of Women in America, Radcliffe Institute for Advanced Study, Harvard University, Papers of Vilma R. Hunt, file 71.6 Writings – The Uranium Merchants, letters to A&E Pregel, 1995–99 and file 72.1 Writings – The Uranium Merchants, research and notes 1990–98.
28 Phillip Merritt, interview by Robert Bothwell, n.d., University of Toronto Archives, Robert Selkirk Bothwell fonds.
29 William McElhone, interview by Bothwell, 5 August 1981, University of Toronto Archives, Robert Selkirk Bothwell fonds.
30 The details that follow are taken from Bateman, letter to Howe, 30 March 1945.
31 The following account is based on Terrence Guernsey, memorandum re National Research Council, Toronto and Hamilton, 4 April 1945, WNW.
32 The RCMP was responsible for investigating offences involving the orders of the FECB, which had its own inspectors but may have relied on the policing organization for muscle. The FECB records on the matter appear to have been destroyed, so the link between the RCMP document raid and Guernsey's routine probe of the newly minted Crown corporation Eldorado has to be reconstructed to a certain extent. One version, based on the personal recollection of one of the individuals involved, suggests that an FECB clerk spotted unusual transactions and alerted his superiors.
33 F.A. Blake, letter to RCMP Inspector W.H. Williams, 25 April 1945, WNW.
34 Guernsey, memorandum, 4 April 1945.
35 W.H. Williams, letter to John Lansdale, 9 April 1945, WNW.
36 Guernsey, memorandum re Eldorado Mining and Refining Ltd., 1 May 1945, WNW. The memo contains letter excerpts as evidence of various sham transactions between supposedly arm's-length companies, such as from Pregel to W. Horn, 12 April 1943, and from Joseph Harris of International Rare Metals Refinery Inc. to Radium Luminous Industries Ltd., 18 December 1943.
37 Guernsey, memorandum, 1 May 1945.
38 Guernsey, memoranda re Eldorado Mining and Refining Ltd., 20 April 1945 and 1 May 1945, WNW.

39 Guernsey, memorandum, 20 April 1945: "On the Balance Sheet at September 30, 1944 this amount [of radium] is shown for a total cost of $135,310.14. It is the only asset owned by the corporation against its capital stock of $150,000."
40 Guernsey, memorandum, 1 May 1945.
41 Guernsey, memorandum, 20 April 1945.
42 Ibid.
43 Ibid; F.J. Mead, Deputy Commissioner, RCMP, letter to Lesslie Thomson, 3 May 1945, WNW.
44 W.H. Williams, memorandum for the Deputy Minister, 30 April 1945, WNW.
45 Memorandum of information desired and points to be established in connection with the proposed new Eldorado sales agency contract, 20 November 1944, Appendix B. LAC, RG 28, Records of the Department of Munitions and Supply, vol 176, file 4-1-491.
46 J.J. Robinette, interview, vol 1, 18 June 1987, Osgoode Society for Canadian Legal History, Oral History Program, 222–26, https://www.osgoodesociety.ca/oral-history/john-j-robinette-1987.
47 "Younger Robinette Unlike Fiery Father," *Sarnia Observer*, 6 February 1968.
48 McElhone, interview, 5 August 1981.
49 Guernsey, memorandum, 1 May 1945; Williams, memorandum for the Deputy Minister, 30 April 1945.
50 McElhone, interview, 5 August 1981.
51 Lesslie Thomson, letter to S.T. Wood, 30 April 1945, WNW; Williams, memorandum for the Deputy Minister, 30 April 1945; F.A. Blake, letter to Commissioner S.T. Wood, 5 May 1945, WNW; F.A. Blake, letter to S.T. Wood, 9 May 1945, WNW.
52 Guernsey, memorandum re Eldorado Mining and Refining, 9 May 1945, WNW. The interview was re-scheduled to May 10th but did not occur at that time.
53 LAC, RG 2 Privy Council Office Records, series 1, vol 2268, PC 3329, 7 May 1945.
54 (1939), 3 Geo VI, c 3 (amended 1940, c 31; 1943–44, c 8). See "Amendment subsection 1 of section 22 of Department of Munitions and Supply Act re inquiries in 'munitions contracts,'" LAC, RG 2 Privy Council Office Records, vol 1848, PC 2989, 8 May 1944.
55 The scope of the investigation involved "any or all matters relating to or incidental to or arising out of the affairs and operations of Eldorado and the sales or disposition of its products (including, without limiting the generality of the foregoing, any or all matters relating to or incidental to or arising out of any sales or sales agency agreements entered into by Eldorado)."
56 RSC 1927, c 99, s 11.
57 As amended by PC 2989, 8 May 1944; PC 3329, 7 May 1945.
58 PC 3329, 7 May 1945. The *Department of Munitions and Supply Act* was amended 8 May 1944 by PC 2989 under the authority of the *War Measures Act* to confer the powers that were relied on to issue PC 3329, to investigate Eldorado under the *Department of Munitions and Supply Act*.
59 "Glassco, J. Grant," *Canadian Who's Who 1952–54*, vol 6 (Toronto: Trans-Canada Press, 1954).

Chapter 8: Follow the Money, Find the Radium

1 "Start Inquiry into Affairs of Eldorado Mine Co.," *Ottawa Citizen*, 10 July 1945, 17.
2 Terrence Guernsey, memorandum re Eldorado Mining and Refining, 29 June 1945, Library and Archives Canada, RG 18, vol Waste Not Wanted Inc. (WNW).

3 Summary of the meeting held in Ottawa on Tuesday, 29 May 1945, Copy No. 4, WNW.
4 Canada, Department of Munitions and Supply, *Canadian War Orders and Regulations: A Consolidation as of January 1, 1944* (Ottawa: Edmond Cloutier, 1944), 202, Metals Controller Order No. 42, 4 February 1943.
5 The contents of the documents, and the conclusions reached, are outlined in the summary of the meeting, 29 May 1945.
6 The group's conclusions are detailed in Guernsey, memorandum re Eldorado Mining and Refining, 1 June 1945, WNW.
7 Lesslie Thomson, letter to S.T. Wood, 5 June 1945, WNW.
8 Guernsey, memorandum re Eldorado Mining and Refining, 7 June 1945, WNW.
9 Leslie Cook, evidence at trial proceedings, *George Heighington et al v Her Majesty the Queen in Right of Ontario*, Action No: 6476/83, Appeal No: 354/88, *Heighington* Transcript of Testimony, 123 (Court of Appeal Record).
10 Ibid, 124.
11 Cook's recollections, including of French's explanation, are from ibid, 125–28.
12 Guernsey, memorandum, 7 June 1945, which included Cook's report.
13 Ibid.
14 See Bruce A. MacFarlane, Director, Legal Services – RCMP, cover memorandum to D.C.I., Re: *Waste Not Wanted Inc. v. The Queen et al*, 21 August 1984, reference to letter dated 8 June 1945 from the Foreign Exchange Control Board to the Deputy Minister of Health, WNW.
15 Guernsey, memorandum re Eldorado Mining and Refining, 4 July 1945, WNW.
16 Guernsey, memorandum, 7 June 1945.
17 Ibid.
18 Guernsey, memorandum re Eldorado Mining and Refining, 9 June 1945, WNW.
19 Ibid.
20 Ibid. The official was Dr. Elson, a physicist working at the Department of Health and also for Carl French at Radium Luminous Industries.
21 J.M. Clish, memorandum re Eldorado Mining and Refining, 27 June 1945, WNW.
22 Guernsey, memorandum, 29 June 1945; Margaret Talbot, "J. Edgar Hoover, Public Enemy No. 1," *New Yorker*, 14 November 2022.
23 Compare Guernsey, memoranda, 29 June 1945 and 4 July 1945, WNW.
24 Guernsey, memorandum, 29 June 1945.
25 Ibid.
26 Ibid. Pregel focused on LaBine's supposedly secret correspondence with Howe, claiming that Eldorado's president had belittled him to the minister because he was unduly influenced by Thomson's views. Pregel complained that Thomson held a grudge against him and was bent on making him pay. He asserted that the RCMP had been lying to Walter Winchell, the American gossip columnist and journalist with a popular broadcast. As Pregel complained to Slaght, Winchell had told his listeners that Pregel had more radium than the enemy, information only the RCMP could have had.
27 The following discussion is based on Guernsey, memoranda, 29 June 1945 and 4 July 1945.
28 An inventory was also taken at the Scarborough farm on 29 June 1945: 3.37 grams of radium in ashes, and a further 1.67 grams distributed between nineteen barrels, nine wooden cases, twenty-six boxes, and a few other containers. See *Heighington v R* (1987), 60 OR (2d) 648.
29 W.E. Kelley, letter to J.G. Glassco, 9 July 1945, Library and Archives Canada (LAC), RG 134, Glassco Commission Investigation, Eldorado Canada fonds, vol 140, file Glassco – Corresp – US Engineers.

30 Slaght liked to say that King had offered him the roles of justice minister and attorney general but he turned them down. That was untrue as well as implausible. The justice portfolio went to the oldest and most important of King's colleagues, Ernest Lapointe, and then to a star recruit from Quebec, Louis St. Laurent, a former president of the Canadian Bar Association. Slaght was not in their league.

31 Charlotte Gray, *Murdered Midas: A Millionaire, His Gold Mine, and a Strange Death on an Island Paradise* (Toronto: HarperCollins, 2019).

32 Ronald Slaght, interview, 2010, Osgoode Society for Canadian Legal History, Oral History Program, 4–7.

33 See, for example, Ian Kyer, *The Ontario Bond Scandal of 1924 Re-examined* (Toronto: Irwin Law, 2023); Katie Daubs, *The Missing Millionaire: The True Story of Ambrose Small and the City Obsessed with Finding Him*; Constance Backhouse and Nancy L. Backhouse, *The Heiress vs the Establishment: Mrs. Campbell's Campaign for Legal Justice* (Vancouver: UBC Press, 2004).

34 Slaght's obituary says he won twenty-nine, based on a comment from his grandson, Ronald Slaght, but other contemporary newspapers put the figure at the more likely nineteen.

35 Slaght, interview, 2010, 3.

36 Ibid, 9–10.

37 "Rupert Davies One of Three New Senators," *Globe and Mail*, 20 November 1942; "John Joseph Bench: Young Senator, Leading Lawyer and Civic Worker," *Globe and Mail*, 10 December 1947.

38 Joseph Sedgwick, interview, 1981, Osgoode Society for Canadian Legal History, Oral History Program, 13.

39 Ibid, 6–7.

40 "A Great Canadian Advocate, Dead at 83," *Globe and Mail*, 28 December 1981, 20.

41 Ibid.

42 The Glassco report indicates that the interviews began 25 June 1945, but the contemporaneous RCMP reports put the date at 10 July, subpoenas having been served on the earlier date. See J. Grant Glassco to C.D. Howe, Report on Eldorado Investigation, 1 April 1947, LAC, RG 134, vol 140, file Glassco – 1947, 3; Guernsey, memorandum re Eldorado Mining and Refining, 4 July 1945.

43 LAC, RG 2 Privy Council Office Records, series 1, vol 2268, PC 3329, 7 May 1945.

44 LAC, RG 2, Privy Council Office Records, series 1, vol. 1649, PC 5782, 5 September 1945.

Chapter 9: Going Public

1 Terrence Guernsey, memorandum re Eldorado Mining and Refining, 14 September 1945, Library and Archives Canada (LAC), RG 18, vol Waste Not Wanted Inc. (WNW).

2 Ibid.

3 Guernsey, memoranda re Eldorado Mining and Refining, 14 September 1945 and 20 November 1945, WNW.

4 Not only did CRUC lack refining capacity, so did International Rare Metals at the relevant time. The Glassco report found no evidence that International Rare Metals operated a refinery at Mount Kisco, New York, when this arrangement was made. The existence of a refining capacity at Mount Kisco in late 1943 is found in the *Minerals Yearbook for 1947*, which was published in 1949. There was no reference to a refining capacity at Mount Kisco in the prior year's publication. See E.W. Pehrson, *Minerals Yearbook 1947* (Washington, DC: Bureau of Mines: United States Government Printing Office, 1949), 1203.

5 J. Grant Glassco to C.D. Howe, Report on Eldorado Investigation, 1 April 1947, LAC, RG 134, vol 140, file Glassco – 1947, 16–20.
6 Guernsey, memorandum, 14 September 1945.
7 Glassco, Report, 1 April 1947, 18.
8 Ibid.
9 Glassco, Report, 1 April 1947, 4.
10 Ibid.
11 "Court Asked to Void Order to Probe Eldorado Mines – Firms Want Ottawa Orders in Council Declared Ultra Vires – Held Drastic," *Evening Telegram* (Toronto), 20 October 1945.
12 Guernsey, memorandum re Eldorado Mining and Refining, 21 October 1945, WNW.
13 "Demands Secrets Disclosed in Eldorado Probe Order, Opposition Wants It Produced in Commons – Powers Granted Said 'Inquisitorial,'" *Evening Telegram* (Toronto), 25 October 1945.
14 H.R. Armstrong, "Ontario Firms Try to Stop Uranium Probe," *Toronto Daily Star*, 25 October 1945, 1.
15 The Star Chamber, a secretive and unaccountable court used in sixteenth- and seventeenth-century England, has come to be associated with arbitrary and oppressive use of state power.
16 "Eldorado Report Near, Howe States, as Suits Brought to Nullify Probe," *Globe and Mail*, metropolitan ed., 26 October 1945, 1.
17 Wellington Jeffers, "Private Enterprise Helped Mightily to Produce Atomic Bomb; Should Its Energy and Initiative Not Be Enlisted to Use Atomic Energy for Good?," *Globe and Mail*, 26 October 1945, 18.
18 "Royal Commission on Eldorado Asked," *Evening Telegram* (Toronto), 26 October 1945.
19 Howe spoke in the House of Commons on 26 October 1945, and the two orders in council were tabled that day. Canada, *House of Commons Debates*, 20th Parl, 1st Sess, vol 2 (26 October 1945), 1520 (Hon. C.D. Howe).
20 J.H. Fisher, "Power of Sweeping Scope Given to Eldorado Prober Orders in Council Reveal," *Evening Telegram* (Toronto), 27 October 1945.
21 Kenneth Wilson, "Court Action Raises Lid on Radium Embroglio," *Financial Post* (Toronto), 27 October 1945, 1–2.
22 Canada, *House of Commons Debates*, 20th Parl, 1st Sess, vol 2 (1 November 1945), 1704–5.
23 The Nation's Business, "Let Us Use Normal Democratic Methods," *Financial Post* (Toronto), 3 November 1945.
24 LAC, RG 2 Privy Council Office Records, series 1, vol 1649, PC 5782, 5 September 1945, s 5.
25 "Who Is This Man Boris Pregel? World Radium Salesman for Belgians, Later for Eldorado," *Financial Post* (Toronto), 3 November 1945, 1.
26 Ibid, 8.
27 Guernsey, memorandum re Eldorado Mining and Refining, 30 November 1945, WNW.
28 Ibid.
29 9–10 Geo VI c 25.
30 "Former Eldorado Official Arrested on Five Charges," *Toronto Daily Star*, 22 December 1945, 12.
31 Ibid; "Ex-Secretary of Eldorado under Arrest," *Globe and Mail*, 22 December 1945.
32 "Former Eldorado Official Arrested," 22 December 1945, 12.

33 "Ex-Secretary of Eldorado under Arrest," 22 December 1945.

34 "Former Eldorado Official Arrested," 22 December 1945, 12.

35 *Criminal Code*, RSC 1927, c 36, s 413.

Every one is guilty of an indictable offence and liable to seven years' imprisonment who, being a director, manager, officer or member of any body corporate or company with intent to defraud,

(a) Destroys, alters, mutilates or falsifies any book, paper, writing or valuable security belonging to the body corporate or company; or

(b) Makes, or concurs in making, any false entry, or omits or concurs in omitting to enter any material particular, in any book of account or other document.

36 Section 504.

In this section, unless the context otherwise requires,

(a) "agent" means any person employed by or acting for another, and includes a person serving under the Crown or under any municipal or other corporation;

(b) "consideration" includes valuable consideration of any kind;

(c) "principal" includes an employer.

2 Every one is guilty of an offence and liable, upon conviction on indictment, to two years' imprisonment, or to a fine not exceeding two thousand five hundred dollars, or to both, and, upon summary conviction, to imprisonment for six months, with or without hard labour, or to a fine not exceeding, one hundred dollars, or both, who

(a) being an agent, corruptly accepts or obtains, or agrees to accept or attempts to obtain, from any person, for himself or for any other person, any gift or consideration as inducement or reward for doing or forbearing to do, or for having done or forborne to do, any act relating to his principal's affairs or business, or for showing or forbearing to show favour or disfavour to any person with relation to his principal's affairs or business; or

(b) corruptly gives or agrees to give or offers any gift or consideration to any agent as an inducement or reward or consideration to such agent for doing or forbearing to do, or for having done or forborne to do, any act relating to his principal's affairs or business, or for showing or forbearing to show favour or disfavour to any person with relation to his principal's affairs or business; or

(c) knowingly gives to any agent, or, being an agent, knowingly uses with intent to deceive his principal, any receipt, account, or other document in respect of which the principal is interested, and which contains any statement which is false or erroneous or defective in any material particular, and which, to his knowledge, is intended to mislead the principal.

3 Every person who is a party or knowingly privy to any offence under this section shall be guilty of such offence and shall be liable upon conviction to the punishment hereinbefore provided for by this section.

4 This section shall not apply to any person liable to punishment under section 412(2) of this Act.

37 RCMP, Brief, "Secret, Eldorado Mining & Refining Ltd.," 1 August 1946, O.G. 146/117 45D 1284-E-1, WNW.

38 See "Former Eldorado Official Arrested," 22 December 1945, 12.

39 Section 444 of the *Criminal Code* provides as follows: "Every one is guilty of an indictable offence and liable to seven years' imprisonment who conspires with any other person, by deceit or falsehood or other fraudulent means, to defraud the public or any person, ascertained or unascertained, or to affect the public market price of stocks, shares, merchandise, or anything else publicly sold, whether such deceit or falsehood or other fraudulent means would or would not amount to a false pretense as hereinbefore defined."
40 William McElhone, interview by Robert Bothwell, 5 August 1981, University of Toronto Archives, Robert Selkirk Bothwell fonds.
41 Alan Edmonds, "S. Tupper Bigelow," *Maclean's*, 1 October 1968.
42 J. Grant Glassco, letter to Pickett, 18 February 1946, LAC, RG 134, Glassco Commission Investigation, Eldorado Canada fonds, vol 140, file Glassco Correspondence – US Engineers.
43 Despite Pregel's claims to have offered assistance, the RCMP's collection of documents relating to this case contains no supporting records.
44 McElhone, interview, 5 August 1981.
45 Robinette relied on section 679(d) of the *Criminal Code:* "A justice holding a preliminary inquiry may in his discretion ... order that no person other than the prosecutor and accused, their counsel and solicitors, shall have access to or remain in the room or building in which the inquiry is held, if it appears to him that the ends of justice will be best answered by so doing."
46 "Eldorado Trial Is Secret," *Montreal Star*, 16 May 1946; "Preliminary Eldorado Hearing to Be in Camera, Court Rules," *Financial Post* (Toronto), 25 May 1946, 4.
47 *Scott v Scott*, 1913 AC 417 at 437 (UK).
48 The magistrate's unpublished decision can be found as "Rex v Pregel, French and Pochon," 16 May 1946, Hoover Institution Library and Archives, Stanford University, Robert S. Norris Collection, box 48, file Boris Pregel (Norris Papers). The appeal before Justice Barlow of the High Court of Justice was reported in *R v Pochon and French*, 1946 CanLII 628 (Ont SC), 10 CR (2d) 143.
49 Boris Pregel, letter to Leslie Groves, 14 May 1946, Norris Papers.
50 L.R. Groves, letter to Marcel Pochon, 16 May 1946, and Snapp, letter to Kenneth Nichols, 27 May 1946, both in Norris Papers.
51 "Preliminary Eldorado Hearing to Be in Camera," 25 May 1946, 4.
52 *Official Secrets Act, 1939*, SC 1939, c 49.
53 Judgment of the Court (unreported), 30 May 1946, Norris Papers.
54 *R v Pochon and French* (1946), 2 CR 143 at 144, [1946] OWN 678. Barlow J dismissed the motion at the end of the argument but wrote reasons only at the request of counsel.

Chapter 10: And Just Like That, Trial and Settlement

1 J.J. Robinette, memorandum for Mr. Glassco, 8 February 1946, Library and Archives Canada (LAC), RG 134, Glassco Commission Investigation, Eldorado Canada fonds, vol 140, file Glassco Correspondence – US Engineers; and memorandum to Eldorado, file 27 Glassco Correspondence 100-A-1-C.
2 W.J. Bennett, interview by Robert Bothwell, 1981, University of Toronto Archives, Robert Selkirk Bothwell fonds, series VI. The interview is one in a series of conversations with Bennett based on the board minutes. On one occasion, former board members Eldon Brown and Bill James joined the interview and pooled their reminiscences. The reference to LaBine's potential testimony derives from these conversations.

3 Robert Bothwell, *Eldorado: Canada's National Uranium Company* (Toronto: University of Toronto Press, 1984), 183–85.

4 Peter C. Newman, "Gilbert LaBine," *Flame of Power: Intimate Portraits of Canada's Greatest Businessmen* (Toronto: Longmans, Green, 1959), 149.

5 Memorandum to file re Eldorado Mining and Refining, Statement of Lieutenant Colonel John R. Ruhoff and Statement of Brig General K.D. Nichols, 13 May 1946, LAC, RG 18, vol Waste Not Wanted Inc. (WNW).

6 Terrence Guernsey, letter to Albert Whitaker, 21 February 1946, Hoover Institution Library and Archives, Stanford University, Robert S. Norris Collection, box 48, file Boris Pregel (Norris Papers).

7 See W.H. Pickett, letters to J. Grant Glassco, 11 and 15 February 1946, LAC, RG 134, Glassco Commission Investigation, Eldorado Canada fonds, vol 140, file Glassco Correspondence – US Engineers; Terrence Guernsey, memorandum re Meeting 3rd April 1946 in Offices of African Metals Corporation, 5 April 1946, WNW; Terrence Guernsey, letter to Lesslie Thomson, 22 March 1946, LAC, RG 134, vol 40, file 23 – Glassco Investigation 100-A-1.

8 Memorandum to file, 22 February 1946, LAC, RG 134, vol 140, file Glassco – Corresp – Tully.

9 "James Tully, 67, Lawyer, Is Dead," *New York Times*, 29 November 1964, 87.

10 Note in Tully's handwriting, 22 February 1946; James Tully, letter to Guy Jarvis, 27 February 1946, LAC, RG 134, vol 140, file Glassco – Corresp – Tully.

11 Tully quoted the US Supreme Court's classic definition of international comity from 1895 as "the recognition which one nation allows within its territory to the legislative, executive, or judicial acts of another nation, having due regard both to international duty and convenience, and to the rights of its own citizens, or of other persons who are under the protection of its laws."

12 On this point, Tully concluded, "The only exception to the foregoing that we can think of might be some treaty between the United States and Canada which would give reciprocal recognition of the acts of either Government in the prosecution of the war in such matters as terminating contract rights for purposes of the better promotion of the war." Tully, letter to Jarvis, 27 February 1946.

13 Ibid.

14 The provision states, "The sales agreement contained an arbitration clause that provided, 'Any and all disputes which may arise between the parties to this agreement shall be decided by arbitration pursuant to the rules of the International Chamber of Commerce.'" International Chamber of Commerce, *Rules of Arbitration*, 1927, art 15; *Civil Practice Act*, 1940, s 1448, art 84.

15 Tully, letter to Jarvis, 27 February 1946.

16 The property had to be personal, the plaintiff had to be entitled to immediate possession, and the defendant had to have wrongfully taken it and still have it in his or her possession when suit was brought. In practical terms, Eldorado would have to prove that it owned the radium Pregel had in his possession and that Pregel held it solely for the purposes of refining it.

17 J. Grant Glassco to C.D. Howe, Report on Eldorado Investigation, 1 April 1947, LAC, RG 134, vol 140, file Glassco – 1947, 11.

18 The letter from Gemmell on behalf of Eldorado to International Rare Metals is dated 2 November 1945 and is quoted in Tully's correspondence but has not been located elsewhere.

19 James Tully, memorandum to J. Grant Glassco, "Re: Contract dated August 20, 1943, between Eldorado Mining and Refining and International Rare Metals Refinery, Inc. for the treatment of 75 grams of radium bearing carbonate concentrate," 11 March 1946, LAC, RG 134, vol 40, file Glassco – Corresp – Tully.
20 Ibid.
21 James Tully, letter to E.B. Richards, 11 March 1946, LAC, RG 134, vol 40, file Glassco – Corresp – Tully. Writing to CRUC on 28 August, Secretary Treasurer Gemmell said the company owned the 28.6 grams of radium sent to International Rare Metals for refining. But the rest was confusing. Gemmell said that Eldorado owned this amount of radium after International delivered 1,751.675 milligrams to African Metals, which was before the shipment of approximately 7 grams of concentrate, as Gemmell noted in a letter he sent just two days later, on 30 August 1945.
22 J. Grant Glassco, letter to James Tully, 13 March 1946, RG 134, vol 40, file Glassco – Corresp – Tully.
23 That meant not just the contract dated 22 December 1942 but also the one dated 19 August 1943 and the letter of agreement of 20 August 1943.
24 The approach "is the disaffirmance or rescission of the co-adventure relationship between Eldorado and CR&U, the contract of December 22, 1942, the contract of August 19, 1943, and the letter of agreement of August 20, 1943, based upon the fraud which was perpetrated upon Eldorado by CR&U and the others acting in concert with it." James Tully, letter to J. Grant Glassco, 19 March 1946, RG 134, vol 40, file Glassco – Corresp – Tully.
25 Ibid.
26 For reference, when White & Case was founded in May 1901, other well-known firms were already well established. These included Davis Polk & Wardwell (founded 1849), Milbank, Tweed, Hadley, & McCloy (founded 1866), Shearman & Sterling (founded 1873 and as of 2024, AO Shearman), and Sullivan & Cromwell (founded 1879).
27 *White & Case: The First 100 Years and Beyond* (New York: White & Case, 2023), ch 4, https://history.whitecase.com/chapter-4-in-the-courtroom.
28 William A. Consodine, memorandum for General Groves, 7 June 1946, Subject: Conversation with Mr. Lowell Wadmond re Boris Pregel; Snapp, cover memo, 13 June 1946; General Leslie Groves, letter to Lesslie Thomson, 21 June 1946, all in Norris Papers.
29 James Tully, letter to General Leslie Groves, 22 August 1946, Norris Papers.
30 General Leslie Groves, letter to James Tully, 5 September 1946, Norris Papers.
31 The court file was technically public at the time, but it is unclear where those records were stored. Efforts to secure a copy from the archives for the purpose of this book were unsuccessful, and we were advised there was no record of this proceeding. Nonetheless, correspondence suggests the files were kept in the lawyers' offices, not the courthouse, and Pregel's lawyer persuaded the court to remove them from public records altogether when a settlement was reached in 1947.
32 T.H. Luhrman to E.B. Richards, 16 December 1946, RG 134, vol 40, file Glassco – Corresp – Tully.
33 The settlement is dated 21 February 1947, but the formal paperwork was not sent to C.D. Howe until mid-April. LAC, RG 134, vol 147, file: Glassco Commission: Trial in New York.
34 Lowell Wadmond, letter to Boris Pregel, 1 April 1947, Norris Papers.
35 Stephen N. Subrin, "Fishing Expeditions Allowed: The Historical Background of the 1938 Federal Discovery Rules," 39 BCL Rev. 691 (1997–98).

36 *White & Case: The First 100 Years*, ch 4.

37 William McElhone, interview by Robert Bothwell, 5 August 1981, Trinity College Archives, University of Toronto, Robert Selkirk Bothwell fonds.

38 James Tully, letter to C.D. Howe, 17 April 1947, RG 134, vol 147, file Glassco Commission: Trial in New York.

39 The contracts were dated 23 October 1942, 24 December 1942, 27 April 1943, and 5 August 1943.

40 A.E. Whitaker, letter to T.M. Guernsey, 11 December 1945; Lesslie Thomson, letter to F.J. Mead, 17 December 1945, WNW.

41 Phillip Merritt, interview by Robert Bothwell, New York, 1981, Robert Selkirk Bothwell fonds.

42 Although Pregel's naturalization file (A004887967 AR-2 Form, 4887967 and Naturalization Certificate C6909787) has been lost or is missing from the US Citizenship and Immigration Services records, his application for citizenship was finally approved by a US District Court judge in New York in the summer of 1950. See Daniel Edgington, letter to Patricia McMahon, 3 October 2019; Petition of Boris Pregel for admission as a citizen of the United States (No. 540687 – United States District Court, Southern District of New York), per Judge Holtzoff, 6 July 1950; Arthur Breuer, memorandum to file, 28 June 1956, National Archives and Records Administration, United States, RG 59, Records of Department of State, folder Pregel, Boris – Claim No. 35761, Confidential Security Material.

Conclusion

1 Glassco finalized his report only after the civil suit settled in the Southern District of New York in mid-April, and delivered it to C.D. Howe on 5 May 1947. James Tully, letter to C.D. Howe, 16 April 1947, Library and Archives Canada, RG 134, vol 147, file Glassco Commission: Trial in New York.

2 James Jefferson and Ross Laver, "Radioactive Traces Found in 2 Scarboro Backyards," *Globe and Mail*, 20 November 1980.

3 Walter Sullivan, "Radium-Soaked Concrete Found in Toronto Building," *New York Times*, 27 February 1975, 14.

4 *Heighington v R* (1987), 60 OR (2d) 648, 649, 653; *Planning Act*, RSO 1970, c 349, s 33(4)(c).

5 Once the battle over legal fees finished two years later, the cost had risen to $625,000. However, Ontario has a loser pays system, whereby the legal fees of the victorious party in a lawsuit are paid by their opponent. The approach is intended to encourage settlement but often results in protracted conflict over what those fees include. As a result, a so-called costs award almost never makes the victor "whole." In the case of *Heighington*, the province challenged the legal fees claimed by the plaintiffs, and an assessor was appointed to review the bill in autumn 1991. Ultimately, the matter was settled out of court at $250,000 plus interest of $75,000. One of the plaintiffs estimated they spent another $150,000 just to collect legal fees after judgment had been rendered. George R.E. Heighington, *A Radioactive Waste Dump in Malvern: A Citizen's Account* (Toronto: GH Technical Services, 2016), s 13.3.

6 *Waste Not Wanted Inc. v Canada,* [1988] 1 FC 239.

7 "Noted Radium Expert Dies at Home in Port Hope," *Daily-Times Gazette* (Oshawa), 2 May 1958, 2; "Pioneer of the Atomic Age," *Cornish Guardian* (England), 12 June 1958.

8 Penny Sanger, *Blind Faith: The Nuclear Industry in a Small Town* (Toronto: McGraw-Hill Ryerson, 1981).

9 Peter Newman, *Flame of Power: Intimate Profiles of Canada's Greatest Businessmen* (Toronto: Longmans, Green, 1959), 165.

10 "Uranium Ore Discoverer Dies," *Ottawa Journal*, 10 June 1977, 5. LaBine had suffered an immobilizing stroke in 1962.

11 Arthur Breuer, memorandum to file, 28 June 1956, National Archives and Records Administration, United States, RG 59 General Records Relating to Atomic Energy Matters, 1948–1962, folder Pregel, Boris – Claim No. 35761, Confidential Security Material. See, also, C6909787 and A004887967, available as part of the Genealogy Program at the Department of Homeland Security.

12 "Dr. Boris Pregel, Ex-head of Academy of Sciences," *New York Times*, 9 December 1976, 50; Serge A. Korff, *Physics Today*, May 1977, 98–99.

13 *BankUnited, N.A. v Merritt Environmental Consulting Corp.*, 360 F. Supp. 3d 172 (SDNY 2018).

14 Frank Giorno, interview by Patricia McMahon, 22 February 2023, on file with author.

15 It may simply have been the recognition that there was no money in the estate, or the claim was too remote. The claim against the province was in negligence for permitting the subdivision to have been built; a claim in negligence against French would have involved the conduct that gave rise to the originally contaminated land. The former was far easier to prove than the latter. Moreover, in 1959, French had merged his three wartime companies – Radium Luminous Industries Ltd., Dial Instrument Finishers Ltd., and Radium Industries Ltd. – into Ceebee Services Ltd., which would have further immunized him personally from a lawsuit.

16 "Carl French Dies, Leader in Fight against Cancer," *Battle Creek Enquirer*, 4 May 1984, 8; "Lawyer Carl French Was among the First to Know of A-bomb," *Sunday Star* (Toronto), 22 April 1984, A10.

17 Robinette represented Steve Suchan, one of the members of the notorious Boyd Gang, who was hanged with Leonard Jackson in December 1952 for the murder of Detective-Sergeant Edmund Tong. The Toronto criminal gang was involved in a series of bank robberies in the city in the late 1940s and early '50s. After breaking out of the Don Jail, they shot and killed Tong when he pulled them over.

18 In the 1960s, the company became Eldorado Nuclear Limited, and in 1988, merged with Saskatchewan Mining Development Corporation to become Canadian Mining and Energy Corporation, which was then shortened to Cameco Corporation.

Index

Note: Page numbers with (f) refer to illustrations.

Printed and bound in Canada

Set in Garamond by Artegraphica Design Co. Ltd.

Copyeditor: Camilla Blakeley

Proofreader: Judith Earnshaw

Indexer: Judy Dunlop

Cartographer: Eric Leinberger

Cover designer: Rafael Chimicatti

Cover vectors: bomb icon by vecteezy.com;
halftone pattern by magnific.com

Authorized Representative: Easy Access System Europe –
Mustamäe tee 50, 10621 Tallinn, Estonia,
gpsr.requests@easproject.com